G

Unl
Do

Withdrawn

An Extraordinary Italian Imprisonment

www.brianlettauthor.com

Other books by the same author:

SAS in Tuscany 1943–45
Ian Fleming and SOE's Operation Postmaster
The Small Scale Raiding Force

An Extraordinary Italian Imprisonment

The Brutal Truth of Campo 21, 1942–1943

Brian Lett

Pen & Sword
MILITARY

First published in Great Britain in 2014 by
Pen & Sword Military
an imprint of
Pen & Sword Books Ltd
47 Church Street
Barnsley
South Yorkshire
S70 2AS

ISBN 978 1 47382 269 6

A CIP catalogue record for this book is available from the British
Library

Typeset in Ehrhardt by
Mac Style Ltd, Bridlington, East Yorkshire
Printed and bound in the UK by CPI Group (UK) Ltd, Croydon,
CRO 4YY

Pen & Sword Books Ltd incorporates the imprints of Pen & Sword
Archaeology, Atlas, Aviation, Battleground, Discovery, Family
History, History, Maritime, Military, Naval, Politics, Railways, Select,
Transport, True Crime, and Fiction, Frontline Books, Leo Cooper,
Praetorian Press, Seaforth Publishing and Wharncliffe.

For a complete list of Pen & Sword titles please contact
PEN & SWORD BOOKS LIMITED
47 Church Street, Barnsley, South Yorkshire, S70 2AS, England
E-mail: enquiries@pen-and-sword.co.uk

Contents

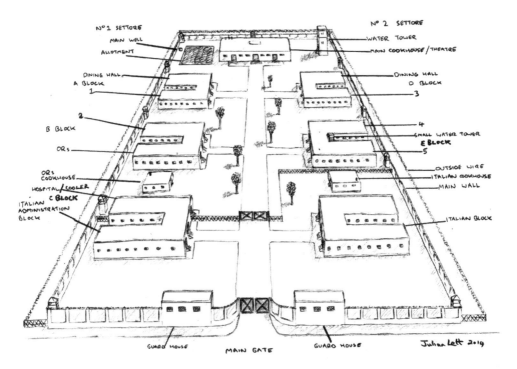

Outline plan of Campo P.G. 21 at Chieti Scalo.

*In memory of my father, Major Gordon Lett DSO,
and all those who suffered with him in Campo 21.*

List of Illustrations

The Americans: Flying Officer Claude Weaver III DFC receiving his wings on 10 October 1941. (*Courtesy of acesofww2.com*)

Flying Officer Bill Wendt. (*Courtesy of his family*)

First Lieutenant Samuel Redden Webster Junior, and his wife Mary. (*Courtesy of their family*)

Flight Officer James E. Beck. (*Courtesy of the family of Bill Wendt*)

Flying Officer James Outerbridge. (*Courtesy of the National Museum of Bermuda*)

Papantonio. (*Courtesy National Archives*)

Group photos. (*Courtesy of the family of the late Captain Arthur Green MBE; and courtesy of the family of the late David Roberts MBE*)

CNA poster. (*Courtesy of the family of the late Captain Arthur Green MBE*)

Tea party invitation, 8 November. (*Courtesy of the family of the late Captain Arthur Green MBE*)

21 Club invitation. (*Courtesy of the family of the late Captain Arthur Green MBE*)

'No Klim' cartoon. (*Courtesy of the family of the late Captain Arthur Green MBE*)

Menu Welsh dinner. (*From the collection of the late Major Gordon Lett DSO*)

Menu Cheren dinner. (*From the collection of the late Major Gordon Lett DSO*)

Larry Allen's noticeboard after the Armistice is announced. (*Courtesy of the late Lieutenant David Roberts, MC*)

Captain Croce, drawn by Lieutenant Jack Hodgson Shepherd. (*Courtesy of Mrs Barbara Shepherd*)

Italian guard, drawn by Lieutenant Jack Hodgson Shepherd. (*Courtesy of Mrs Barbara Shepherd*)

Officers' living quarters, drawn by Lieutenant Jack Hodgson Shepherd. (*Courtesy of Mrs Barbara Shepherd*)

A class at the water tower, drawn by Major Gordon Lett DSO.

Plan of Tunnel 3, as in September 1943. (*Courtesy of the family of the late Captain Arthur Green MBE*)

Wall of Campo 21 in November 2013. (*Author's collection*)

The author with the current Commandant of Campo 21, Colonel Marco Mochi, in November 2013. (*Author's collection*)

Introduction

Imagine: you are imprisoned in a room containing 39 other men. You sleep on one of a pair of wooden bunk beds, with nowhere to put any personal possessions except on a small shelf by your bunk, or in a cardboard box underneath it. You have no privacy. Apart from the three men who occupy the bunks beside, and above or below yours, there is a gap of only 20–24in. between your bunk block and the next one on each side, where four more men are trying to sleep. For warmth at night, you have only two sheets, two thin woollen blankets, and what clothing you wear. It is early January, and there is snow on the mountains that tower over your prison compound. You have no warm winter clothes, only shorts and one shirt which are nearly worn out, so during the daytime you wear your blankets in place of a coat. Your shoes or boots have long worn through and your feet are cut, but there are no proper bandages. There is no heater in your room and after dark falls, at about 1630hrs, the electric light is so dim that you can't see to read or write. You have had no hot water to wash in for months and the stench from the lavatories, which do not flush, is appalling. Your diet is monotonous and the food barely adequate.

You have been in this prison for nearly six months. The guards all speak a foreign language and the interpreter is unwilling to translate any of your requests or complaints accurately to the prison governor. There have been no visitors or phone calls from home; any letters that you write never seem to reach your loved ones. Rarely does a letter from them reach you. Your loved ones themselves are threatened by an enemy against whom you can no longer defend them. Your home is far away across the sea and even if you could manage to escape from your prison, you would be in a hostile land, surrounded by enemies. If you were seen trying to escape, you might lawfully be shot dead. You are in your early twenties, and you are facing a sentence of unknown duration. Life is passing you by.

You are in Campo Prigioneri di Guerra Number 21, at Chieti, Italy. It is January 1943.

This book is intended as a tribute to the many thousands of men, some young, some not so young, who were imprisoned by the enemy during the Second World War. These men had committed no crime, but had been captured while fighting in defence of their country. Today, our society in the United Kingdom marks its disapproval of crime with fixed-term prison sentences of which a prisoner will serve half or less, or, if the crime is extremely serious, with indeterminate life sentences. Prisoners will be well fed, provided with adequate warmth, bedding and clothing, will be allowed family visits, and family contact by post and telephone, and will have access to such luxuries as television.

The lot of a prisoner of war was very different. The sentence was of indeterminate length, since no one knew how long the war would last (or, in the early years, who would win it). Conditions in the camps were often very harsh, with inadequate food, bedding and clothing. In Campo 21, whose story this book tells, shortage of water was an acute problem. No visits from family or friends were allowed, and post was either very much delayed or non-existent. Illness, both physical and mental, was often inadequately treated – usually because there were few medicines or medical instruments available. The only crime the prisoners had committed was that of being captured, or worse, of obeying an order to surrender.

Campo 21 was a large camp, containing at various times up to 1,600 prisoners of various nationalities. It was designated for officers, but also held over 200 other ranks who performed the necessary more menial tasks within the camp. A complete cross-section of society was there, all of them entirely at the mercy of their guards. For those who read this book, most of whom, I would guess, have never been arrested and remanded in custody, the story may be difficult to fully understand. Arrest or capture means the immediate imposition of a total lack of liberty. You no longer have any right to choose where you go or what to do with your life. You must do exactly what you are told at all times. For some of the new arrivals in Campo 21, imprisonment came as a total shock. The starkest of contrasts was for shot down airmen. A few nights before they might have been celebrating in the hotspots of Alexandria, Cairo, or even London's West End, only to find themselves, abruptly, prisoners in the squalid conditions of Campo

21, with the most depressing of future prospects. For pilots and aircrew, who enjoyed the vast freedom of the open sky, imprisonment in a walled camp was purgatory. So, too, for those whose lives before the war had been lived in wide-open spaces such as the Australian outback, many parts of the United States of America, or the moorlands of Britain.

After the retreat to, and evacuation of Dunkirk in May/June 1940, thousands of British troops were taken prisoner. For the vast majority of them, imprisonment would last for five years, the equivalent of a ten-year prison term in modern Britain. I remember well as a young barrister in the 1970s, appearing for the defence before His Honour Judge the Lord Dunboyne at the Inner London Crown Court, knowing that he had been captured at Dunkirk, and had served five years as a prisoner of war. In fact, having himself experienced the pain of incarceration for so long, Lord Dunboyne was far from being an unduly harsh judge.

My own father, Major Gordon Lett DSO, was one of the 35,000 Allied troops captured at the surrender of Tobruk in June 1942. He was 31 years of age when he reached Campo 21 at Chieti, in August 1942. He had been an Acting Lieutenant Colonel when captured at the fall of Tobruk, and had been a regular soldier before the war. In a sense, the danger of being taken as a prisoner of war was part of his full-time profession. However, since progress in his career depended upon rising in rank, time behind the wire was lost career time, and he would now be overtaken by many of his juniors in the hurly-burly of war. Many other prisoners were appreciably younger, and were soldiers for the duration of the war only. They came from all walks of life, some voluntarily, some because they were conscripted. Most had left families behind them, and the vast majority wished only to return to their peacetime professions once the war was won. Some were little more than schoolboys, who in happier times might have been carefree university students, or travelling around the world for a year before taking their degrees. Others were mature married men, who had left wives and children at home. These were the men who had to face life behind the walls and wire of Campo 21.

Much has been written about the German prisoner-of-war camps, such as Colditz and Stalag Luft III, from which the Wooden Horse and Great Escapes took place, about the horrors of the German concentration camps, and about the inhumanity of the Japanese towards their prisoners. Relatively little has been published about the Italian camps, which operated from June 1940, when Mussolini took Italy into the war on Germany's side to form the Axis alliance, until the Italian Armistice in September 1943, by which time it is estimated that over 80,000 Allied prisoners of war were held in Italian camps. Although nominally run along similar lines to German ones, the Italian camps were in many ways different, and, after Rommel's victories in North Africa and the fall of Tobruk in June 1942, they became very overcrowded. Various other factors adversely affected conditions in the Italian camps, and the Italian administrators in any event lacked Teutonic efficiency. Campo 21 was one of the biggest, and one of the worst: after the war, a number of its Italian personnel were considered for prosecution for war crimes.

This book traces the life of Campo 21 from the time that it was opened on 3 August 1942, until it closed following the fall of Sicily to the Allies and the resulting Italian armistice in September 1943. It follows the lives (and deaths) of many who endured imprisonment at Chieti. It is a story of capture, suffering, and – for some – escape. It is also a story of courage, inventiveness and durability, and of how to make the most of whatever circumstances a man might find himself in.

For the reader, I should add this: the account of what happened in Campo 21 may initially and inevitably create the impression that the Italians during the Second World War were a cruel and unattractive people. Of the Fascists this is absolutely true, particularly when it seemed that, thanks to their German allies, they might win the war. However, as virtually every escaped prisoner of war discovered, the ordinary Italians were of a totally different character, particularly the peasant farmers, the *contadini*. The courage and self-sacrifice of many of those who helped the escapers was quite extraordinary, based on a simple humanity and respect for their fellow man. The success of most of those who escaped through to Allied territory was thanks to the food, shelter and guidance provided to them by the Italians that they met, despite the rewards that were offered for the handing over or betrayal of Allied prisoners, and the threatened penalties for helping them. An escaped prisoner of war who was recaptured would simply be returned to the camp. An Italian who had helped him, or was suspected of helping him, would usually be shot, and his home often burned to the ground. This was well known to the Italian people and yet still they helped. Thus, those reading this book are entitled to judge the Fascists harshly, but not the ordinary Italian people. To drive the point home, I should add that my father, Gordon Lett, dedicated his second book to the Italian Military Police, the *carabinieri*.

Brian Lett
Somerset 2014

Month 1

August 1942

THE BEGINNING

In early 1942, the Second World War was being fought between two power blocks. One comprised the Axis powers, essentially Germany and Italy, together with Japan, after she had attacked Pearl Harbor in December 1941. The other was known as the Allies – the British, Canadians, Australians, Indians, and New Zealanders, together with the smaller British Empire nations, South Africans, the free forces of the various countries that the Axis powers had occupied, and, since Pearl Harbor, the United States of America. Until the arrival of Field Marshal Erwin Rommel in North Africa, there were a relatively modest number of Allied servicemen in Italian prisoner-of-war camps. The Italian campaign against the Allies had been generally unsuccessful, and most of the prisoners taken during it were Italians captured by the Allies. However, once the Germans gave their support to bolster the weakening Italian position in North Africa, that position changed. Rommel and his Afrika Korps won a series of victories that resulted in the taking of Allied prisoners. Since nominally the Italians remained in charge of the North African campaign, prisoners taken by them or by their German allies were an Italian responsibility. The surrender of Tobruk in June 1942 resulted in an enormous increase in the number of prisoners for whom the Italians had to find accommodation. An estimated 35,000 Allied personnel were taken at Tobruk, and the Germans were only too happy to leave the task of housing them in suitable camps to the Italians. The Italians knew perfectly well what their duties were, since so many of their own men were prisoners of the Allies. However, their immediate logistical problem was an enormous one – many thousands of prisoners but nowhere to put them.

The rights of prisoners of war had first been recognized by the Hague Conventions of 1899 and 1907, which had held effect during the First World War. On 27 July 1929, the Geneva Convention was signed by 47 countries – members of the League of Nations and a number of others – creating a bill of rights in international law for prisoners of war. The Convention was later ratified by most of the signatories, including Great Britain, Germany, Italy and the United States. Japan signed but never ratified the Convention. Russia was viewed at the time as something of an international pariah, and neither signed nor ratified it. Any nation embarking upon a war would expect to take enemy prisoners, but also to have a number of its own servicemen captured by the enemy – most countries were therefore keen to ensure fair treatment for their own nationals at the cost of committing to fair treatment for the enemy prisoners that it took. The Swiss, traditionally neutral, were to umpire a prisoner's rights.

The central provisions of the Geneva Convention can be summarized as follows:

• Prisoners were to be treated humanely.
• No constraint was to be applied to those who refused to give any information beyond their name and rank, or service number.
• Prisoners were to be allowed to keep all their clothes, including metal helmet and gas mask if carried, and any personal papers. They must surrender arms, military equipment and service papers. If insufficiently clad, they were to be clothed by the holding power.
• Prisoners were to be kept in fixed camps, away from the battle area, which were to be dry, clean and warm, and no less sanitary than the holding power's normal barracks.
• The prisoners had the right to correspond with their families, and to practise any religion that they chose. Inward post could include food, clothes and books.
• Rations were to be no worse than those of the depot troops of the holding power.
• Each camp was to include a hospital.
• Officer prisoners were to salute their equals and seniors in their captor's forces.
• Pay as appropriate to rank was to be provided by the holding power. Officers would not be required to work, warrant and non-commissioned officers were to work only in a supervisory role.

- No prisoner could be put to warlike, unhealthy or dangerous work, or made to work excessively long hours.
- Prisoners were subject to the civil laws of the holding power, and might be punished judicially according to those laws, but might not receive corporal punishment, excessive penalties, or be place in noisome cells.
- For escape or attempted escape, the maximum disciplinary penalty that a prisoner might receive was 30 days' solitary confinement. Of course, if he committed an offence of assault or theft as a part of his escape, then he would be liable to judicial penalties in addition to any disciplinary penalty.
- Warring nations might communicate with each other through the International Red Cross, and an appointed Protecting Power (in Europe usually Switzerland) would ensure, by means of inspections of the prisoner of war camps, that any nation was complying with the Geneva Convention.

Prisoners also remained subject to their own country's military discipline. Within the prison camps a Senior Officer, usually British (SBO), would be appointed to be in overall command of the prisoners and responsible to the camp Commandant for their conduct. It would be his job to maintain discipline within the camp and to ensure that military law was obeyed by his men. Of course, the extremely difficult circumstances in some of the camps rendered this a difficult task and a wise SBO would exercise considerable discretion according to the situation his men were in. The SBO would appoint a camp Adjutant, and each hut or prison building would have its own hierarchy, each reporting up the chain of command to the SBO, and passing on his orders to the men.

However, in North Africa in late June 1942, the practicalities of the situation meant that the Geneva Convention was at least temporarily unenforceable. Captain Charles 'Bonzo' Burdon-Taylor, a 23-year-old from the Durham Light Infantry, was captured by the Germans when his position was overrun. He did not remain in their hands for long, since all Allied prisoners were to be handed over to the Italians. Burdon-Taylor described being brought across the desert towards what looked to him, from a distance, to be a brown sea, but which turned out when he got closer to be thousands upon thousands of Allied prisoners in khaki battledress. He recalled that when he was finally despatched by the Germans to walk into Italian hands, friends of his from the Durham Light Infantry spotted him and called out, 'Good God, they've got Bonzo!'

There was no interrogation by the Italians of their prisoners, it was simply a question of finding somewhere they could be caged up, until it was possible to ship them over to the Italian mainland. Although triumphalist and jubilant, the Italians were totally unprepared and the prisoners were transported to a number of vastly over-crowded compounds, where water was in very short supply, and sanitation at its most basic. The prisoners came from a wide cross-section of different countries and races representing all corners of the British Empire and South Africa. There was also the odd American, but the United States were as yet playing no significant part in the North African and Middle East campaign. It had been a South African, Major General Klopper, who had been the senior officer in command of Tobruk at the time of its fall, and who had given the order to surrender, taking many by surprise. Tobruk had been unsuccessfully besieged for many months in the previous year, when defended by mainly Australian troops. Some were already grumbling that the South African support for the Allied cause was half-hearted, and that the Boers amongst them really sided with the Axis powers. However, for those who had been in action in the desperate defence of Tobruk, the overriding feeling was one of exhaustion. They suffered the deprivations of the temporary North African camps in a daze and hoped that they would eventually reach mainland Italy safely.

The Italians were experiencing enough difficulty supplying their own forces. They were just not capable of supplying their prisoners properly, or in accordance with the Geneva Convention. Major Gordon Lett, who was to become a long-term prisoner at Campo 21, described the lack of water, vital for survival in the heat of the desert: 'Most of the troops were desperately thirsty, and it was a horrible thing to see soldiers actually crying for water, and, when they could, crawling round the water point licking the tops of the containers for any spare drops that had collected there during filling. The water was brought from a point in the harbour, which under [Italian] sketchy organization only managed to make two trips per day, which was barely sufficient for a single issue.'

Lance Bombardier Frank Osborne, 72 Field Regiment, Royal Artillery, an economics graduate of London University and another future inmate of Campo 21, was captured at the Knightsbridge Box at the end of May 1942, and as a prisoner in North Africa was soon swamped by the influx of prisoners from Tobruk. By the time he was passed by the Germans into Italian hands, his physical condition and that of his companions was dangerously low. Osborne described the moment when a large water carrier arrived, carrying hundreds of gallons of liquid by then regarded as more precious than diamonds: 'Multitudes of thirst frenzied beings clawed and bit, kicked and snatched for a vantage point.

Friends became mortal foes and croaked vile deprecation on their enemies. The vehicle possessed numerous drain cocks – they were peak points of panic. The circular caps atop the tanker were also besieged. Steel helmets were shorn of their rubber padding and used as drinking bowls. Lying in wait under the chassis, with cool cunning, were the helpless unfortunates who trapped the inevitable spillings of the human maelstrom above. Gloating on the outskirts, with shining and clicking cameras, were our Axis tormentors. Propagandists had a field day, though such revelations would be unhesitatingly discredited today.'

All the Allied prisoners had to be transported to Italy either by air or sea, and the danger of being shot down or sunk on the journey was a real one. Ships were sunk and many lives lost. Once in Italy, most of those destined for imprisonment in Campo 21 were first held for a few weeks at a Transit Camp at Bari and then taken by train north to Chieti. Conditions at Bari were far from good, but it was the first chance that some of the prisoners had to begin to recover from the trauma of capture. For most it was a very sudden and dramatic change of status. Captain J. E. Kenwyn Walters, Royal Tank Regiment, commented: 'As far as I was concerned this must have been the lowest point of my life. Until then [capture], I had been an officer in the British Army with all the backing that that gave. Now, I stood up with practically nothing and was dependent on the enemy for everything – including my life.'

Lieutenant John Speares, Royal Signals, recorded: 'I was completely dazed, in a state of shock, incapable of thinking very much for a long time … one had to exist, that was the primary objective. At Bari, when we first saw a Red Cross parcel, there was immense excitement – it was the first demonstration that our side cared and could help. The sight of a Rowntree's cocoa tin was the first thing that woke me up from the state of shock and isolation that I was in.' However, Speares was one of ten men who had to share a single Red Cross parcel – it contained amongst other things a packet of raisins, which they counted out amongst them raisin by raisin, to ensure that everybody got their fair share.

For prisoners of war arriving at PG 21 Chieti, the first impressions of the camp were excellent, particularly after the horrors of life as a prisoner in North Africa. Although not built as a prisoner-of-war camp, Chieti was relatively well designed. It comprised a series of brand new buildings encircled by a high wall, and had apparently originally been intended for use as a barracks for Italian soldiers, and later as a prison concentration camp for anti-Fascists. However, the flood of Allied prisoners of war pouring into Italy following the surrender of Tobruk meant that plans for the almost finished camp at Chieti had to be changed. Prisoners, when they arrived at Chieti in the early days, would be held outside in the compound whilst their Italian guards sorted them out. Each was thoroughly searched again, having to strip partially or fully naked in front of the assembled Italian guards for the purpose. Many covertly buried their treasured possessions in the earth of the enclosure where they were first held, in the hope of being able to retrieve them later – only to see the entire holding area dug over by the Italians after they had been allocated to their barracks, and all those precious possessions found and confiscated, never to be seen again.

Gordon Lett, who reached Chieti at the end of August, was one of many new arrivals upon whom the camp initially made a favourable impression: 'At first sight, the camp appeared to conform with civilised convention, and doubtless our neutral visitors thought so too. It consisted of a walled enclosure, approximately 700 yards by 300 yards in area, in which were six barrack blocks, a single storey high, and an impressive looking cookhouse at the end of a broad asphalt roadway. The buildings were new, and their appointments modern. There were neat metal door handles, glazed white tiles in the washrooms and lavatories, many shining taps, innumerable water cisterns, newly planted trees, and – at first – expanses of grass and vestiges of a garden. A high water tower … dominated the south-west corner.'

The wall that surrounded the camp was 4 metres (about 13ft) in height and went a further 2 metres underground. Estimates of the precise size of the camp vary – Captain Trippi, the Swiss Inspector who visited in October 1942, gave its measurement as 197,000 square feet (the equivalent of about 150 × 150yd), considerably smaller than Lett's estimate. The walls of the camp still stand today and the author's estimate is that the total area within them measures about 300 × 400yd, but only part of this was for use by the prisoners. The Italian guards and administration had their own quarters. There were eight main buildings – the guardhouse on either side of the main gate, the cookhouse at the opposite end of the camp, and six U-shaped bungalow blocks, three on each side of the central path that ran from the main gate to the cookhouse. Four bungalow blocks were to accommodate the prisoners, one was for the Italian garrison (the first on the right), and one was for the Italian administration and the camp hospital (the first on the left). Each bungalow block comprised two separate L-shaped bungalows, joined by an arched and open doorway at the front of the building that led through to a rear courtyard. Standing at the main gate and facing into the camp, the buildings on the left were known as *Settore* (Sector) One, and those on the right as *Settore* Two. All the bungalow blocks except that occupied by the Italian garrison were given letters: A–C in *Settore* One, D and E in *Settore* Two. The officers barrack wings of the blocks were given individual numbers 1–5. There were two wings used for dining halls. The other ranks had their own wing of Block B. The northern aspect of the compound looked towards the town of Chieti, standing on its hill, with the cathedral prominent. Looking southwest, there was a magnificent view of the Gran Sasso range of mountains.

From a large entrance gate, an asphalt roadway led down the middle of the camp, between the solidly built bungalow blocks, towards the cookhouse. On either side of the road there were some small trees, and a grassed area that would not long survive use by thousands of prisoners' feet. The cookhouse at the end of the roadway was a long low building, which eventually was also to house the camp theatre. In the first block on the left beyond the entrance gates were not only the camp hospital and the administration offices, but also the 'cooler' – the punishment cells for prisoners who misbehaved. The 'legs' of the U-shaped barrack bungalows each comprised two large dormitory rooms, and two large washrooms. The crosspiece forming the front of each bungalow contained smaller rooms and one of the bungalows contained a shower room, with 60 showers. The other ranks had their own cookhouse, between the hospital and their wing. The barrack bungalows and the cookhouses were divided by barbed wire from the remainder of the camp, which was used by the Italian garrison. Relatively new, the camp was potentially an excellent facility.

Campo 21 first opened its gates on 3 August 1942, in full summer. The camp was close to the village and railway station of Chieti Scalo, just outside the town of Chieti in the Abruzzo, about 12 miles from the east coast of Italy and the Adriatic Sea at Pescara. Chieti is about halfway down the boot of Italy, and very approximately level with Rome on the west coast. As mentioned, the view from the camp was an enticing one of fields, mountains and the attractive hilltop town of Chieti, as well as the mountain range of the Gran Sasso. The camp was under the control of the Italian IX Armoured Corps. Lieutenant Colonel Mario Barela, the first commandant of the camp, indicated at the first inspection by the Swiss Protecting Power, that its capacity was 1,800 men. This was a wild exaggeration. The camp had in fact originally been designed to hold 350 men. Italian records state that at the time when its intended use was changed to that of prisoner-of-war camp it was to hold a maximum of 1,000 men, but by 1 September 1942 it already contained 1,489. At the time of the first inspection by the Protecting Power on 7 October 1942, the total had risen to 1,603. The prisoners slept in dormitories of 40 bunks, or in the smaller rooms at varying rates of occupancy. The beds were what the Italians call *castelli* – wooden two-bed bunk units (officers were meant to be given individual beds). In some of the dormitories, two-bunk units were placed side by side, creating a 'castle' of four bunks, with each such castle a mere 20–24 inches from the next. In reality, the camp was grossly overcrowded. It was probably fit to hold 600–750 long-term prisoners at most. The main problem, however, was that the smart modern complex was extremely short of running water, rendering its showers and lavatories virtually useless.

The modern façade and fittings, which initially fooled the arriving prisoners, also had an effect on the first Swiss inspector to visit the camp. Gordon Lett describes the inspector, one Captain L. Trippi as, 'an elderly gentleman of Swiss nationality, who spoke good English and insisted on speaking in English all the time, but was slightly deaf.' Captain Trippi was clearly impressed by the superficial gloss of the camp, reporting back that the installations in all the bungalows were quite up to date, and in some instances luxurious. He described the shower room as 'most excellent'. Trippi's report will be dealt with more fully later.

As far as the prisoners were concerned, however, it was not long before they realized that the appearance of luxury and modernity was merely a mirage, something that all desert soldiers understood. Lieutenant Ronald C. W. Hill, Royal Artillery, who arrived in Campo 21 on 5 August, recorded in his diary that on his first day he sat at tables equipped with tablecloths and serviettes, and that he enjoyed his food much more under such decent conditions. Lieutenant George Hervey-Murray's reaction was much the same. But the tablecloths and serviettes never appeared again, and as the camp filled up the food became worse and worse.

Major Lett described the realities of the camp:

The unfortunate inhabitants of PG21 soon discovered that the glazed tiles were mere camouflage for the most primitive of sanitary systems, that the water cisterns had never worked since the day that they were installed, and that the impressive water tower produced the very minimum of water. The rooms which had been built to house twenty men in each had, in many cases to hold forty officer prisoners. The beds were of wood, and built in double bunks, one above the other – as used in the barrack rooms of the garrison soldiery – and the mattresses consisted of old sacking stuffed with dry grass which in the words of one senior officer: 'would not be fit to feed cattle upon', and which was never renewed. The cookhouse, too, proved but a whited sepulchre, for apart from the large cauldrons with which it was furnished for cooking the eternal Italian macaroni stew, or pasta, there were no other utensils available, not even ladles for serving out their contents – hence the food tins which were eventually obtained from Red Cross parcels had, perforce, to serve a double purpose as saucepans, or drinking vessels, for individual officers. Everything else connected with this luxurious establishment – as certain optimists at home believed it to be – was of the same standard.

With 1,600 prisoners eventually crammed into six wings of the bungalows, facilities out of doors became of great importance. Paths ran off the central asphalt road to the bungalows. There was space outside sufficient for some games, but the trees, paths and road got in the way, and there was a trip wire and 'forbidden zone' in front of the surrounding walls, together with signs in English warning the prisoners not to cross the wire and approach the wall. These read: 'FORBIDDEN ZONE. PASSAGE AND DEMURRAGE NO ALLOWED. DANGER' at the wire, and: 'WARNING It is forbidden to approach the wall. The sentries have orders to fire without warning', on the walls themselves. Similarly, across the asphalt road that led through the centre of the camp, near to the gate out of the prisoners' compound, there was a white line painted, beyond which the prisoners were not allowed to go. Here also was the notice: PASSAGE AND DEMURRAGE NO ALLOWED. The poor quality of English reflected the modest ability of the senior interpreter and security officer in the camp, Captain Mario Croce. The word 'demurrage' was researched by the prisoners, and found to be a technical term relating to the length of time that a railway goods wagon was left idle. The sign was therefore taken by the prisoners to mean: 'no crossing of the line or hanging about allowed'. Nobody ever told Croce how poor his English was.

Captain Dominick 'Toby' Graham, Royal Artillery, arrived in Chieti on 4 August, as one of a batch of about 500 junior officers. The shortage of water was acute in the summer heat, and at that stage (with the camp nowhere near as full as it would be later), the water to the taps was turned on only twice a day for one hour. The lavatories did not flush. In the courtyard of his bungalow, number 5, Graham describes a well, and a water tank mounted on stilts with an antiquated pumping machine which used to break down regularly. He commented that the water tank had an alternative use – if you climbed up onto it, it was possible to see over the wall of the camp to the outside world. For the first week, Graham and his fellow prisoners had nothing but Italian rations to eat. That meant rice, macaroni, tomato puree, bread and cheese, and all portions were sparse. Wine was provided and occasionally a little marsala, in accordance with the ration supplied to the Italian soldiery. For Italians, wine is part of the meal. Some prisoners would swap their cigarettes for extra wine from those who did not want it, and some would then attempt to distil a more violent spirit from it. However, on any occasion when the Italians found a prisoner drunk, all wine was stopped for the foreseeable future and any wine found hoarded in the camp was poured away. At the end of the first week, the SBO arranged to buy fruit and vegetables outside the camp, so the situation was eased a little. A trade rapidly sprang up amongst the prisoners, and those lucky enough to have arrived in Campo 21 with any personal possessions were able to trade with them. Graham commented that in the early days one of the most prized possessions was a book. Reading passed the time and was a form of escapism from the uncomfortable realities of the camp. Books might be divided into quarters and each quarter leased or sold to a reader in exchange for food, cigarettes or clothing. It was not until much later that any books were received through the Red Cross.

Many of the prisoners arrived still wearing their desert uniforms of shirt and shorts in which they had been taken prisoner. It was all they had, but in the Italian summer, except for cleanliness, the light clothing was not a problem. It would be different when winter came. Toby Graham, like many others, had problems with his boots. When he first arrived at the camp he had been told that if he handed in his damaged boots, a cobbler would mend them. Graham duly handed his boots over to the camp authorities and went barefoot, believing that he would soon get his boots back. In August, with fine weather, that was not too great a hardship. However, the boots did not return in a few days, or a few weeks. The weather changed to rain in late September, and for those without boots going outside became very uncomfortable. The officers' feet became covered in blisters and sores, often with cuts that would not heal. Graham's boots were finally returned in November, but by then his feet had spread to such a degree that he could not wear the boots even without socks, and his feet were covered in sores. It was a further two months before he was able to put them on again.

When the camp first opened, the officers were provided with a small number of Cypriots as servants. They were a part of a mule company that had been captured on one of the Greek islands before the British had evacuated them. However, Graham complained that these men carried lice, which inevitably spread quickly to the officers, until all forty men in his barrack room were infested. The inadequate water supply substantially aggravated the problem. The Cypriot servants were in due course replaced by Allied other ranks, but getting rid of the lice was a more complex problem. Graham and his companions had been wearing the same clothes since their capture, day in and day out. In order to de-louse their clothes, they had to wash them every day for a week in a substance called Creosole. At this stage, with the camp filling up, the water was turned on for only half an hour, twice a day. The clothes were in any event becoming worn and fragile from overuse, and whilst they were being washed and then drying, the officers had nothing to wear except their blankets. Even this was no good, as their blankets required similar de-lousing treatment, and in the end most men simply stayed in bed under their sheets until their clothes and blankets were dry.

Another of the more senior officers to arrive in the camp was Major Harold Sydney Sell, Durham Light Infantry, who was a few months older than Lett. He described Campo 21 as undoubtedly the worst camp in Italy, but commented, 'Prison life is a test of moral fibre.' Sell noted that the greater number of inmates had been captured at Tobruk, and that many were young and fresh from home, without the discipline and toughness of front-line troops. Lett made a similar comment about those who had had the misfortune to be captured before they could learn anything about discipline or British Army traditions. Sell also commented on the number of 'base wallahs' from Tobruk. Facing the difficulties of life in the unpleasant conditions of Campo 21, Sell stressed that 'the answer to such problems is Guts Guts and more Guts.' The overall situation in the camp was extremely difficult. Sell noted in the early days: 'Over 1,000 men are in this den, no organization and all bolshy. Everyone is unshaven, filthy and verminous, and a sprinkling of the usual skin diseases. The best clad have shirts and boots. Food is delivered to an ill equipped cookhouse and there is no means to check the ration scale. The preparation and distribution is left to us, but with what? There is no sign of any news from home or even that anyone knows our whereabouts.'

Sell recorded that in August, about one in six of the inmates was suffering from jaundice. As the month went on, the situation deteriorated rapidly, with all sorts of pilfering going on between the prisoners. Some of the thieves were caught and beaten up. Even one of the chaplains succumbed to pangs of hunger and was caught stealing a piece of bread from a sleeping comrade. The reaction was swift and violent – the cleric's bedding and belongings were thrown down a well, although threats that the cleric would follow were not in fact carried out. Lieutenant George Hervey-Murray recalls another chaplain who made a habit of getting to breakfast early in order to steal the bread intended for other men. Harold Sell's own bunk was raided and he lost his fork and his fat ration, after which he and his bunk companion set up a sentry rota for their bunks. The first few months without proper food were the most difficult, until the prisoners' stomachs shrank. Once they grew used to their very restricted rations, it became somewhat easier.

Lieutenant Colonel Mario Barela, the first Commandant of the Camp, was, unfortunately for his future charges, an enthusiastic Fascist. A number of commandants of other Italian camps were First World War veterans, who had fought alongside the British against the Austrians, and were sympathetic to their British prisoners. Barela was the opposite. He was about 45 years old, no more than 5ft 6in. in height, fat, clean shaven, of upright bearing, arrogant and extremely pompous. Barela's own opinion of himself was that he was too good for the task to which he had been assigned, and he wished to remain in post for as short a period as possible before moving on to something better. No doubt he was delighted to be lording it over numerous Allied officers rather than fighting them in North Africa, but he was quite content to leave all the real work in the camp to others, and quite happy to delegate decisions to those who were prepared to take them. Although his prisoners were to be almost all English speakers, Barela apparently spoke no English. In order to communicate with his charges, he would have to rely on the senior camp interpreter, Captain Croce. Lett recalls that apart from Barela and Croce, there were five other Italian officers, and a large body of soldiers and *carabinieri*.

Captain Mario Croce was another ardent Fascist, violently anti-British. Through Fascism, he found a way to further his own career and almost certainly to enrich himself. He was a 'Special Service officer' and Gestapo trained. Croce claimed to have lived in the United States before the war, and to have worked for the Lloyd Triestino Shipping Company. He was a bully, and thoroughly dishonest in the way that he performed his job as an interpreter. He was also the head of security. It soon became clear that he had the power to overrule any decision made by the Commandant, and Lett records that Croce was in direct contact with the Fascist Special Intelligence Service in Rome. Campo 21 was Croce's first appointment as a camp interpreter, and since Barela spoke no

English and had no interest in the camp, Croce found himself in a position of very considerable power. Every communication from the Senior British Officer to the Commandant had to come through him, as did all complaints about ill-treatment. He was in charge of censorship of the prisoners' outgoing mail, and also seems to have had total control over whether any letters were actually despatched to their intended recipients. Incoming mail also came under his aegis. Although the camp Commandant changed from time to time throughout its existence, Croce was to remain a constant presence in all camp affairs, and a painful thorn in the side of the Allied camp leadership. He was deeply involved in everything that the Italians did or did not do with respect to their charges. Lett was to say of him: 'To a great extent he ran the camp – he supervised the mail, conducted searches, watched over the duties of the *carabinieri*, arrested officer prisoners of all ranks when he felt like it and shut them up in detention cells, and was present at all meetings with the representative of the Protecting Power. As far as he was concerned, the Commandants of the camp were only figure heads. Nevertheless, they certainly found him useful as a screen when they had an unpleasant duty to perform. Although he was fully aware of the contents of the Geneva Convention, of which a copy was available in the camp, he took pleasure in ignoring it, and often deliberately tried wrangles of his own in the hope of causing a little extra discomfort, or obtaining a little extra money from prisoners of war.'

The camp was guarded by a detachment of Italian soldiers, in addition to whom there was a modest squad of *carabinieri*. The soldiers were a mixed bunch. Some were active Fascists, but rather more were reluctant combatants, simply grateful that they were at home in Italy and not fighting in North Africa, or worse, in Russia. Generally speaking they were low-grade troops. Some were perfectly willing to shoot at their captives if given an excuse. They are described as being generally very short of stature, with rifles that seemed too big for them, and often outsized uniforms. The *carabinieri* , who were an honourable force with a considerable history, and nominally served the king of Italy and not Mussolini, were again not of the highest quality. Their commanding officer was an elderly second lieutenant in his early fifties, Demetrio Zena. He was stationed in the camp from 10 August 1942 until 2 October 1943, and may well have had Fascist sympathies, since he was later to make a statement to British authorities saying: 'The general conditions in the camp were of the best ... Captain Mario Croce, who was the Chief Interpreter of the Camp, treated the prisoners of war with every consideration and did all he could to please them.'

In contrast, Lieutenant Freer Roger, Argyll and Sutherland Highlanders, said: 'Croce's mission in life was to make our life as uncomfortable as possible, and his ability in that direction amounted almost to genius.'

The camp had received its first prisoners on 3 August 1942. The initial batch was of about 250 South Africans, some of the many captured when Tobruk surrendered. Their senior officer, who initially became the senior officer of the camp, was a Captain Mansergh. The South African numbers eventually rose to 337 officers and 49 orderlies (privates and non-commissioned officers), making a total of 386 men in all by early October. One of the bungalow wings, in D block, was filled exclusively with South Africans and predictably became known as South Africa House. One of Croce's tasks in the weeks ahead would be to try to drive a wedge between the South African and the British prisoners – in this he failed. It did not take long for the first inmates to discover that the gleaming shower block was useless since there was virtually no water, and that the lavatories would not flush for the same reason. To obtain water the prisoners were reduced to queuing for access to a well, into which they would lower a tin can held by a string. This can had to provide water for washing bodies, eating utensils and clothes, and for flushing the lavatories. Besides this, there was an extreme shortage of drinking water.

The first 500 British prisoners arrived from the transit camp at Bari shortly after the South Africans, on 4 or 5 August. They were mainly junior officers and included Toby Graham, Lieutenant Stuart Hood, Highland Light Infantry, and Lieutenant Ronald Hill, who like a number of others kept a daily diary of events. Hill was born on 11 May 1918, and was therefore 24 when he arrived in Campo 21. He had been schooled at Purley High School, becoming head boy in 1936. He went on to King's College, London to study physics, but as a member of the Officer Training Corps there he was called up on the outbreak of war, and therefore did not graduate. He was a good sportsman, excelling at rugby and water polo. Hill joined the 4th Durham (Survey) Regiment of the Royal Artillery. He served in the British Expeditionary Force in Greece, and was evacuated with them when that campaign turned into a disaster. Returning to North Africa, Hill was captured at Tobruk on 21 June, when his unit was surrounded. He arrived in Campo 21 as an experienced young soldier.

The camp Commandant, no doubt with Croce's encouragement, refused to allow the British, now comfortably in the majority and including more senior officers than the South African Captain Mansergh, to elect their own senior officer. Nonetheless, the British officers organized themselves and the camp, and imposed their own command structure. Only when a batch of officers appreciably more senior in rank, including a number of colonels, arrived on 22 August, did the Commandant finally agree to the appointment of a British Senior Officer (SBO), and the new SBO was Lieutenant Colonel Charles E. Gray, of 3 Gurkha Rifles. Gray adapted and expanded the command structure as the population of the camp grew.

Gray appointed an adjutant and staff officers, and each bungalow and each room was placed under the command of its own senior officer. Matters were organized along military lines. Gray controlled a 'Cabinet' of officers, senior and junior, representing the various groups and interests in the camp. In due course this embodied representatives from education, hospital, sport, music, theatre, religion, other ranks, and various others. As their activities expanded, so did the requests for funding, which was available by means of levies on the officers' pay, and as a result of various fund-raising efforts in the camp. As is the way of Cabinets, there was much competition between the various departments for funds – education wanted textbooks, sport wanted footballs, and so on. Amongst the officers who arrived on 22 August was Colonel Gooler, a US tank expert also captured at Tobruk. He in due course took charge of the small contingent of US officers, mainly pilots, who later arrived in the camp.

Initially, there were no British orderlies at Campo 21, only the Cypriots, who were expected to perform all the menial tasks. On 19 August, these were replaced by some British other ranks, who had volunteered to act as the officers' batmen. Frank Osborne joined them in September. Osborne had volunteered to come to Campo 21 from an other ranks camp at Gravina, which he regarded as far worse. Osborne was given a job as a waiter, which he initially regarded as a rather too lowly for a University of London Economics graduate. However, he soon came to realize that he had one of the best jobs in the camp, since it meant that he was in regular contact with the kitchen, as a result of which he never went short of food. The reaction of other NCOs was similar. K. J. Bowden, Ordnance Corps, was a married man with a child who had been a resident inspector with the Scottish Provident in Sheffield before the war. He volunteered to come to Chieti from Sulmona to work (this was later on, in April 1943). Bowden's reaction on being told he would be a servant to the officers was to ask for a transfer back to Sulmona – until he, like Osborne, realized the enormous benefits of working in the officers' mess.

As the August days passed, more and more men arrived as prisoners in the camp, and it became horridly overcrowded. The total of 1,603 men noted on

7 October was well above the number that the place could properly hold, more than four times the original intended capacity when it was built. The fall of Tobruk saw men of all ages and from all types of background pass into enemy hands. Very many arrived with little or no personal possessions. What they had had been taken from them by their Italian guards early in their captivity, with the promise of later return, but never appeared again. Their clothing was generally the African desert kit – uniform shirts and shorts. Many, particularly those captured in the front line, had no spare clothing, and by the time they reached Campo 21, their desert boots or shoes were well worn, often badly in need of repair. With the onset of winter this would cause great hardship. In contrast, some of those who were not front-line troops had left their staff flats in Tobruk well dressed and with suitcase in hand. These were the 'base wallahs' of whom Harold Sell was so dismissive.

Young bachelors and mature family men all found themselves in the same cage, and paced unhappily behind the walls and wire of Campo 21. This was to be their home for the foreseeable future, unless they could find some way to escape, or the war ended unexpectedly. Frustratingly, the prisoners could look out to the adjoining higher ground and the nearby mountains of the Gran Sasso, yet were no longer able to enjoy their freedom. The walls of Campo 21 had become the boundaries of the lives of 1,603 Allied prisoners. Many commented then or later on the effects of their dramatic change of status. Most had been in shock after capture and it was only now, settled in to their permanent camp, that the reality of their situation hit them. K. J. Bowden said: 'If you were a criminal prisoner in England, you would at least know the length of your sentence, and could calculate the date of your release. Also you got three square meals a day. Not so here. We lived in hope, but also in fear of being shot against the wall, or [later] being killed in an air raid.' Bowden says that the overwhelming cry of the prisoner was always, 'How much longer?'

Lieutenant Jack Hodgson Shepherd, Royal Engineers, a talented artist, who was 24 when he came to the camp, wrote: 'No one who has never been a prisoner of war can ever be able to really understand the life of incarceration. Some will imagine life to have been much worse than it was, and many will imagine it to have been far better than it was. Maybe after a long period of time, you will get very near to understanding without ever understanding the whole.' Shepherd quoted from the American Nobel prizewinning author, Sinclair Lewis: 'There are no good prisons. There can no more be a good prison than there can be a good murder, or a good rape or a good cancer.'

PASSING THE TIME

Theatre

As the camp began to fill up and settle into a routine, its occupants looked for ways of passing the enormous amount of time that they had on their hands. Numerous societies and clubs were set up – most with the object of entertainment or education. One of the earliest was the Dramatic Society, of which Tony Maxtone Gaham became the first chairman. Lieutenant Anthony James Oliphant Maxtone Graham, 16th Laird of Cultoquhey in Perthshire, had been born in 1900, and was aged 42 when he arrived in Chieti. Before the war, he had worked for many years as a Lloyd's broker, and it was relatively late in life, therefore, that he became a soldier upon the outbreak of war. He had married in 1923, Joyce Anstruther, a writer and poet who wrote amusing pieces for *Punch* magazine and for the *Spectator*, as 'Jan Struther'. She became the creator of 'Mrs Miniver', initially a *Times* newspaper column in the 1930s, then a book of the same name published in 1939 and eventually a very successful film. In modern times, *Mrs Miniver* might be described as a light-hearted look at English family life. The Maxtone Grahams had three children: James (born 10 May 1924), Janet (born 24 April 1928) and Robert (born 6 May 1931). The separation from his family caused by war and imprisonment was devastating for Tony. He had left England for North Africa in 1940, when his children were 16, 12 and 9, and was separated from them and his wife for five years until his eventual liberation in 1945. At the time of his capture at Tobruk in June 1942, he had already been away from his family for more than two years. He was missing vital years of his children's company as they grew up, and he was not there to advise or help them. James, his eldest son, reached the age of 18 in May 1942, whilst his father was in the desert. Although in those days eighteenth birthdays were not celebrated as they are now, it was still a significant birthday, since young men over the age of eighteen were eligible to serve in the Armed Forces. It is difficult to fully appreciate the anguish that family men such as Tony Maxtone Graham must have gone through during their imprisonment, particularly if there were difficulties in receiving post from home, as was the case in Campo 21. His happy family life before the war did not survive the five-year separation. After the publication of her book, shortly after war was declared in 1939, Joyce Maxtone Graham was invited to lecture in the then still neutral United States, and travelled there with her children. There she remained for some considerable time and was awarded an Honorary Doctorate of Literature by Pennsylvania University in 1943. She eventually came back to the United Kingdom, but after the war, when Tony Maxtone Graham finally returned home, the couple divorced. That was in 1947, and Joyce subsequently left England to live in the USA, where she remarried in 1948.

At their London home in Wellington Square, just off the King's Road, the family had had a stage in the playroom, and had regularly enjoyed amateur theatricals and charades. Maxtone Graham therefore knew more about staging plays than many. He suffered the hardship of being very junior in rank, despite his relatively advanced age, but most younger men in Chieti respected his maturity and experience. Having been elected Chairman of the Dramatic Society, he, like many others, was to find that the theatricals within Campo 21 provided some solace during his incarceration. Maxtone Graham wrote a number of revues and plays himself, using his middle names of James Oliphant, and he was always on the lookout for writing talent. Many of the prisoners had experience of amateur theatricals, particularly at school, but good writers were difficult to find. Later, it would be possible to obtain the scripts of plays through the Red Cross, but for the first few months, the prisoners had to write their own. Lieutenant John Pelley, Coldstream Guards, who arrived in Campo 21 on 22 August 1942, remembered being approached by Maxtone Graham almost at once, and being asked if he could provide scripts for any sketches that he remembered. Initially, he wrote out two that he recalled from his Sandhurst days, and later became involved in one of them as an actor. This was entitled Broadway Backstage, and Pelley played a female part, which he was to follow up with others once bitten by the theatrical bug.

Maxtone Graham himself does not appear to have performed on the stage, but worked in the all-important props and make-up department, and wrote scripts for shows and plays. The first requirement, of course, was to create a theatre. This the Dramatic Society achieved by building a makeshift stage in a room off the canteen. They used a number of then vacant bunk beds and covered the board floor of the stage with curtains and blankets. The stage curtains were tablecloths. By the time John Pelley arrived, the theatre was up and running, and on 26 August, Pelley attended a one-act play written by James Oliphant (Maxtone Graham himself), entitled *Vanity Star*. The play was set in 1938, in 'Watney's Bank, High Street, East Tooting'. They had a cast of eight. The first two to appear on stage were Geoffrey Lewis, an aspiring professional actor who had given up his career as a solicitor to graduate from RADA just before war broke out, and Geoffrey Bateman. Captain Geoffrey C. Bateman, Royal Army Service Corps, was a member of the well-known family who owned a chain of opticians. He had arrived at Campo 21 with one English blanket from Tobruk and a torn Italian blanket acquired at Bari, which he later wore as a poncho in bad weather. He was better clad than many. Bateman enjoyed his stage performance, but complained that the Italian Commandant, Lieutenant Colonel Barela, came to a matinee and talked loudly throughout it. Of course, since the play was in English, Barela had only a very limited understanding of what was going on. Bateman recalled that in the early days the plays were improvised with very little by way of props or costumes. Make-up was made from margarine and charcoal, red ink and chalk.

Campo 21 provided the opportunity for new talent to emerge. A little later on, Lieutenant Paul Hardwick arrived, having been captured in North Africa like the vast majority of the prisoners, but having initially been incarcerated at Campo 5, the Italian Colditz at Gavi. Gavi was a castle prison, later designated as for 'bad boys' – those who had previously escaped or caused trouble. It was probably the most secure prison camp in Italy and Hardwick was only there for a short time before being moved on to Chieti.

Commissioned into the Green Howards, Hardwick had been born in Bridlington in the East Riding of Yorkshire on 15 November 1918. He had been 20 when the war started, and a student of modern languages at Birmingham University. When he arrived in Chieti he was 23. Within the camp, he was to discover a love of and talent for acting which would carry him through the rest of his life. He remained a prisoner until the end of the war and afterwards developed a professional career on the stage, joining the Royal Shakespeare Company and acting in many plays in the West End of London. He became internationally recognized and appeared in a number of films (including the James Bond movie, *Octopussy*) and on television. At Chieti, he excelled in a multitude of different parts, demonstrating his versatility in comedy, Shakespeare and the 'whodunnit'. Lieutenant W. M. G. 'Bill' Bompas, Royal Artillery, a fellow inmate in Campo 21 wrote in his diary: '[Hardwick] displayed enormous talent both as a comedian and straight actor. He has a vital ability which can grip you as few others. If he becomes a professional he may go far...' Sadly, Hardwick was to die in harness at 64, today regarded as a relatively young age. He collapsed with a heart attack at Wyndham's Theatre in London, one Saturday night in October 1983, whilst preparing to go on stage in a play called *Little Lies*.

Another talent in the camp was Lieutenant Ian Tennant, Scots Guards, who would eventually become Sir Ian Tennant, head of Grampian Televison. Born on 11 March 1919, Tennant went to Eton College and after school had gone up to Magdalene College, Cambridge. He had left at the end of the first year of his degree to work in film production at a studio in Welwyn Garden City. He was commissioned into the 2nd Battalion, Scots Guards in 1940, serving as an intelligence officer until his capture at Tobruk. Arriving in Campo 21 at the age of 23, Tennant dedicated much of his time to theatrical and musical productions. Lieutenant David Smith-Dorrien, Sherwood Forresters, and Captain A. C. Glover, Royal Tank Regiment, also worked as producers.

Many people enjoy amateur theatricals, but the theatre in Campo 21 served a far greater purpose than in civilian life. Apart from the actors, a play would provide worthwhile occupations for a considerable number of others. The backstage staff would number many more than the actors, involving a stage management team, props, costumes, scenery and make-up teams. Charles 'Bonzo' Burdon-Taylor became one of the stage managers, and described reading the scripts and studying the set, before training the teams to ensure that the right props were in the right places at the right time. Working on a production gave those involved a focused objective, a sense of team spirit, and it brought a real sense of satisfaction when the play was successfully staged. All these things were difficult to find and foster in the bleak conditions of Campo 21, particularly as winter approached.

A second benefit was simple enjoyment and escapism. The actors and stage staff could become absorbed by the play from an early stage of rehearsal, while the audience could look forward to an evening of enjoyment, and during the performance might escape for an hour or two into a happier world, far from Campo 21. The existence of a thriving theatre also meant a busy costume and scenery department, able to supply costumes and props for other escapist activities, such as fairs, pretend circuses and brass bands.

There was a third, secret, benefit. A theatrical company had a legitimate need for various items which could also help a prisoner to escape. Scenery had to be built, for which tools, timber and paint were needed, and costumes had to be created. Some of the timber might find a secondary purpose shoring up an escape tunnel. Tools were always in demand for all sorts of illicit purposes. Civilian clothing was vital for escapers. Make-up, even of the homemade variety, also had an obvious value. Although inevitably the Italian guards would endeavour to keep a careful eye on the theatrical department, the prisoners became skilled in fooling them and smuggling away the things they needed. From humble beginnings, the Chieti Dramatic Society was to become a major contributor to life in the camp.

Music

Throughout history, and throughout the world, music of all kinds has proved to be a major contributor to the 'feel good' factor of any society. So it would be in Campo 21. Arriving tired, sick and demoralized, the prisoners were uplifted to find that, from the earliest days, there was music in the camp. Tommy Sampson had managed, throughout the trauma and deprivation of the early days of imprisonment, to retain possession of his cornet, and as soon as he arrived in Campo 21, he began to play. Second Lieutenant T. D. 'Tommy' Sampson, Royal Artillery, was another captured at Tobruk. Born in 1918 in Newhaven, Scotland, he came from a Salvation Army background, and began by playing the cornet, and then the trumpet. By the age of 14 he was already in demand as a cornet soloist, and by the age of 18, he was a deputy bandmaster of the Leith Corps Band. He joined up within a few days of war being declared in September 1939, and in 1940, Sampson was sent to Egypt. He took his cornet with him, and was soon playing in local radio broadcasts under the name of 'Sammy Thompson', using the alias so as not to unduly annoy his superior officers. When the order came to surrender, Sampson had slipped his cornet under his battledress, realizing that if he did not take it with him, it might be a very long time indeed before he got his hands on another. Somehow, he managed to keep hold of it – perhaps because of the fact that the Italians loved music. He still had it when he arrived at the transit camp in Bari; he began to play and in no time found himself giving concerts to hundreds of men. Captain A. O. McGinlay MC, Royal Tank Regiment, had been wounded at Tobruk, but was sufficiently recovered to be in the Bari camp at the same time as Sampson. McGinlay could play the piano accordion, and was introduced to Sampson, who was keen to meet him. Sampson asked McGinlay to join him in entertaining the prisoners and McGinlay found himself loaned a padre's piano accordion, which the padre had used to conduct services in the desert. When transferred to Chieti a few weeks later, still in possession of his cornet, Sampson just kept on playing. His was the big band sound – after the war he became a famous bandleader – and as soon as possible after arrival at Campo 21, Sampson began putting together a group of singers and a band. His choir sang close harmony rather than traditional church music. In the stressful and depressing atmosphere of the camp, his Salvation Army background served him well. Others were deeply grateful for the music that he and his singers provided in the early days. McGinlay had also been transferred to Chieti and was delighted to work with Sampson again. He describes Sampson as 'pumping out' handwritten music from which others could work.

There were others with musical talents. Second Lieutenant Anthony Cuthbert Baines, Royal Armoured Corps, was born on 6 October 1912, thus aged 29 when he arrived in Chieti. Baines was a notable musician. His ability had been identified by Sir Thomas Beecham in 1933, when he was only 20, and he had been offered and had accepted the job of bassoon and contra bassoon player in the London Philharmonic Orchestra. He was an expert on all types of wind instruments and was also, by 1942, an experienced orchestral conductor. After the war, he became the world's leading authority on woodwind instruments, and the Curator of the Bate Collection at Oxford University. Baines brought with him a great memory for music and was able to recreate whole symphonies for the emerging camp orchestra. Lieutenant Horace Crabtree, East Surrey Regiment, who arrived in Chieti in February 1943, remembers that the entire score for *HMS Pinafore* was written out from memory, presumably by Baines, and that it was put on with great success. Baines spent most of his time as a conductor and for him one of the greatest luxuries in Campo 21 was the fact that he had, quite literally, a captive orchestra. Everybody had as much time as might be required to rehearse any piece and of course they did not have to be paid a penny for their time. In Campo 21, Baines composed his first symphony. It became possible to buy musical instruments from the Italians and eventually pianos were obtained on hire for the camp. John Speares recalled that so talented were the musical team that when new arrivals came into the camp, they would be asked to whistle or sing any popular new tunes of the day, and those listening were able to write down the music for them.

By late August, enough musicians and instruments had been gathered to enable a weekly outdoor concert to be held. This took place on Saturday evenings at 2000hrs, and was known as 'Saturday Night at Eight'. John Pelley enjoyed his first Saturday night concert on 29 August. Another musician in the camp, a pianist, was Lieutenant John Lepine, Royal Artillery. Lepine became the director of dance and variety music on the Entertainments Committee, and also publicity manager, a job which he said occupied him 24 hours a day, and made life much more bearable.

Art

Campo 21 was particularly fortunate to have amongst its inmates a highly skilled artist, Gordon Horner. Second Lieutenant J. G. E. Horner, Royal Artillery, had been an established artist before the war, and had worked for a time in the North African desert as an official war artist for the *Sunday Chronicle*. He was captured in the desert and transported to Italy, where he bunked with the actor Paul Hardwick – first at Gavi, where they started their career as prisoners because of overcrowding elsewhere, and then at Chieti. After the war, during which he spent nearly three years in captivity, he was persuaded to publish a delightful book of his wartime and prisoner-of-war sketches, which he did privately, entitled *For You the War Is Over*. In Chieti, Horner founded and was the leading light of the Art Club. Initially, of course, it was difficult to obtain the materials to draw or paint with, but once these began to come through in next of kin parcels, or from the YMCA or other charities, art became a growing passion for many in the camp. Second Lieutenant W. E. 'Bill' Bowes, Royal Artillery, wrote: 'Although I do not profess to be either artist or art critic, I have been particularly interested in the doings of our Art Club. They gave us some wonderful exhibitions, and from the first the work of Gordon Horner aroused general admiration. He specialised in charcoal portraits in the early days when we had no paints, and I had the pleasure of sitting for him.' Many of the inmates of Campo 21 joined Horner's art classes, Gordon Lett being one of them. As a result, there still exists a number of drawings and paintings of Campo 21's landmark buildings, such as the water tower and the main compound. Both Horner and his bunk mate, Paul Hardwick, were apparently notorious for being incurably untidy: their double bunk became known to their roommates as 'Slum Corner'. Although Horner blamed Hardwick, he conceded that his own attempts to make fig pudding, together with the odd bits of sketching paper and dirty charcoal littering his bunk did not help. Horner and Hardwick's neighbour was running a food trading business, and complained that Slum Corner lowered the tone of the area!

There were many talented artists in the camp. Their difficulty, however, was finding new subjects to draw and, later, to paint. For a brilliant cartoonist like Horner there were always people to sketch, but for the landscape artist subjects quickly became exhausted. Jack Shepherd soon tired of the few landscapes available to draw in the ample time he had available. There was the view within and without the camp looking north, south, east and west, and various features of it, which could be depicted as they appeared in the different seasons. Having covered these possibilities, Shepherd was grateful to a friend, Lieutenant Dennis Clapp, RASC, who suggested one day that he should imagine he was outside, sitting on the hill below Chieti town and looking down on the camp, and that he should draw it from that perspective, essentially as a feat of imagination. The result was one of the best drawings of the layout of Campo 21 that still exists.

Sport

Sport would eventually become a major part of life in the camp. Many of the prisoners were young, and although the very poor diet substantially reduced their energy, sport could provide them with both a means of keeping fit and a way of passing the time. It was also good, of course, for team spirit and morale. Into Campo 21 arrived some notable sporting figures, at various stages of their careers. The now notorious 'bodyline' cricket tour of Australia in 1932/3 was relatively recent history in 1942, and two of the England cricket squad who had fought and won that series became residents in the camp – Lieutenant Bill Bowes, Royal Artillery and Captain F. R. 'Freddie' Brown, Royal Army Service Corps. Although England teammates, Bowes and Brown were two very different men.

Bowes was a little older, at 34, having been born in Yorkshire in July 1908. Although in the modern era of super-fit cricketers that would be regarded as old, in the 1930s and 40s a cricketer's career would last until he was 40 or more, provided he could avoid injury. Bowes was a big man, standing 6ft 4in. tall, and was a fast bowler by trade. He had first played for England in 1931 and had already enjoyed a distinguished career for the MCC, Yorkshire and England before the war interrupted play. In the 1932 edition of the *Wisden Cricketers' Almanac*, Bowes was named as one of the five cricketers of the year and had the very rare distinction of having bowled out the great Australian batsman Don Bradman, first ball. A railwayman's son, Bowes had been educated at West Leeds High School, followed by a short spell in an estate agent's office, before being signed up as a professional cricketer. Bill Bowes was a married man with children, separated from his family by his captivity. His youngest child had been born in October 1939, just after the outbreak of war, and he had joined up shortly afterwards. Thus Bowes's career in professional cricket was cut off in 1940, at the age of 32, while he was at the top of his game. He faced the frustration of his remaining good years being wasted in captivity. In the daze that followed the surrender of

Tobruk, Bowes emerged to find himself first in the transit camp at Bari, and then in Campo 21. One of the grimmest factors for him was the food ration that the prisoners received, totally insufficient to support his substantial frame. Bowes, however, came of good durable Yorkshire stock, and once in Chieti soon buckled down to combat the mind-wracking, demoralizing boredom of prison life. He was appointed Sports Officer, in charge of organizing camp sporting activities – the only problem being that there was absolutely no sports equipment. He also threw himself into the theatre, taking on a wide variety of parts.

A young Yorkshire colleague of Bowes's, Harold Beaumont, also found himself in Chieti. Beaumont was not an officer, but one of the other ranks (ORs) who worked in the camp. He was eight years younger than Bowes, born in October 1916. He had been a Yorkshire Colt, and was struggling in the hope of establishing himself as a County professional when the war came along. He was a right-hand bat, and a right-hand medium pace bowler. Now in August 1942, having already lost two years of his cricketing career to the war, Beaumont found himself trapped in Campo 21, with no immediate prospect of returning to the game to establish himself. Bowes had at least enjoyed a very successful cricketing career, Beaumont had yet to begin his. Like all professional sportsmen, he knew how competitive his chosen trade was, and that whilst he languished in Chieti, other young and talented cricketers were coming to maturity, who would be his rivals if he was ever released.

At the other end of the scale to Beaumont was Lieutenant C. G. 'Tim' Toppin, Royal Artillery. He was 36, having been born in April 1906. Toppin was a very talented all-round amateur games player. He had briefly played first-class cricket for Worcestershire in the 1926 and 1927 seasons, as a right-handed bat and occasional off spinner. He had also played for the Musketeers, a well-known, wandering Sunday side for whom a number of amateur first-class cricketers turned out (including Freddie Brown of Surrey and England). He was a fearless player, who scorned the use of a box or batting gloves even when facing fast bowling. However, he had never had any pretensions to making a life of professional sport. For him, cricket was just an enjoyable part of life, amongst many other things. A fellow member of the Musketeers, Captain John W. Bowley, Royal Artillery, was also a prisoner in Chieti.

So, too, was Freddie Brown, the England all-rounder. Brown was 31 when he arrived in Chieti; he was born in Peru in December 1910. He had been awarded an MBE in January 1942 for his gallantry in the evacuation of the British Army from Crete. Brown was a single man and very much an amateur cricketer, in the days when cricket still divided itself into 'Gentlemen' and 'Players'. He was schooled privately in England and then attended St John's, Cambridge, where he won a cricket blue. Brown was an aggressive right-hand bat, and a right-arm bowler capable of bowling spin or medium pace. He joined Surrey, where he played under Douglas Jardine, did the double of 1,000 first-class runs and 100 first-class wickets in 1932, and became one of Wisden's Cricketers of the Year in its 1933 edition. Brown had been selected for the 1932/3 MCC (England) tour to Australia and New Zealand, the 'bodyline' tour, but he did not play in the Australian Tests, though he played the two Tests in New Zealand. After the tour, Brown fell out of favour with the selectors, and played less cricket in the following years, concentrating more on his business career. He was recalled to play in the Second Test against New Zealand in 1937, but then dropped again. He achieved his career best bowling figures of 8/34 in a county game against Somerset at Weston-super-Mare, two weeks before war was declared. After the defeat at Dunkirk, a number of one-day matches were arranged at Lord's cricket ground in aid of the Red Cross. On 31 August 1940, Wisden tells us that F. R. Brown opened the batting for the Buccaneers against a British Empire XI at Lord's, because other members of his team had been delayed by the Battle of Britain. He scored 77, including two sixes and eight fours. Bowling spin, Brown then took all the six Empire wickets that fell, before the match was curtailed, again due to the Battle of Britain. Bill Bompas says that Brown was known in the camp as 'Ma' or 'Bruin', and noted in his diary, 'Very kind hearted, big chap, fond of sleep and mah-jong, plus quite a bit of exercise. Has absolutely no side at all, and seldom mentions cricket.' Freddie Brown did agree to give talks on cricket when asked, and later captained one of the sides that played in Chieti, but he was clearly modest about his abilities.

Apart from the cricketers, Chieti held some men well-known for other sports. Captain A. D. S. 'Tony' Roncoroni, Royal Artillery, was an England rugby international, having been capped against Wales, Scotland and Ireland in 1933. He had played as a second row forward, and according to his friend Toby Graham, also a prisoner in Campo 21, was 'the biggest man I have ever seen'. (This did not in due course prevent Roncoroni, also known as 'the Ronc', from joining a tunnel-digging team.) Tony Roncoroni was born in March 1909 and was just 23 when he was first capped for England against Wales at Twickenham in January 1933. He was playing club rugby for Richmond. Ironically, bearing in mind the time he was later to spend in prison camp, the Ronc's captain in his first international was the wing Carl Aarvold, later to become the senior judge at the Old Bailey, and an expert on imprisonment. Playing for Wales that day at centre was an 18-year-old schoolboy, Wilfred Wooller, who later became a renowned cricketer. Wales won the low-scoring game by 7 points to 3 – the first time that they had won at Twickenham for twenty years. The Ronc stayed in the side for the next two internationals, winning one and losing one. Now in his early thirties, he was still a very energetic man.

From the world of boxing came Eddie Wenstob, known as the 'Viking Assassin', a Canadian heavyweight and light heavyweight professional. Born in 1914, Wenstob was 28 when he arrived at Campo 21 and in his physical prime. He had fought in Canada, the United States and in England, and at one stage was rated third in the world as a light heavyweight boxer. His last fight had been on 28 November 1941 in Canada, when after defeating Packy Paul he had announced that he would not fight again, and had gone to war.

It was for the senior sportsmen in the camp to do their best to help and encourage the youngsters, and indeed all the others who were wasting away their lives in Campo 21. Internationals like Bowes, Brown and Roncoroni became role models for them and would often enthral a group of prisoners with reminiscences and anecdotes from their lives in international sport. Reading through the memoirs of those who were imprisoned in Chieti, the name of Bill Bowes in particular stands out. Bowes, a determined and devastating cricketer when he so chose, was described by all those who knew him in Chieti as a genuinely nice man, and the job he did as Sports Officer was much praised. Bowes faced all sorts of problems. There was initially a total lack of equipment and a lack of suitable space for most ball games. The compound was dissected by the main tarmac road, with paths off to the various bungalows. The young trees planted on the open ground further restricted the games that could be played. Men seeking exercise would walk endlessly up and down the central roadway, or around the wall on the safe side of the tripwire. When it was possible to arrange an organized game of some sort, the periods of play had to be kept very short, since their diet denied the men any real energy.

However, mankind will always play games and most games can be adapted to circumstances. So games evolved in Campo 21 which were probably not seen anywhere else in the world. The Italian guards would not initially supply the prisoners with any tools, wood or nails that might be used to make sports equipment such as bats or goals, and in the early days little came through from the Red Cross. A game called 'tenniquoits' evolved, which as its name suggests was a cross between tennis and deck quoits, played with rings over a net. However, at that time the Italians even refused to give them the string they needed to create some sort of net. Also, the prisoners had no balls to play any games with, so Bowes and those working with him were obliged to make their own. To start with, they gathered together a stock of all the cast-off, torn or damaged clothing they could find – though there was precious little of it. Using this, they began to make cloth balls. An old torn shirt was transformed into a rugby ball – Bowes and his team having carefully shaped and stitched it, and stuffed it with more cloth. They then evolved a game which was a cross between rugby and basketball; a goal was scored when the ball was deposited in a fruit basket at either end of the small playing area. Sadly, the cloth ball, fought over by twenty-odd men, did not last long, and when Bowes made other balls in this way, including footballs, they suffered the same fate. Then Bowes discovered that amongst the prisoners in the camp, there was a competent leather worker. Recruiting his services, Bowes then scoured the camp for prisoners wearing leather boots (many had only light desert boots or were barefoot). When a pair was found with proper leather uppers, its owner was persuaded to allow the boots to be cut down to shoes, so that the severed upper sections could be sewn together to make durable, leather-clad balls. In this way, Bowes was able to create suitable balls for most sports – though not yet cricket. In August 1942, these schemes were still in their infancy. Illness swept through the camp with the onset of autumn, and cold and lack of food also reduced the number wishing to play outdoor games. It would not really be until the spring of 1943 that organized sport became a major pastime in the camp. In the meantime, Bowes personally did his best to keep the men as fit as possible and every morning he led a physical training session for his bungalow.

Escape

The duty of every prisoner was to try to escape. The official thinking was that all escape attempts would be likely to tie up extra enemy troops. The chances of any escape being successful were small – they were after all in enemy country, a very long way from home. However, manning the prison camps was a drain on enemy resources and any bid for freedom that got beyond the boundaries would involve more troops to hunt down the escapees. If a few actually succeeded in making a 'home run' so much the better, but the main aim officially was simply to cause the enemy as much trouble as possible.

Of course, for the prisoners, the hope of returning home was the real motivation for escape. Hope was in short supply in prison camp and time was plentiful. Boredom and consequent depression were significant dangers. For regular officers, there was often an additional reason for wanting to escape. As Lieutenant A. A. M. Gregson, a young officer of the Royal Artillery whose training at the Royal Military Academy, Woolwich, had been accelerated by the outbreak of war, put it: 'The fact of being taken prisoner rankled beneath the surface and I spent many hours night and day contemplating how and why one should have fallen captive – it seemed a trifle disgraceful. Consequently the desire to escape was ever present. One was conscious of the fact that this war was "the be all and end all" of life for a regular soldier and to be locked out of it was disgraceful.' Gregson and many other regular soldiers longed to get back to the action.

Thus, as soon as prisoners began to arrive at Campo 21 plans for escape began to be laid. Most, if not all, of those arriving at the camp were quite recently captured and therefore had no experience of captivity, and of the potential weaknesses of prison camp regimes, but nonetheless many had already tried to escape. The motto was 'the sooner the better'. Lett, for example, had been involved not only in an evasion and escape attempt in North Africa, but also a 'through the wire' escape attempt at the transit prison camp at Bari. Most favoured were escape attempts whilst travelling – pragmatic efforts when a suitable opportunity seemed to present itself. A later arrival in Campo 21, Captain Michael Gilbert, Royal Horse Artillery, had escaped from the train bringing him from a transit camp at Capua to Chieti. He had disguised himself in a mocked-up German desert uniform, but unfortunately damaged his ankle when jumping from the train and was quickly recaptured. Gilbert was a little older than of many of Campo 21's inmates, born in July 1912. He had been schooled at Blundell's School in Tiverton, Devon, and later attended the University of London. He had worked as a schoolteacher for a few years before deciding to become a solicitor. Captured in the Western Desert, Gilbert was one of those who intended to do everything that he could to escape.

Once in Chieti, for a hard core of the prisoners, escape remained their main objective – the challenge that eased the burden of captivity. In essence, there were four ways of escaping from a prison camp: over the wire or wall, through the wire or wall, under the wire or wall, or out of the gate. The high walls that surrounded Chieti generally ruled out the option of going 'through the wire' (although there were a few exceptions as we shall see), and going over it would be very difficult. The wall was a high one and there were guard towers at regular intervals. Thus the real options were to somehow get through the main gate, or to go under the wall by means of a tunnel. Since Chieti was a brand new camp, and not originally built for the purpose to which it was now being put, some of the new arrivals in the camp hoped that they would be able to take advantage of the 'bedding down' process to bamboozle their way through the gate. Also, there was a potential advantage, denied in many camps, arising from the solidly built bungalows that the prisoners were to inhabit. In purpose built camps, such as the German Stalag Luft III from which the famous Great Escape was mounted, the prison huts were deliberately built on stilts to prevent tunnelling. In Chieti, the bungalows were solidly built from ground level, so in theory it would be possible to dig straight down into the ground from within.

Escapes from prison camp were usually the result of a team effort. In Chieti, before long an Escape Committee was set up to oversee all escape attempts. Since internally the prisoners remained under British military discipline, all would be escapees had to apply for permission for their attempt to the committee, and to present an outline of their plan for approval. Sometimes a plan would be approved, sometimes it would not. The Escape Committee had to consider how practical the plan was, its chances of success, and whether it might compromise other escape attempts. Also, the committee had to bear in mind that escape attempts usually brought reprisals from the camp guards in the form of extra parades, aggressive searches of prisoners' personal possessions, and sometimes worse. As in most prison camps, there were many in Chieti who succumbed to lethargy and inactivity, and who resolved simply to 'sit it out' until the end of the war. These men resented any interference with their routines and would be most unhappy if feckless escape attempts resulted in trouble for them.

The Escape Committee was in a position to provide considerable help and support to those whose plans it approved. From a would-be escaper's point of view there were two distinct stages to be dealt with: first, how to get out of the camp itself, and then how to get home. Once beyond the walls, unlike High Command in London, the prisoners had no interest in how many enemy troops might be redeployed from other duties to search for them – they were just looking for a realistic chance to get out of enemy territory. Thus, very careful preparation was required both for the escape itself, and for the subsequent journey home. The Escape Committee organized and utilized an extensive support network for escapees. Escaped prisoners would need civilian clothing, food, a map, a compass, identity papers and passes for the journey –

and if possible, money. These would usually be prepared by others with the necessary expertise. Maps were the responsibility of Captain Pat Spooner, Royal Armoured Corps, and were usually copied from the silk maps smuggled into the camp by arriving aircrew. Aircrew, who obviously always faced the danger of being shot down in enemy territory, were trained in evasion techniques and supplied with escape kits. These would include a map of the relevant part of Europe or North Africa printed on a silk handkerchief, with all significant towns marked. When shot down, they could either use these immediately to try to evade capture and get back to friendly or neutral territory or, if captured, conceal them to assist in a future escape. Some aircrew managed to smuggle such maps into Campo 21 and, later, parachutists who arrived in the camp as a result of the Tunisian campaign also brought maps with them. Spooner's job was to get them copied as accurately as possible, and he ran a network of artists with the necessary skills. Lieutenant John Joel, Green Howards, was one. By way of a preliminary examination, he was asked to copy a silk map onto paper. His effort was considered up to standard, so he returned the original and began making more copies of his master copy. Joel explained the difficulties of his work – three lookouts were needed: one at each end of the corridor that ran through the bungalow where he was working, and one outside the window. If the alarm was raised, everything had to be hidden away. It was slow work. Another who worked on maps was Lieutenant Gordon Norbrook, Royal Worcestershire Regiment. Norbrook was 21 years old when captured in North Africa. He had been schooled at St Paul's School in London, and had only just started at the Midland Bank (now a part of HSBC) when war broke out. His service had included sand-bagging Falmouth and Gyllynvale Bay in Cornwall in the early months of the war where he met the sweetheart who was to become his wife after the war. When Norbrook was posted to North Africa, their romance had to be continued by post. The Norbrook family was one of the few lucky ones. Following Gordon's capture they were informed that he was missing on 28 July 1942, but within days received notification that he was a prisoner in the hands of the Italians. Eager to get out of Campo 21, Norbrook became a member of a tunnel team, disposing of the soil that was dug out.

George Hervey-Murray was one of those who made compasses, using broken razor blades, a pin and the base of a Gillette razor which contained a magnet. Hervey-Murray was a good craftsman and an experienced sailor. He was asked by the Escape Committee to instruct other prisoners on how to sail the sort of craft that they might be able to steal from the Italian coast after escaping from the camp. Hervey-Murray duly built a model of such a sailing boat, and during sessions of the Chieti Yacht Club used it to teach novices how to sail – in theory, at least. As it turned out, he learned of no prisoner who successfully escaped and was able to put his teaching into practice.

Assistance was also gained from MI9, the British Intelligence department whose duty it was to help escapers. This department was under the command of Colonel Norman Crockatt DSO, MC, an experienced and heroic soldier of the First World War. Its charter made it responsible for: a) facilitating escapes of British prisoners of war, thereby getting back service personnel, and containing additional enemy manpower on guard duties; b) facilitating the return to the United Kingdom of those who succeeded in evading capture in enemy territory – mainly aircrew who had crashed or been shot down; c) collecting and distributing information; d) assisting in the denial of information to the enemy; and e) maintaining morale amongst the British prisoners of war in enemy prison camps. MI9 was founded early in the war, and grew in line with the size and complexity of its task as the war progressed.

As time passed, MI9 would try different methods of sending escape materials into the camp secretly, concealed in parcels for the prisoners. Crockatt issued an embargo on any of his team sending such items in Red Cross food parcels – nothing should jeopardize these, so vital were they to the well-being of the prisoners. However, the Red Cross acted as a neutral post office to forward all parcels, including those sent by families and charitable organizations, and it was in these that the escape materials would be concealed. Alongside organizations such as the YMCA, which often sent sporting equipment and books into the camps, MI9 invented a variety of family members for the prisoners, who would send 'next of kin' packages containing exciting items. They also invented a number of charitable organizations and sent 'doctored' parcels under their names. If a baseball or cricket bat arrived in camp, it might be found to have a doctored handle, in which it was possible to conceal a screwdriver or other small tool. Tins of Canadian powdered milk, called KLIM (milk spelt backwards) might carry a silk map or other useful document secreted under its ordinary label. The many items sent covertly by MI9, included blankets which could be shaved down to look like ordinary civilian checked cloth and could be used to make suits. A number of such items reached Campo 21. Another example was a magnet which could be used in the making of compasses, something which together with the maps was vital for a successful escape.

In some ways, the battle between the prisoners of war and their captors was an unequal one. The camp guards, and indeed the Commandants, were second- or third-rate troops who were unsuitable for one reason or another to serve in the front line. In contrast, many of the prisoners were very able men indeed. Two significant advantages that the Escape Committee had were the huge pool of highly talented individuals within the camp, and the amount of time that they had available. The prisoners in Chieti came from every walk of life, and as in any community of more than a thousand people, their skills were extremely varied. They included artists, engineers, miners, electricians and cooks. Artists became forgers of documents, miners and engineers became tunnellers, and cooks prepared the 'escape cakes' – a form of consolidated, high-energy ration designed to sustain a man on the run. Further, as the months passed, those intent on escape often took the opportunity to learn some Italian. Classes were given by Italian speakers as a part of the academic side of Chieti life. Thus, if an escape plan was approved by the committee, considerable resources could be employed to increase its chances of success. On occasion, since it was an official camp committee and the camp was subject internally to British military discipline, the Escape Committee could order people to help a team of escapers by performing essential tasks. This was rarely necessary, but when large support teams were required, for instance watchers or spoil disposal men for a tunnel, if a man was 'asked' to help, he did not really have an option.

MI9 also developed a method of communicating with prisoners of war by means of codes, and later radio messages – many of the camps eventually managed to construct a secret radio receiver. The second SBO at Chieti, Lieutenant Colonel William Marshall, 5 Mahratta Light Infantry, was later to confirm that Chieti had acquired such a radio. Gordon Norbrook remembered the secret radio, which he referred to as 'our canary'. So far as codes were concerned, pilots, particularly of fighter planes, were instructed in MI9 codes as a part of their training. Other selected personnel also went into prison already armed with codes to enable them to communicate secretly with MI9. One was Captain D. S. Carmichael, Indian Army, who was captured while out with an advanced fact finding unit supporting the Long Range Desert Group. There were different codes of course, and they changed over time – the one he was given involved the use of every fourth and sixth word written into a letter home. He used the code to report anything he saw which he thought might possibly be useful to the Allies – for instance, a large concentration of enemy vehicles in a particular place, or significant troop movements. These things might be observed by him, or others, when travelling between camps. In reply, Carmichael received words of encouragement and general information as to how the war was going, but in his case never anything that proved to be of significance. Additionally, some prisoners had taken the precaution of having already instructed their families in a simple code of their own, so if need arose they could send messages that would get past the censor. Information sent secretly to a prisoner's family by such means would often then be passed on by the family to MI9. As we shall see, the prisoners also developed other methods of obtaining up-to-date information on the outside world.

Once outside the camp, the first question for an escapee would be which way to go. For those in Chieti, in the late summer and autumn of 1942, there were limited options: go north and attempt to cross into neutral Switzerland, or perhaps into Yugoslavia to join the partisans there, or head for the coast and try to steal a boat to get away by sea. Another option was to head for the Vatican State in Rome, which remained neutral, but that would probably simply have swapped one prison for another, in the sense that getting home from there would have been extremely difficult. Once decided, the escapee would then have to consider how to travel. The coast could be reached on foot, but for greater distances the popular method was the train. Thus forged papers would need to be in order and cash would be required.

Cash presented a problem, which in due course MI9 tried to address. Although officer prisoners continued nominally to receive their pay whilst in prison camp, it was really a book-keeping system. The only cash officially allowed to prisoners was a camp currency, which was worthless outside the walls. When Red Cross parcels eventually began to arrive, their contents would become of considerable value for barter purposes, particularly cigarettes and chocolate. However, an escaper couldn't buy a rail ticket with cigarettes. MI9 therefore tried to send in hidden cash wherever possible.

An additional difficulty that an escaped prisoner always faced in Italy was that a *straniere*, a foreigner, always stood out. This was far less of a problem in Germany, where there was a substantial labour force drawn from many occupied European countries. In Italy, however, there were few foreign workers and the Italians, with their strong sense of style, always seemed able to tell if an outsider was amongst them. Also, Italians were habitually inquisitive, and would ask all sorts of questions of their fellow travellers as a matter of course. As a result, it was preferable to stay under cover and to travel on foot at night, rather than risk being unmasked by fellow passengers on the trains. Even on foot, escapers faced the considerable danger of bumping into civilians, or alerting the dogs as they passed by a village. Very few indeed had a command of Italian good enough to fool a village population. This situation would not change until after the Italian Armistice of September 1943.

In August 1942, as the inmates arrived in batches by railway at Chieti Scalo station and were marched along the road to the camp, all such considerations lay in the future. As the camp settled down, the simple objective for most was to adjust to the life that they now faced, and to find a way of coping. There were a few, however, for whom the prospect of escape was all that mattered, and they began straight away to plan how they might breach the security of the Italian guards. It was not very long before the escape attempts started.

Month 2

September 1942

SETTLING IN AND THE *RIVOLTA*

With the coming of September, things were beginning to settle down in Campo 21, although new prisoners continued to arrive and the camp became increasingly full. The greater the numbers, the more acute the shortage of water became. It is perhaps difficult for the modern reader to identify with such a problem, since except in a time of national or local disaster, the availability of water for drinking and washing is automatically assured. It is only when we suddenly lose such a benefit, that we realize how vital it is. Some of this book was written at the author's house in the village of Chiesa di Rossano, high in the Tuscan mountains, where the population of the village rises dramatically in the hot summer months, when many Italian families come there to escape the heat of the plains. The water supply becomes overstretched, and from time to time the supply is turned off for six to eight hours. All of a sudden, one realizes how dependent we all are now (at least in the West) on having running water – to wash, to flush the lavatory or to fill a glass when one is thirsty. This is what the inmates of Campo 21 simply did not have. Consumption of drinking water had to be carefully planned. Queues for the taps during the short period when they functioned were long. Water from the well could be used for washing one's body or clothes, but that too had to be queued for, and if you only had one pair of shorts (often the case) then washing them would leave you near naked, or perhaps wrapped in a blanket. The everyday problems caused by lack of water were acute.

The command structure amongst the prisoners was now well established. Lieutenant Colonel C. E. Gray, 3 Ghurka Rifles, was the SBO, the camp adjutant was Major A. D. MacKenzie, Camerons, and the assistant adjutant was a Captain Hall. The important role of chairman of the internal Red Cross Committee, who dealt with Red Cross parcels, was filled by Captain J. MacKenzie, Royal Artillery, who soon became known as 'Red Cross Mac'. As has been said, Red Cross parcels were of vital importance to the prisoners. Rations supplied by their captors proved to be very basic, and the Red Cross food supplies were formulated to give the best dietetic value. It was intended that each man should receive one parcel per week, but that virtually never happened in Campo 21. A typical British parcel would contain a ¼ lb packet of tea, a tin of cocoa, a bar of chocolate, a tinned pudding, a tin of meat roll, a tin of processed cheese, a tin of condensed milk, a tin of dried egg, a tin of sardines or herrings, a tin of preserve, a tin of margarine, a tin of sugar, a tin of vegetables, a tin of biscuits, and a bar of soap. Cigarette parcels were sent separately. Parcels would also come from other Allied countries – the Canadians would include tins of KLIM powdered milk, much valued both for their content and for the size and shape of the tin. Tins from Red Cross parcels (apart from their contents) proved a very useful source material for the prisoners, as did the boxes themselves and the string used to tie them up.

The theatre was in full swing, the Saturday Night at Eight concert was a regular fixture for many of the prisoners, and the education classes were going from strength to strength. Nonetheless, John Pelley noted in his diary on 6 September that the cigarette situation was getting quite desperate, and on 8 September that there was less and less food. The lack of good food had obvious effects, but the significance of a lack of cigarettes in the war years was out of all proportion to what it would be today. In 1942, nobody suggested that smoking was not good for you and the large majority of servicemen smoked, as did their Italian guards and most of the civilian population. Cigarettes were considered one of the essential comforts of a prisoner of war, and specific cigarette parcels were despatched to all the camps. Smoking is addictive under any circumstances and was made more so by the boredom of the camp. Thus in Campo 21, as in many other camps, cigarettes became a form of currency both for trade between prisoners and also for bribing the Italian guards. However, the supplies were irregular and unpredictable and when cigarettes were in short supply tempers would become easily frayed. Heavy smokers would eternally be on the scrounge for discarded cigarette butts and the prisoners tried smoking other things such as dried tea leaves, which apparently smelt dreadful. The artists were those men who could break down a factory-made cigarette and re-roll it into two or more 'greyhounds' – thin self-rolled cigarettes often made using pages from books. September was a particularly bad month in Chieti; Pelley recorded on the 25th, 'Cigarettes now extinct in the camp.' This may well have been the doing of Captain Croce, who would simply hold parcels and post in the office until he felt like distributing them. Also, although there is no clear evidence of this, it is likely that Croce would keep back mail for a particular prisoner whom he did not like, or had identified as a troublemaker. Certainly, Gordon Lett, whom Frank Osborne was later to describe as Croce's Public Enemy No. 1, suffered from a lack of post and parcels from home for many months.

Each bungalow had its own noticeboard, used for many different communal purposes such as to advertise events, or to post messages seeking news of friends or colleagues. One of the slightly older prisoners, Captain Arthur Green, Adjutant of the 11th Regiment, Honorable Artillery Company (HAC), compiled an archive of these notices and messages which illustrates many aspects of camp life. Arthur Green was born on 5 November 1911, and was therefore 30 years of age when captured at Mersa Matruh on 28 June 1942, whilst trying to rescue a wounded soldier. He was a chartered surveyor who had served as a territorial in the HAC since 1932 and had been commissioned in 1939. Green got married on 12 September 1941, exactly two weeks before he sailed with his regiment for North Africa. Now, nearly a year later, he faced an indefinite period of imprisonment many hundreds of miles away from his bride. For her part, she would know nothing of his fate for many months, having been informed that he was missing, believed dead.

One of the notices that Arthur Green kept concerned an officer of the Hussars, and said simply: 'Information is being sought by the parents of 2/Lt F.L.Coleman, Hussar, who is suffering from a head wound and is believed to be in hospital in Italy. Will any officer who may be able please furnish details to 2/Lt D Grimblett E5/4/39 or Captain F Earle, E 3/2.' Coleman does not appear in the list of prisoners still held in Italy in August 1943. Sadly, it seems he never made it out of North Africa. The Commonwealth War Graves Memorial at El Alamein records that Second Lieutenant Francis Laurin Coleman, of the Royal Armoured Corps, died aged 21 years on 2 June 1942.

A more common use for the noticeboards was for trade. A prisoner would list what he had to 'sell' and what he wanted in exchange. On a sample list kept by Arthur Green, Lieutenant Richard Edmonston Low, Royal Artillery, wanted to exchange Canadian biscuits for milk, D. Buckley: Klim (Canadian powdered milk), condensed milk or Canadian biscuits for English tobacco, C. Meehan:

Canadian biscuits for cigarettes. Cigarettes were always the most sought after item.

The diarist, John Pelley, also suffered from the shortage of cigarettes, but was throwing himself into theatrical life. On 9 September, his diary records that there was a dress rehearsal for his sketch: 'During the passionate love scene, my brassiere broke, and my false bosoms rolled nonchalantly across the stage, closely followed by the couch breaking, depositing Mac and myself in a struggling heap … it was a screaming success with the critics.' Despite his comment on 8 September that food was getting less and less, Pelley enjoyed 'an enormous birthday tea' on the 11th. For occasions such as a birthday, a prisoner and his closer friends would save up some rations, going even hungrier for a few days, and scrounge others, in order to have a decent celebratory meal on the day.

Food generally was sparse and of poor quality. Captain Douglas Flowerdew, Royal Artillery, who was in charge of mess arrangements until he was transferred out of the camp just before Christmas, said simply: 'The food was rotten, cooking facilities were very bad, fuel was short and the Italians unhelpful.' In queues for food and water, democracy prevailed. Senior officers had no precedence over their juniors. If a lieutenant colonel found himself at the back of a queue behind a group of subalterns, that is where he stayed. A significant part of the ration was the rice issue, which was always full of weevils. In September, the rations issued by the Italians could be supplemented with fruit bought into the camp from local traders. Figs and grapes were particularly plentiful but they, and other fresh fruit, caused bowel problems amongst the prisoners. There was always a variety of forms of dysentery in the camp, not helped by the dreadful latrines, swarms of flies and generally insanitary conditions. A lot of the men suffered bouts of illness with distended stomachs, a form of oedema. But when the fruit season was over at the end of September, they became extremely hungry. Lieutenant G. B. Fisher, Royal Armoured Corps, commented that with the lack of protein in their diets many prisoners suffered from sores caused simply by malnourished skin and which failed to heal. Medical supplies in the camp 'hospital' were few. There were no antibiotics and a shortage of bandages. If a bandage was taken off a wound so that it could be treated or inspected by a doctor, the same soiled bandage would have to be re-used after the treatment. For many, there were no bandages at all, and in winter, this would cause considerable discomfort. George Hervey-Murray arrived in Campo 21 with minor injuries to his legs which did not heal, but developed into very nasty 'desert sores' or ulcers. They became so large and deep that it was very painful for him to walk or even stand.

He attended the hospital, and for a time was an inmate, but there was little that the doctors could do. Hervey-Murray was unable to stand during roll calls, and with other injury cases was allowed to sit on the steps of the bungalows. He suffered throughout the winter and his wounds only began to heal properly the following spring.

Pelley notes that on 7 September, a hundred of the inmates were allowed to go for their first walk in the countryside surrounding the camp, under heavy escort. The officers had to give their parole, promising not to try to escape whilst they were outside the camp. This parole was never broken, but apart from the pleasure of going outside the walls such walks also provided very valuable intelligence for future escapes. The 4-metre-high wall around Campo 21 meant that the prisoners could learn little from inside about the immediate terrain that they would have to face, if and when they got out – they could see only the hills and mountains that rose above the wall far in the distance. Walks were stopped shortly after this, however, when the escape attempts began.

Another young officer, Freer Roger was one of many finding the conditions of Campo 21 hard to endure. He commented that there was absolutely no comfort or privacy, and that the prisoners had to keep such clothing and possessions as they had in old Red Cross boxes under their bunks. There was no furniture in the rooms for storage. A convention grew up that if a man sat down and covered himself with a blanket, then he should not be disturbed because he needed some privacy. This was the only way an inmate could retreat into a world of his own, however briefly. The tension in the camp continued to rise through the first half of September. Men such as Harold Sell resented the way that, in their view, the SBO, Lieutenant Colonel Gray, was too accommodating with the Italians. This was not an uncommon complaint in the camps and was often unjustified; the SBO had to judge for himself how to get the most out of a camp commandant, and sometimes an apparent policy of appeasement would result in more opportunities for escape or better facilities for his men. Gray was feeling his way in his new and challenging command.

Toby Graham recalled that it was in September that the Italians started a canteen, where the prisoners could buy extra food. He described it thus:

Prices were exorbitant and only a small quantity of food was sold. On one occasion they produced some condensed milk for us at a cost of about a shilling a mouthful, knowing at this stage that we would have paid anything to get it. [In 1942, a labourer's wages would often be just shillings a day, and the average wage was £6 a week. In modern currency, a shilling represents 5p]. Another time, some powder like Horlicks appeared at quite a reasonable price. After about a month, when everyone had been gorging on it, they suddenly announced that owing to a misunderstanding about the decimal point the price was ten times as much as they had originally stated. In this way the Italian commandant and his henchmen made a very good living out of us, for it cost us practically our whole income to keep alive.

Jack Shepherd remembered that the Italians wrapped biscuits that were already rotten with weevils in shiny silver paper and sold them to the unknowing prisoners for 10 old pence (just under a shilling) each. Lieutenant Arthur Gilmore wrote home to his brother in England giving his new address of Campo 21, in a letter that slipped by the censor, begging for food. His brother, the Reverend Norman Gilmore, sent the letter on to the Admiralty, saying; 'Coming from one who has always been quite exceptionally uninterested in this subject [food], it would seem to indicate that the Red Cross parcels are probably not getting through to P.G.21.' The Admiralty passed the letter on to the War Office, asking to be kept informed, and expressing the hope that the problem was simply due to PG 21 being a new camp.

Toby Graham was a would-be escaper and describes the difficulties that faced prisoners who were trying to gather together an escape kit – maps, a compass and so forth. Many of these items would be created covertly in the camp but they then had to be successfully concealed somewhere, so that they would not be found during the regular random searches by the guards. For a while it was noted that the South African bungalow was spared these searches, as the Italians tried to drive a wedge between the South Africans and the other Allied prisoners in the camp. Therefore, a lot of maps and compasses were concealed there. Sadly, after about a month the policy changed and the South African bungalow was also searched, resulting in a large haul for the Italians. The guards were always alert to possible hiding places in the compound and it was common to see the *carabinieri* digging, under the direction of a sentry who had seen a prisoner apparently burying something. Hunting for mapmakers, they would mount surprise raids, running into the camp at the double, surrounding a bungalow and commencing a search before those working on maps could hide them away.

Baiting the guards and making their life as difficult as possible became a fine art, risky though it often was. The younger prisoners in particular drew a childlike pleasure out of this. Toby Graham describes how he and his roommates in bungalow 5 always tried to confuse the Italian who took their roll call, springing a new trick on him virtually every day. They would stand in five rows when being counted, and if each row swayed, first, third and fifth from left to right, and second and fourth from right to left, it would become almost impossible for the guard to count those present without entering between the lines of men. Alternatively, all the tall men would stand in the front row, blotting out any real view of those behind. The guard tried to get around these problems by counting pairs of feet, since these did not move and could be seen by bending down. The prisoners counteracted this by producing an odd boot to place in the line, so that the guard ended up counting half a body to spare. They were undoubtedly juvenile, but these little games brought Toby Graham and his companions a lot of pleasure. In a small way, they could feel they were striking back.

Generally, the prisoners looked to do anything that would keep them occupied and pass the time. Captain N. L. 'Mac' MacLucas, Cameron Highlanders, was one of many who spent much time playing cards. Any game would do, although bridge gradually became a favourite, because of its complexities and the time that it took. MacLucas recalled learning a different sort of card-playing lesson, however – never play snap with pilots, their reactions would be far quicker than yours!

Commandant Barela was keen to impose his authority on the Allied officers now in his charge. He adopted a habit of riding through the camp on his bicycle, expecting all the prisoners to stand and salute him as he went by – these salutes he acknowledged with a casual wave of the hand. This was enormously irritating for the Allied prisoners. Unfortunately, the Commandant had not made himself very popular with his own men, and one of the *carabinieri* dropped a friendly hint to the prisoners that Barela was being carefully watched from Rome, and if he made a single mistake in running the camp, he was likely to be relieved of his command and sent to fight in North Africa. Thus armed, the men watched for an opportunity to embarrass the Commandant.

The first escape attempt from the Chieti camp came on 13 September. Captain John Meares, Indian Armoured Corps, had been sizing up the chances of getting out of the main gates and found a way he thought would work. After more than five weeks, there had as yet been no attempt at escape and the guards were perhaps a little over confident. John Meares had noted a supply lorry that brought fruit and vegetables to the camp every day. It would pass through the outer gate (shared with the Italian garrison) and the inner gate (guarding access to the prisoners' compound) without hold-ups. Meares believed that, since it was still relatively early days and both the guards and the prisoners were still settling into their routines, there were flaws in the security systems of which the camp guards were not yet aware. The fruit and vegetable lorry duly entered the prisoners' compound on Sunday, 13 September, and offloaded its cargo at the cookhouse store. Whilst the lorry was stationary, Meares managed to crawl unseen beneath it, and wrap himself around its undercarriage. His plan was to drop off the lorry once he was well clear of the camp and make his bid for freedom. He had collected together enough food to sustain himself for some days once he was out. The lorry duly pulled away and moved slowly out of the camp, passing through the inner and outer gates without challenge – moments of unbearable tension for its concealed passenger.[1]

Nearby the gates was the small village of Chieti Scalo, which stood around the railway station of the same name and, unluckily for Meares, since it was Sunday (always a festival day in 1940s Italy) the driver of the lorry, his work done, decided to stop at a local hostelry for a glass of wine. Thus in the middle of a village, the unfortunate Meares was left trying to hang on to the undercarriage of the lorry whilst its driver relaxed and refreshed himself. How long Meares was there is not clear, but not surprisingly he was soon spotted by a local, who drew the military's attention to his presence under the vehicle. Being still no real distance from the camp, he was quickly re-arrested and marched back through the gates, destined for 30 days in the 'cooler', which was the standard maximum sentence for an escape attempt. Unfortunately, he was carrying a number of tinned foods from Red Cross parcels to sustain him on the run and of course these were discovered. Accordingly, Lieutenant Colonel Barela, the Commandant, and Captain Croce, the all-controlling Interpreter and camp Security Officer, took the view that allowing prisoners to have Red Cross parcels unopened was a risk to security – they decreed that in future all parcels and the individual tins that

---

[1] I should note here that one of the problems with all records of events is that for the inmates the camp was undoubtedly something of a gossip factory, plagued by rumours of all kinds. Thus, there are differing accounts of virtually every major event that occurred, and it is often difficult to identify the real eye witnesses. In telling the story of Chieti I have done my best to identify and distil an accurate account of each major event.

they contained should be opened by the guards and their contents distributed to the prisoners, so that the food had a limited life and could not so easily be hoarded. This measure affected all the prisoners and led to much resentment. From that time, each man was allowed to possess only two used tins – one as a drinking vessel and one to act as a feeding bowl. When the contents of a Red Cross tin were tipped out into a feeding bowl by the camp guards, the food had to be consumed almost at once, and if the prisoner were lucky enough to receive two Red Cross tins at the same time, the contents, whatever they might be, were simply dumped into the bowl together.

The frustration of the prisoners at the behaviour of their captors increased by the day. Harold Sell noted, 'The day of challenge is approaching fast.' It arrived after the failure of the first escape. As usual, there was a morning rollcall on the following day, 14 September. It was a hot sunny day. The men lined up outside their bungalows, facing outwards, backs to their block. The Senior British Officer, Lieutenant Colonel Gray, and his adjutant, stood in front of the parade, to greet the Commandant when he arrived. On this particular morning, after the rollcall had been satisfactorily completed, Commandant Barela decided to instruct the Allied prisoners on the Italian method of bringing a parade to attention. Through Interpreter Croce, Barela told Lieutenant Colonel Gray that upon the sounding of a bugle call in the Italian fashion the parade must come to attention, and that they would practise the procedure there and then. Grey explained to the men what was about to happen, to much disgruntlement but some laughter from the prisoners. Barela's order was in fact contrary to the Geneva and Hague Conventions, which stipulated that prisoners should respond only to orders given by their own officers. Proper procedure was that the Commandant should ask the SBO to call the prisoners to attention, not attempt to do it himself. The bugler duly sounded the Italian equivalent of the general salute and the parade came raggedly to attention. Unwisely, rather than leave matters there, Barela insisted that the parade must do it again to a better standard. Again the bugle sounded and the parade shuffled even more raggedly to attention. Captain Croce picked out one of the prisoners whom he apparently felt was not making sufficient effort, a British lieutenant who belonged to Bungalow 4, and went over to rebuke him. Just what was said between the two is not certain. Lett, in his diary, describes the incident as follows: 'The officer… told him bluntly that he had no intention of obeying any orders that were not given to him by a British Senior Officer. Croce became very angry, and fixing his monocle in his eye…made the rather inane remark: "I don't like nasty things,

I like nice things" and then went and complained to the Italian Commandant, whereupon the officer was placed under the escort of five soldiers armed with rifles and bayonets and marched off to the punishment cell.' The lieutenant's departure was accompanied by applause from the remaining prisoners, and shouts of 'Good luck', and 'We'll be joining you'.

Barela then announced that the parade's movements were not smart enough and that they would have to try yet again. The third attempt was predictably even worse than the first two, as the prisoners' patience ran out. Barela then said, through Croce, that the parade must come to attention at the bugle call smartly, and that if they did so at once he would dismiss the parade. He also made promises that if they behaved he would do what he could to remedy various defects in the camp, such as the poor sanitation and lack of water. Otherwise, Barela warned, the men would have to stay on parade until he was satisfied with their performance.

Bungalow 5, the nearest to the Italian quarters, was already known as the Bad Boys Bungalow. From their assembled ranks came the cry: 'We'll stay!', which was quickly taken up by the rest of the parade. All the men stood at ease and began to chat amongst themselves, to the fury of Barela. He now lost all self control, and shouted out, 'Rivolta!' – revolt or mutiny. He ordered the camp alarm to be sounded and the whole of the guard turned out. They arrived at the double, surrounding the men on parade, with bayonets fixed. Knowing that if things got really serious he and his guards were outnumbered, Barela also sent a message to the garrison in Chieti town, requesting reinforcements. Lieutenant Colonel Gray then held a conference with the bungalow commanders, that ended in a warning from him to the prisoners that they could go on doing what they were doing, but must be careful not to use violence or insulting language. The men on parade then decided to sit down.

Commandant Barela now saw that he might lose this battle, and made an offer to the South African contingent that they could return to their hut. The Italians knew that after the surrender of Tobruk there had been some suspicion and bad feeling among the rest of the Allies against the South Africans, a feeling that the surrender had not been necessary and that South African support for the Allied cause was half-hearted. Barela was using this knowledge to try to drive a wedge between the South Africans and the other Allied prisoners. The South Africans, however, were having none of it. They announced that they preferred to stay where they were, and did so. For the prisoners, this was the first real test of the authority of Barela against their collective will, and a most important psychological moment for them. Barela, on the other hand, realized that he was in danger of losing control in front of his own men. It was an impasse. After another half an hour nothing had changed, so Barela and Gray were forced to reach a compromise, which was in reality a victory for the prisoners. Gray announced to the men that, as SBO, he would now give the order for them to come to attention, and once they had done so, they could dismiss. The prisoners rose to their feet and upon the order from Lieutenant Colonel Gray they came smartly to attention, then returned to their bungalows. Barela had lost the battle and thereafter never again tried to impose his bugle call. On future parades, the officers would be brought to attention by an order from their own commanding officer, and would not be expected to respond to orders to do so from Colonel Barela.

Barela's arrogance and stupidity had given the prisoners a very valuable opportunity to demonstrate their solidarity and collective will. In normal life it would seem a very small victory, but in the oppressive conditions of Campo 21 it was an important declaration that they remained a united Allied force and that, though held captive, they would not allow themselves to be diminished by trivial and unnecessary orders. Morale amongst the camp inmates had received a notable boost and the incident of the *rivolta* is one that most prisoners remembered for years afterwards.

FARRELL'S ESCAPE

Despite the failure of John Meares' escape attempt on 13 September and the trial of strength between Barela and his prisoners on the morning of 14 September, the next attempt took place later that same day. A young lieutenant from the Durham Light Infantry, Joseph Farrell, had been laying his plans for some time. Farrell apparently spoke good Italian, but had deliberately kept that fact secret during his imprisonment, foreseeing that to do so could bring him certain advantages. His captors might, of course, speak amongst themselves more freely if they thought that the prisoners could not understand, and there were other potential bonuses. Farrell had watched the comings and goings at the main gates with great care over the few weeks he had been in the camp and he had learned the guards' routine. He knew that the guards were as yet not familiar with the appearance of most of the prisoners, or even of their fellow guards. Following the fall of Tobruk, and during the transit period which had included a period in the Bari Camp, a number of the luckier Allied prisoners had been supplied with items of Italian military clothing to replace their own worn out desert kit. Without great difficulty, Farrell was able to gather together a complete Italian uniform. Dressed in this, he planned to use his good Italian to bluff his way out of the camp. After the morning revolt on 14 September, he duly put on the uniform and simply walked out, apparently talking his way through the prisoners' gate, and then passing through the main gate on to the road. No doubt the hairs on his neck stood up as he walked down the road towards the railway station, listening for shots or shouts from behind him. He knew, as they all did, that escapers could be lawfully shot in the attempt. Neither shots nor shouts came, and Joseph Farrell walked calmly out of sight of Campo 21 and on to the station. For the time being he was free.

For many escapees, the greatest problems were likely to be met outside the camp. Italy was an enemy country and in September 1942 its morale was still relatively high. The battle for North Africa was in full swing and Rommel had scored a number of significant victories, including Tobruk. The most obvious option for an escaper was to head north, in the hope of being able to cross the border into Switzerland and the quickest way to get there was by train. The rule of thumb was to trust no one and to travel by as direct a route as possible. Nonetheless, the Italians recognized foreigners with surprising ease, and Allied escapees were in great danger of being spotted – the trains carried substantial risks, particularly for those who spoke no Italian. Farrell's Italian was good, however, so the train offered an opportunity to put many miles between himself and Campo 21 in a short space of time. It seems Farrell stole a bicycle to get himself to Pescara station, about 12 miles away, rather than risk trying to board a train from Chieti Scalo, which was the local station to the camp and would have been riskier. It was always possible that a guard would turn up there who would recognize him, and it was not a very busy station, which did not suit Farrell's plan.

Farrell had decided he would make the main part of his journey north (to Switzerland) by train. He had carefully worked out a plan which required confidence and verve for its execution. On reaching Pescara station, Farrell dumped his stolen bicycle and waited for a suitable moment to enter the station and reach the platforms. When it came, he dashed past the barrier like a passenger in danger of missing his train – nobody stopped him. Now clear of the initial security barrier, Farrell had still to find a train that would carry him in the right direction. To solve this problem, he would wait until a train was beginning to leave a platform and then rush up, calling out in Italian: 'Is this for

Milan?' Eventually, after a number of attempts, he got the answer 'yes' and was helped onto the departing train. There is no account available of what money or papers he was carrying if any, but it must be assumed that he had by now dumped his Italian Army uniform and changed into 'civilian' clothes (no doubt manufactured in Campo 21).

So Joseph Farrell took the train, and successfully travelled more than 200 miles north to Parma. He had no ticket, dodging the ticket inspectors by working his way along the train ahead of them, then hopping off when the train stopped at a station, moving back along the train and getting on again behind the inspectors before the train moved away. He kept his nerve admirably, the method worked well, and finally the train reached Parma. Here, Farrell got off the train, and attempted to pass through the exit barrier, but now his luck ran out. He was challenged at the barrier by the *carabinieri* on duty there. He punched one of them on the chin and vaulted the rail, but although he managed to sprint out of the station, he was pursued and arrested in the streets nearby within minutes. After a struggle, Farrell was handcuffed, and taken to the *carabinieri* headquarters in Parma. He was held there overnight and on 16 September escorted back to Campo 21, arriving at 0230hrs on the 17th. His bold attempt at escape had failed.

Farrell had been free for rather less than 48 hours, but he had succeeded in getting a long way from the camp. Despite the frustration of his recapture, he had gathered very valuable intelligence on conditions in the outside world, which in due course he would be able to pass on to his fellow prisoners. Lieutenant Colonel Barela was furious. He had had a bad two days, and however much he twisted the truth Barela could claim absolutely no credit for Farrell's recapture. A prisoner had got clean away and it was only the sharp-eyed *carabinieri* at Parma Station who had brought about his arrest.

Farrell was stripped and searched thoroughly by the camp *carabinieri* upon his return to Chieti. Whilst he was standing naked in front of the guards, the duty officer offered him a cigarette, which Farrell gratefully accepted. Farrell then asked for a light, which the duty officer refused. He also forbade the two *carabinieri* who were carrying out the search to give him a light, and clearly thought the 'joke' was highly amusing. In fact, it was a gentle beginning to the psychological and physical torture that was to follow. After the search, Farrell's shirt, trousers and boots were returned to him and he was placed in a cell inside the Italian guardroom in their section of the compound. The cell had a single barred window. About an hour later, the Commandant, Lieutenant Colonel

Barela, and the Interpreter, Captain Croce, arrived. Barela, through Croce, asked Farrell how he had managed to escape from the camp. Farrell, who had every hope of using the same method again, and may have known that a similar escape was being planned by others in Campo 21, told him nothing.

Colonel Barela was already in serious trouble with his superiors for not preventing the escape. The Commander of the Zone, General Belgrano, had visited the camp whilst Farrell was on the loose to find out how it had happened and Barela had been unable to tell him. Barela was awaiting some form of disciplinary action and hoped to improve matters somewhat by discovering from Farrell how he had breached the camp's security. When Farrell refused to say, Barela became extremely angry. He had Farrell taken out of the cell and out to the rear of the guardroom. Farrell was then placed against the back wall and Barela began to threaten him, saying, through Croce: 'None of your friends know that you have arrived back. It would be very easy for me to have you shot, and your body placed as if you were shot whilst trying to escape.' Barela continued to utter these threats for about ten minutes, making clear that if Farrell did not tell him how he had escaped, he would very probably shoot him. Barela then announced that he was going to leave Farrell for a while to think about it. He had the guards mark out a rectangle of about 15ft by 3ft, bounded by the wall against which Farrell stood, and indicated to him that this was his exercise area. Barela posted a guard with rifle at the ready at either end of the rectangle and ordered that if the prisoner stepped outside the rectangle, or even touched the wall, he was to be shot as attempting to escape. Farrell was kept within his 'exercise rectangle' until 0500hrs, then taken back to his cell. For the next few days, the process of threats and very limited exercise continued.

Tension amongst the Italian guards was running high. Barela was demanding to know how Farrell had escaped and they could not answer. Inevitably, Barela held the guards to blame. In contrast, the prisoners had been celebrating Farrell's escape. Following his disappearance, there had been numerous rollcalls and searches, as the Italians struggled to find out how he had got out. On the morning of 17 September, there was yet another rollcall, and the men were kept standing on parade in the sun outside their huts for two hours. Perhaps inevitably, they grew restless. The patience of one man finally snapped when a squad of guards, on their way to search his bungalow, foolishly decided to march straight through the assembled ranks outside it rather than go around them in the normal fashion – perhaps a sign of their own frustration. It was a dangerous mistake. As the guards pushed their way through, one of the prisoners who is named either as Captain Philip John 'Pip' Gardiner VC, Royal Tank Regiment (who subsequently denied that it was him), or Captain R. G. Borradaile, Cameron Highlanders, stuck out a foot and tripped one of the guards, sending him flying face down on the ground. His companions reacted swiftly, one of the guards swinging his rifle butt as hard as he could against the head of one of the British officers, Captain Richard J. Finch, Indian Army Frontier Rifles, who was the adjutant of the bungalow. Finch was trying to maintain some order, foreseeing the potentially very dangerous consequences of tripping the guard. He was knocked out and suffered a nasty injury to the head. Bleeding badly he was carried off to the hospital, where he stayed for three weeks. The doctor there informed him that his skull had been fractured, but Finch was later to say that he did not blame the Italian guard, who had struck him during a very tense situation. The guard was quickly disarmed by the substantial figure of Bill Bowes, the England cricketer.

Harold Sell described what happened after Finch was knocked to the ground: 'A confused battle was in progress, with some of us struggling for possession of the soldiers' weapons ... we remained ready to start in earnest.' Sell's frustration at all that had happened to him since his capture rings through his words and no doubt many of his fellow prisoners felt the same. John Pelley, who seems to have been quite enjoying himself with his acting (despite the shortage of cigarettes), commented in his diary: 'Really serious incident this morning. Extra roll call. My bungalow was surrounded by guards as is usual in a hut search. One of the guards was tripped by an officer, this led to a fight and general melee, and Dick Finch [Frontier Force] was hit over the head with a rifle butt and taken to hospital unconscious. There is little doubt that it was entirely our fault. It was very lucky that the guards had not got their bayonets fixed, as I am sure that they would have used them with relish.' Second Lieutenant John Jenkins, Royal Engineers, commented: 'Things looked extremely dangerous. It is no fun having a score or so rifles pointed at you at point blank range.'

For a moment or two, it must have seemed as if serious violence would erupt, but happily the Senior British Officer on parade, Lieutenant Colonel G. P. Kilkelly, 8th Hussars, called the men to attention, and the Italian officer in charge of the guards, a Captain Dell'Aquila (the Italian quartermaster of the camp) also kept his head, and called the guards to order. With the situation temporarily stable, Captain Dell'Aquila escorted Captain Finch to the hospital. The situation had indeed been a dangerous one, perhaps not surprisingly in the pressure-cooker atmosphere that was Campo 21. Bill Bowes, who was to prove himself to be one of the more mature and sensible inmates, had put himself into mortal danger by disarming the guard. Had any prisoner succeeded in grabbing a weapon from one of the Italian guards and actually used it, or even had the Italian guards thought he was about to use it, there would have undoubtedly been a bloodbath, with numerous Allied casualties. The Italians manning the machine-gun posts on the walls would not have held back, and those soldiers still armed with rifles would also no doubt have begun firing. Commandant Barela, who could not have got much sleep after his interrogation of Farrell, shortly afterwards joined the parade – hearing of Finch's injury, he commented: 'He has broken his head has he? Good!' He probably did not realize how close the incident had come to outright conflict. The parade was dismissed and it was made clear to the prisoners by the SBO and his command team that they could make no complaint about the assault on Captain Finch. The Allied assault on the Italian guard (tripping him) that had started the near riot had robbed them of the protection of the Geneva Convention. Prisoners of war were entitled to their rights because they were no longer combatants and were at the mercy of their captors, but any prisoner of war who fought back crossed the line and became a combatant again, thereby losing his rights under the Convention. The incident had demonstrated how dangerous the frustrations experienced by prisoners could be. An important part of the SBO's job was to keep these frustrations under control and it was in this that theatre, music, education, sport and escape plans helped the most.

Barela and his henchman Croce were having a very bad time. From their point of view, they had narrowly avoided a riot on the morning of 17 September, which would have cost them both their jobs. They realized that although their armed force would inevitably have prevailed over 1,600 unarmed prisoners, there would most likely have been some Italian casualties once the shooting started and that would not have been acceptable to High Command in Rome. It was surely no coincidence, therefore, that on the afternoon of 17 September, after the danger of riot had been avoided and perhaps realizing that their regime had gone too far in its treatment of the prisoners, 100 Red Cross parcels were released into the camp (one between every 16 prisoners), a mixture of the popular Canadian parcels and New Zealand parcels. Neither of these countries was suffering from the rationing that was in force in Britain. Post was also handed out, always a significant event, and Pelley was delighted to receive three letters. It is probable that Croce had held all of these items for some time, but felt it useful to release them now, to calm the tensions in the camp. Extra roll calls continued, however, as the Italians were understandably frightened that more prisoners might escape. Further, all walks outside the camp had now been stopped. The Italians still did not know how Farrell had got out. They suspected (rightly) that the walks were providing the prisoners with the opportunity to learn more about the geography and conditions outside the camp. The vigilance of the guards was heightened and bungalow searches and extra roll calls imposed.

Meanwhile, for Barela and Croce the problem remained that two prisoners had succeeded in getting out of the camp on two consecutive days and it was still not known how one of them, Farrell, had escaped. Farrell himself may have been unaware of the near riot on the morning of his return to camp, but he was still holding out. He continued to face down the threats from both Barela and Croce. Farrell was still being held in the guardhouse and his presence there was known only to the Italians, which gave Barela considerably greater freedom in the way he chose to treat his prisoner. So long as the SBO did not know that Farrell was there, he was vulnerable: Barela's threat that he could have Farrell shot and then pretend that he had been killed while attempting to escape, was all too feasible. Happily for Farrell, the news of his presence in the Italian guardhouse leaked out on Sunday, 20 September. The Church of England padre, the Reverend Major Chutter, had been to visit prisoners held in the cooler to offer them communion, and the *carabiniere* who had escorted him asked afterwards if he now wished to see the prisoner in the guardhouse also. Although he knew nothing about any prisoner being there, Chutter at once said yes. He was taken to Farrell, who was having an exercise period outside his cell. Chutter found Farrell too upset to take communion, but talking to him discovered that Farrell was in fact a Roman Catholic – he therefore promised that he would arrange for the Roman Catholic padre, Father G. W. Forster, to come and see him. Now it became clear, however, that the Italians did not actually want Chutter anywhere near Farrell – he was asked to leave the guards' compound. The invitation from the *carabiniere* had clearly been a mistake, given contrary to Barela's orders.

Chutter returned to his quarters in the prison compound, but no sooner had he arrived back than he was summoned to see Commandant Barela. Croce (whom Chutter referred to as the 'blackshirt interpreter') was also present. Barela coyly asked Chutter not to tell anyone else that Farrell was in custody in the camp, which placed Chutter in a difficult position. He had only learned of Farrell's presence there as a part of his spiritual duties and had been offered the chance to see him as a part of his ministry. There was an argument therefore that the information should remain confidential. Nonetheless, Farrell's welfare was all important, and thus there was a balancing act to be performed. Chutter responded by saying that provided Father Forster was allowed to see Farrell every day, he would not tell the other prisoners. Barela agreed to the condition and Chutter returned to the prisoners' compound to give his instructions to Father Forster. Forster duly attended the guards' compound to see Farrell. He was taken first for a meeting with Barela, who tried to ingratiate himself with Forster, emphasizing that they were, after all, both Roman Catholics and telling him that after he had taken Farrell's confession, he should advise him that his present treatment would continue if he refused to say how he had escaped. Forster point blank refused to do anything of the kind, whereupon he was sent straight back to his quarters without being granted access to Farrell. He reported his failure back to Chutter. Over the next few days, Father Forster kept trying to gain access to Farrell, and each time it was refused. At this point, neither the Reverend Chutter nor Father Forster had told anyone else of Farrell's situation.

Barela and Croce continued to step up the camp's security measures. On 22 September, Ronald Hill commented on a very intensive search of his bungalow. On 23 September, there were five roll calls, causing considerable disruption to the prisoners' lives. Also on 23 September, the Italian guards discovered a tunnel, but it was still under construction and could not possibly be the means of Farrell's escape. Nonetheless, it was a depressing moment for the tunnel-digging team and for the prisoners as a whole. Tensions still ran high and conditions were day by day getting worse. On 24 September, John Pelley recorded in his diary: 'Had a good sleep in the afternoon, this is a difficult feat as it must be done under a sheet owing to the ferocity of the fly population who share our living quarters.' The flies were no doubt attracted by the unhygienic conditions caused by lack of water and proper sanitation. The population of the camp was still growing and food supplies grew shorter than ever.

When it became clear that Barela was not going to relent on his decision to refuse visits to Farrell, the Reverend Major Chutter realized he must take some decisive action. He wrote out a full report of what had happened and what he knew of Farrell, and left it with a fellow officer, with the instruction that if he, Chutter, did not return within an hour, it should be handed to a senior officer, Lieutenant Colonel R. H. Wheller, Royal Artillery. Clearly, Chutter feared that Commandant Barela might swallow him up into the guardhouse along with Farrell if he thought it necessary to keep him quiet. The report was his insurance policy.

Chutter now walked up to the white line across the tarmac road that marked the end of the prisoners' permitted zone and demanded that he be taken to speak to the Commandant. Once in Barela's presence, he announced that if the Roman Catholic padre were not allowed to see Farrell, he, Chutter, would tell all that he knew to the SBO and his fellow prisoners. He also informed Barela of the existence of the report that he had already written. Barela found himself cornered. Eventually, he agreed that Forster could, after all, visit Farrell. The Reverend Major Chutter had won a small victory. Chutter returned to his quarters, and immediately sent Father Forster to make a pastoral visit. This time, Forster was allowed in to see Farrell and spent some time with him. However, it seems that for whatever reason, Farrell made no complaint to Forster that he had been ill-treated. Chutter had intended that Forster should make regular visits to check on Farrell thereafter, but unfortunately it seems that Forster was far from well (as was the case with so many of the prisoners), and his visits to Farrell thereafter were extremely sporadic.

By granting Father Forster access to Farrell, Barela and Croce had gained a little breathing space, but the clock was ticking and still they had not discovered how Farrell had escaped. By the end of the first week following his recapture, it was clear to Barela and Croce that mere threats were getting them nowhere: Farrell still refused to tell them what they badly needed to know. So on the night of Saturday, 26 September 1942, Barela moved from threats to actual violence. Farrell was asleep in his cell when he was awakened at midnight by the same duty officer who had taunted him with the cigarette when he was first returned to the camp. The officer opened the door and, speaking in French, which at that time all Italians studied at school, asked Farrell: 'Tres bien?' A surprised Farrell replied yes, he was fine. The man left and Farrell went back to sleep. Sometime later the same night, Farrell was violently awoken by the mattress being pulled from under him on the board that served for his bed. Two *carabinieri* had come into his cell. Farrell saw that one of them was holding a pistol like a club. As he began to ask what was happening, he was punched in the mouth by one of the *carabinieri*. Suspecting that there was a beating to come, Farrell reacted quickly. His boots were beside the bed and he grabbed them, swinging them round his head to keep his attackers at bay, while yelling at the top of his voice. The two *carabinieri* retreated to the door and Farrell hurled the boots after them – they hit the glass fanlight above the door, shattering it and showering the *carabinieri* with glass – one of them screamed out and both retreated, locking the door again.

Farrell's victory was a temporary one. A few minutes later, the Commandant, the duty officer and Croce entered the cell, accompanied by a squad of guards with their bayonets fixed to their rifles. Farrell was forced against the wall at bayonet point. Commandant Barela was carrying a 6ft bamboo cane, wielding it with both hands, with which he then set about beating Farrell on the arms and body. Farrell could not tell if the cane was weighted so that it would do more damage, but when he raised his arms to defend himself, the first blow deadened one arm, rendering it useless. Barela, clearly in a fury, proceeded to thrash Farrell about twenty times with the cane himself, before handing it to a *carabiniere* to finish the job. The *carabiniere* delivered another twenty or so lashes, before Barela called him off and they left Farrell alone and in considerable pain in his cell, locking the door behind them. Both the initial attack and the beating from Commandant Barela were totally unlawful.

On the Sunday morning, 27 September, two of the guards nailed a blanket over the only window to the cell, leaving Farrell in the dark. Shortly afterwards, Barela and Croce visited Farrell again. The blanket was lifted for the duration of their visit, but returned to position after they left. Barela, through Croce, told Farrell that he believed that he (Farrell) had suffered a nightmare the night before – referring to the beating that he, Barela, had delivered – and that he was sorry to hear that, but he assured Farrell that such nightmares would continue until he had confessed how he had managed to escape and reach Parma. Barela also said that he intended to arrest Farrell's friend, Lieutenant Robert Wilders, Royal Engineers, as an accomplice in the escape, unless Farrell gave them the evidence that they wanted. If arrested, Wilders would no doubt receive similar treatment to Farrell.

Faced with a combination of the threat to his friend and the threat of continued beatings, Farrell changed his tactics. He purported to confess to the methods that he had used, and made a signed statement to Barela. The statement was mainly lies, but seemed finally to satisfy Barela and Croce. In the statement, Farrell said that in order to reach Pescara and Parma as quickly as he had done, he had stolen a bicycle. However, he kept the essentials of his escape, particularly the fact that he had disguised himself as an Italian soldier, to himself. He still hoped to use the same method again. For a week after his 'confession' all went quiet. Farrell continued to serve his time in solitary confinement without further threats or beatings. Meanwhile, in the outside world of Campo 21, life went on.

Since their capture, for most prisoners news of the war had been very restricted. Their captors were at first triumphant, and because of the fall of

Tobruk, many Allied prisoners feared that Rommel's forces would roll on and take Alexandria, the British headquarters in Egypt. The failure of the Allied raid on Dieppe in August reinforced the optimism of the Italians, who described it as an abortive attempt by the Allies to open a second front. There was no good news for the prisoners, but as the weeks passed and there was still no word of the fall of Alexandria, many inmates of Campo 21 became more hopeful. In September, a number of RAF aircrew had arrived in the camp, having been shot down flying from Malta, and they brought encouraging news that things were not quite as bad as the Fascist press was suggesting. They put the failed Dieppe raid into perspective. Then, on 29 September, prisoners arrived in the camp who had been captured at El Alamein. They confirmed that the Allied line was holding and also brought news that Japan had suffered setbacks. The Japanese invasion of Port Moresby, Papua New Guinea, had failed with an apparent loss of 20,000 men and 14 ships. United States forces had begun operations for the recapture of the Solomon Islands, and it was said that 70,000 Japanese prisoners had already been taken. Gordon Lett gathered together all the information he could obtain and began to analyse the Italian papers which were allowed into the camp, sometimes able to read between the lines of what was deemed suitable for public consumption.

Towards the end of his sentence, Barela and Croce came to see Farrell again. Barela clearly was worried that his ill treatment of a prisoner of war would leak out after Farrell had completed his solitary confinement. He knew he had gone far too far. Barela therefore told Farrell that his headquarters in Rome were now demanding to see the report of Farrell's escape, and that Barela would have to say that Farrell had committed the two civilian crimes of a) stealing a bicycle, and b) assaulting a *carabiniere* at Parma Station. Barela said that if he did so, Farrell would be taken before a civilian court and would undoubtedly receive a long sentence in jail. However, he said he was prepared to do a deal. If Farrell agreed that upon his release from solitary confinement, he would make no mention of the ill treatment and beating that he had received, he, Barela, would omit the allegations of civil crimes from his report to Rome. Farrell refused, but two days later Barela and Croce came to see him again, saying it was his final chance to reach a deal. Farrell had by this time had plenty of time to think about it and had decided to negotiate. He wanted to impose his own condition – that after he had completed his 30 days of solitary confinement, he would not be moved to another camp, but would remain in Campo 21. Farrell still believed that the method he had used to escape would work again and that therefore it was essential he stay where he was. Barela agreed and the deal was made. Farrell was not charged with any civilian offences and he was released from solitary confinement on 16 October 1942. However, despite the condition that Barela had agreed to, Farrell was transferred out of Campo 21 a few days later and sent to the 'bad boys' camp at Gavi, the Italian equivalent of Colditz. Too much had gone wrong under Barela's command, including another escape attempt whilst Farrell had been in solitary, and before he got out Barela had been sacked as Commandant and a replacement brought in.

Month 3

October 1942

THE FIRST INSPECTION

For a very few of the prisoners in Campo 21, the month started reasonably well. John Pelley was given, at very short notice on 1 October, a burlesque part in a new show opening that same night at the theatre. It was written by John Lepine and entitled, 'Evening at the 21'. Pelley described it as a skit on the already famous Shakespearean actor Lawrence Olivier. The 21 Club became a regular feature of the theatrical world at Campo 21 and offered pure escapism both for the actors and stage staff and for the 'guests' – the inmates of the camp who were all invited to the shows.

But for most of the men, the depression of their indefinite imprisonment was becoming less and less bearable. Food was getting shorter and the weather less warm. For those without boots or shoes, rain made the stony ground of the compound muddy and painful to walk on. George Hervey-Murray described their state:

> The nights were long because we didn't lead an active life, and there was little to tire us and make us go to sleep quickly. Also, being hungry made sleep difficult and one might just lie awake thinking of all the lovely food one would give anything to have, but knowing only too well that it might be years before one might ever have another proper meal, if ever again. Many of the more sensitive types would lie on their beds most of the day, facing the wall, and just feeling really miserable, and they would not respond if someone kindly enquired if they were alright … There were, however, many who seemed not to have a care in the world and would for

ever be busy and active, playing volley ball, walking furiously around the perimeter and spending hours washing their meagre clothes.

The essential challenge was to find something to pass the time, otherwise a prisoner would almost inevitably slide down into an abyss of depression.

The prisoners continued to try to get back at their captors and guards by baiting them. The methods varied – on one occasion it is said that the Commandant accepted an invitation to a theatrical show and the leading 'lady' came down into the audience after the show, presented him with a bunch of flowers and kissed him on both cheeks. The Commandant's reaction is not recorded, but the incident undoubtedly caused the prisoners great amusement. When Croce and his 'tapping' team (sounding the floorboards to locate tunnels) visited Stuart Hood's bungalow, he and his colleagues would pretend to be terribly helpful, rushing around saying things such as: 'Try there…this sounds a bit suspicious…here's one.' On a purely childish level, Hood recalls that from his bungalow people used to make faces through the windows at the guards (one side of their bungalow faced the guard's quarters), or make obscene gestures to provoke them. The Italians responded by whitewashing the windows of the bungalow, whereupon the prisoners put derogatory slogans on them, such as 'Finito Benito' (Benito Mussolini is finished). Hood describes it all as a way of keeping their spirits up, a game that could be played against the detaining forces. Sometimes, it made their enemy extremely cross. The guards were poor-quality soldiers, easily provoked – and of course if they lost control it could be dangerous, as they were armed and the prisoners were not.

A game which almost without fail got the guards excited was to show them a drawing of a hammer and sickle, or a clenched fist, references to the very unhappy times that some of their troops were having on the Russian front. A number of ex-prisoners have told the story of one of their most dangerous games. The men of two of the bungalows agreed that they would play a trick on the guards by dressing up a dummy as a prisoner, and then, in the dark after curfew, they would tow the dummy on a length of Red Cross string across the distance between the windows of the two bungalows, creating the impression of a real prisoner on the loose in the compound. They thought the guards would be tricked into firing at it, which would be amusing. The scheme was duly put into effect, with some success. Then a more sophisticated version of this ruse was devised after a thunderstorm one night. The guards had apparently thought the camp was under attack and had started firing wildly in various directions, including straight up at the sky. Some of the Sappers in the camp, with more than enough time on their hands, began working out angles at which the machine-gun posts might be persuaded to fire at each other or, even better, at an Italian foot patrol in the camp. A sophisticated scheme was worked out, involving carefully positioned dummies to be manoeuvred at night, to attract a cross-fire from the sentries that might result in them hitting each other or a passing patrol. However, the SBO decided it was just too dangerous, and put a stop to it.

On 6 October, a number of items ordered by various societies and paid for by the prisoners finally arrived. All prisoners of war continued, on paper at least, to receive their military salaries, so the Campo 21 inmates had the means to buy things. However, the Italians controlled the accounts and prisoners would find that ridiculous sums were deducted from their pay in order to pay for trivial items. Later, such items were sent as gifts from the Red Cross, but Croce interfered with the flow of parcels and if the prisoners could be coerced to buy things locally there was an enormous profit to be made. For example, 6 October saw the arrival in the camp of a proper football ordered by the Sports Committee, at a cost of an exorbitant £6 – the equivalent of a week's wages – and regular games could at last commence. This football was apparently the only one to survive among the 1,600 occupants of the camp for the next three months.

Also, there appeared a number of musical instruments ordered by the Entertainments Committee, which would transform the quality of music in the camp. (Again, instruments arrived later on via the Red Cross, free of charge.) However, with the Italians controlling the market, Pelley recorded that to pay for the first consignment of instruments there was a levy on all officers of 15 lire. If that is right, then the total cost could have been as much as 17,000 lire. Two pianos arrived on hire, together with a selection of band and orchestral instruments purchased. Tommy Sampson had drawn up a careful list of what was needed to equip an orchestra and a variety of bands. From now on a number of musical groups began to be set up – there was a concert orchestra (conducted by Tony Baines), a dance orchestra of twenty pieces (which McGinlay 'squeezed into' on bass), bands, ensembles, sextets and quartets. The concert orchestra rehearsed in separate sections, with Tommy Sampson taking the brass section, Tony Baines the reed section, John Lepine the rhythm section, and so on. McGinlay commented: 'After we had all rehearsed enough, we were brought together. I can remember the thrill to this day: the tune was 'Japanese Sandman' [a popular 1920s piece by Richard A. Whiting]. When I heard the combined orchestra, if they had opened the gates of the prison that night, I would not have gone out ...' Tommy Sampson led his own band, Tony Baines had the full orchestra, and amongst the smaller groups were Claude Goodwin and his Accordion Band, Pitso's Gipsy Orchestra, John LePine's Jiving Cats, and Nat Fotheringay's Sextet. Other musical groups would form and disband for particular occasions.

An interesting footnote is that when 'Mac' MacLucas finally received the cello he had asked for, he found that the pin (almost essential to enable the instrument to be played) had been removed by the security conscious camp administration. Like all prisoners of war, MacLucas found a way to improvise when playing the instrument and also discovered that the niche on the cello that should have held its pin was ideal to hide the length of metal that he was in fact using for tunnelling. Tunnel teams were at work in various parts of the camp and tools that might be used for digging were much sought after. The Italians had worked out a way of neutralizing the advantage that the prisoners might otherwise have gained from the fact that their bungalow blocks stood in direct contact with the ground and were not on raised on stilts. A squad of guards, either led by Croce personally or under the command of a lieutenant of the Alpini, would make regular visits to the huts and would tap all the floors with hammers in the hope of hearing the hollow sound indicating a tunnel. This proved a successful tactic. The prisoners soon learnt to recognize the squad when it entered their compound, always in single file, all rather short of stature, and nicknamed them Snow White and the Seven Dwarfs. Whenever the team was spotted, prisoners would burst into song with 'Hi ho, hi ho, it's off to work we go'.

Toby Graham commented that one's view on life depended what one was involved in: 'If a man's work depended on supplies from outside, then he was inclined to be in favour of peaceful relations with the Italians, from whom supplies of books and other materials for running courses and the arts could be obtained. On the other hand, the escapers reckoned that a hammer stolen for tunnelling was a fair exchange for the discomfort caused to everyone when the Italians retaliated by a bout of searches and the removal of privileges, including the withdrawal of Red Cross parcels.' There was a division between those who thought that the war should as far as possible be continued in the camp, and those who thought that prisoners should start preparing for the future by improving their education, as though the war was, for them, over. Pelley notes that on the same day the football and instruments arrived, 6 October, a number of officers read essays to the bungalow inhabitants. Bill Bowes, the England fast bowler, read a piece on cricket.

Then, on 7 October, there was an event which caused great excitement and hope amongst the prisoners. The first of the Protecting Power's representatives to inspect the camp arrived. His visit came as a complete surprise to the Allied personnel. Croce and the Commandant had kept it to themselves until the representative actually appeared, no doubt hoping that as a result the prisoners' complaints would be less organized and more muted than would otherwise have been the case. It may also be why the football and the musical instruments were supplied to the prisoners the day before his arrival. Captain L. Trippi was an elderly, somewhat deaf individual, who spoke good English and indeed would speak no other language whilst in the presence of British officers. In the presence of the representative of the Protecting Power, the attitude of the Italian authorities in the camp superficially changed. Towards Dr Trippi, they were smarmy and eager to please, putting on a very different face to the one they normally showed the prisoners. Still, Lett reports that Trippi was given a full report of the prisoners' requirements, and seemed impressed in particular by the obvious deficiencies of their clothing. The weather in early October was mainly fine, but it was wetter and already getting colder, and winter was bound to bring the need for warm clothes and plenty of them. Some of the officers wandering around the compound had nothing to wear but tattered shirts and shorts – not even shoes. Others were swathed in blankets, which represented the only warm clothing that they had. An extreme example was Captain Bob Walker Brown, who had been wounded in North Africa when captured, and initially was in prison hospital in Lucca. A strong young man, he survived his wounds, but arrived in Chieti with nothing but a pair of damaged and blood-stained shorts and a blanket. The list of complaints was long. Lett notes in his diary that the prisoners had not been supplied with mugs to drink from, but still had to make their own out of used biscuit tins. The future looked bleak, with no heating whatsoever provided for the bungalows for winter time, and a dearth of Red Cross parcels. In the late summer and early autumn, fruit and vegetables had been easy to buy from the locals, but once the harvests were over Red Cross parcels would become completely essential to the prisoners' survival.

Trippi's report confirmed that there were currently 1,605 prisoners in Campo 21. Of these, 1,200 were British, 386 South African, and there was a sprinkling of others including two Americans. Three men were in the 'cooler' at the time of the inspector's visit. The report can perhaps be fairly described as a masterpiece of appeasement. The tone is set by an introductory paragraph in which Trippi states: 'The camp is situated in a plain, 148 feet above sea level, at the foot of a mountain with a city on its elevation. It is removed from the danger zone, the climate is healthy and the sojourn here is pleasant at this time of year.' He goes on:

> Five of the six bungalows are at the disposal of the prisoners of war, the sixth is occupied by depot troops. All the installations are identical, quite up to date and luxurious in some instances ... The camp is provided with first-class sanitary installations. Along the walls of a large, well-ventilated room with large windows are sixteen water-flushed, closed-in Turkish water closets [known to the British as 'squatters']...the walls are covered with majolica tiles and everything is sanitarily first rate and clean....The shower-bath installation with sixty showers is luxuriously installed; there are single rooms for shower baths with adjoining dressing rooms. The majolica tiled walls of the showers are two metres high.

After these glowing remarks, when Trippi came to deal with the failings of the camp, his remarks lack any bite whatsoever. He notes the overcrowded forty-bunk dormitories, the fact that there were no stoves for the winter, the lack of enough Red Cross parcels, the inadequate clothing, the lack of medical supplies and dental instruments in the camp hospital, and the absence of any regular water supply. About the latter, which totally undermined the alleged excellence and luxury of the lavatories and showers, he says:

> Unfortunately, the water supply is not equal to these most excellent installations. The region receives its water from the neighbouring town, which is well provided with water, but, as we were informed, the diameter of the conduit which conveys the water to the camp is not large enough so that the camp does not get more than 24 cubic metres of water in 24 hours. Additional water is obtained from ground-water fed cisterns but in spite of the two centrifugal pumps, even this does not cover consumption, and water for the toilets is carried in pails to the house. We were told that the water conduit will be enlarged, we presented a request to this effect to the War Ministry and hope that the excellent sanitary installations will soon be able to fulfil their purpose.

Major Sell comments that his bungalow had actually had to buy a bucket from the Italians in order to carry the water from the well to flush the lavatories.

Whilst not being a complete whitewash, the report totally failed to place a realistic emphasis on the deficiencies of the camp. It undoubtedly did not reflect the feelings of many of the prisoners. To many who read it, the report was taken to say: 'The camp is satisfactory, although certain things need to be sorted out.' Trippi no doubt nodded and smiled as much when meeting Commandant Barela and Captain Croce as he did when meeting the unfortunate Allied prisoners, but he failed to address the urgency of the situation in his report, or to look into the future. To rectify the lack of water major work would be necessary, since presumably the entire pipeline from Chieti town to the camp would have to be replaced. Italy had a broken economy and was in the middle of a war that it could not afford to fight, so there was in reality no chance that the pipe would be replaced. The Italian Ministry of War had far more pressing matters to consider than the supply of water to some of its prisoners. Matters such as the lack of any form of heating, and the inadequacy of clothing and Red Cross food parcel supplies, would rapidly become urgent with the onset of winter. Trippi's report was passed from the Protecting Power at their office in Berne, Switzerland, and then to the British diplomats there. A summary of his report reached London on 23 October 1942. Unfortunately, the summary concluded: 'General impression satisfactory'.

Had Lieutenant Colonel Gray or the other prisoners in Campo 21 known how lukewarm Trippi's report was in respect of any kind of criticism, they would have been enormously frustrated. However, at least it did alert the Swiss authorities to the fact that improvements needed to be made, and it is said that they duly reported the camp's shortcomings to the Italian military authorities who were responsible. Further, Trippi's visit had the immediate effect of persuading the camp administration to issue a second blanket to every man. Nonetheless, illness amongst the prisoners was increasing. Due to the Spartan conditions, lack of proper sanitation and overcrowding, colds and minor illnesses spread through the camp like wildfire.

CAPTAIN CROCE LEAVES CAMP!

Whilst the first Camp Commandant, Mario Barela, alias the Trick Cyclist, was deeply unpopular, Captain Mario Croce, the Camp Interpreter, was universally hated. He was something of a peacock in appearance, with a small pointed beard, a distinctive strutting walk and highly polished boots. His uniform was of very fine cloth. He was tall, with wide shoulders and a narrow waist, favoured strong male scent, and wore a monocle attached by a black silk cord. He had the habit of carrying his head listing to one side. He would customarily appear in company with at least two orderlies, who no doubt were there to boost his sense of self importance, as well as to give him the confidence to act as outrageously towards the prisoners as he sometimes did. He was also often accompanied by a dog. The men believed that Croce positively enjoyed making their lives as difficult as he possibly could. In fact he was a bully, who enjoyed bullying not only the Allied prisoners but even his own junior staff. Gordon Lett, who had numerous encounters with Croce, described the ordinary Italian soldiers as being frightened of Croce, and as 'cringing' whenever Croce appeared. Croce expected to be feared and could not understand why the Allied prisoners did not behave towards him in the same way. He never really appreciated that much of the time the British prisoners were making fun of him.

It was probably with some enjoyment, therefore, that three of the more senior officers in the camp, Major Holden DSO, of the Royal Tank Regiment, Captain Aubrey Whitby, of the Royal Artillery, and Captain George Duncan MC, of the Special Boat Section (SBS) and the Black Watch, hatched their plan of escape. As related above, James Farrell had successfully walked out of the camp dressed as an Italian soldier, and though he was still in solitary confinement at this time it was believed that he had resisted interrogation and the Italians still did not realize how he had escaped (as was in fact the case). Holden, Whitby and Duncan decided to emulate Farrell and to walk out of the camp dressed in Italian uniforms. Aubrey Whitby was close to Croce in height, build and colouring, and they decided that he, who spoke good Italian (he had relatives who lived in Pisa), should impersonate the odious Croce, while Holden and Duncan pretended to be his orderlies. The three would then march out of the gates together – the presence of 'Croce' hopefully deterring any guards from challenging them. Once outside, they would ditch their uniforms for civilian clothing and make for the coast on foot. There, they hoped to steal a small boat and cross to the Balkans, where they could join the partisan freedom fighters. Duncan, the SBS small boats expert, could take charge once at sea.

Gathering together and adapting the necessary articles of Italian uniform was not difficult. There were still many bits and pieces being worn by the prisoners and the theatrical department included a number of skilful tailors. Croce's long military 'top boots' presented a problem, but the theatrical department produced a very passable imitation. Finally, the theatrical make-up department was able to create a 'Balbo' beard and moustache for Whitby to match Croce's. Whitby had carefully studied Croce's mannerisms and believed that he could carry off the part. It took time to complete the preparations, but by the second week of October, with Farrell still languishing in the cooler, all was in place.

The attempt took place two days after the visit of the Swiss delegate, Captain Trippi, on 9 October 1942. At about 2000hrs, as dusk was falling, there was a lecture in progress in the courtyard outside Bungalow 5, the one nearest to the gate. One of those listening to the lecture on a subject now long forgotten was Gordon Lett. He was standing on the edge of the audience when he noticed an Italian orderly walk out of the bungalow and down the steps to the path, carrying a cardboard box on his head, in the customary local manner. The orderly's appearance was followed by the exit from the bungalow of Captain Croce, though Lett did notice that Croce did not give off his customary strong smell of perfume. Lett also noted that Croce's complexion was not quite pallid enough, though his head was tilted at exactly the right angle. It was of course, Whitby. A second orderly now emerged from Bungalow 5, and followed 'Croce' and the first orderly down the path towards the compound gate. The acting was superb. Lett describes the party arriving at the compound gate, where 'Croce' was of course recognized by the sentry, who saluted. 'Croce' returned the salute in his usual dilatory fashion and he and his two orderlies passed through the gate under the noses of the watching guards without any action being taken against them. They walked on, out through the main gate and down the road away from the camp. It was a bravura performance.

Most unluckily, a short way down the road from the camp the trio passed an Italian private coming in the opposite direction. The private recognized one of 'Croce's' orderlies as a prisoner of war from the camp. He immediately began to question the three, despite the apparent presence of Captain Croce. Whitby now excelled himself. Using his fluent Italian, and relying on the fear which Croce had instilled in all the Italian soldiery, he faced the man down and managed to cow him, at least for the time being. Whatever his surprise and suspicion at what was going on, the private did not dare continue to challenge the authority of 'Croce' to his face. Ordered on his way, he proceeded to walk on into the camp and only reported his suspicions when he was safely inside. That gave Whitby and the others just enough time to get out of sight off the road and to change from their Italian uniforms into civilian clothing (which presumably was in the box that the 'orderly' had been carrying on his head). Their plan was to head southeast, and hopefully to reach the coast in the area of Francavilla.

Back at Campo 21, the alarm was raised as soon as the private reported his suspicions. It quickly became obvious that the real Croce had not just walked out of the camp and that therefore the three men who shortly before had passed through the gate were escaping prisoners of war. Gordon Lett says that fifteen minutes after he saw Whitby and the others leave the camp, the bugle was sounded for a roll call. Darkness had descended and the courtyard was lit by the perimeter searchlights. The occupants of the bungalows took up their parade positions under the watchful eyes of the sentries in pill boxes on the walls, whilst the camp guards searched Bungalow 4, which was normally occupied by the men it was now thought were missing. The bungalow commanders checked their men, and waited for the Commandant to attend and to dismiss the parade. Time passed slowly, and after a while, the prisoners ceased to stand on parade, but sat down and began to have some fun at their captors' expense. They started singing various Axis patriotic songs, whose tunes were of course very familiar to their guards, but in this case using extremely rude English words. The Italians could not quite understand what was going on. It then began to rain.

An element of farce was added to the situation when three prisoners arrived from the camp theatre, late for the roll call. Lett describes their arrival as follows: 'There were sounds of ribald mirth from the end of the parade ground nearest to the "theatre" block, due to the late arrival of two maidens clad only in brassieres and the briefest of panties, chaperoned by a motherly peroxide blonde ... they were three members of the theatrical company who happened to be rehearsing for that weekend's cabaret.' Events now having descended into farce, the prisoners were eventually allowed to drift back into their bungalows, as the rain became heavier.

Meanwhile, the Italians had attempted to throw a cordon around the countryside outside the camp. Whitby, Holden and Duncan, believing themselves surrounded, lay down in the middle of a ploughed field and relied on the darkness to give them the cover that they needed. Happily for them, it seems that the Italians did not employ dogs in the search. Eventually, the sound of searching died away. Whitby and his companions were soaking wet, but still free. It was now, no doubt, that George Duncan's expertise in concealment and evasion came into its own. Although officially a member of the Special Boat Section, at this stage of the war the SBS was simply an extension of the Special Air Service, and Duncan's training would have embraced all the skills he needed on the run in Italy. For three nights, the escapees made their way southeast towards the coast, concealing themselves in deep cover and lying up during the day. They lived off the rations they had carried with them out of the camp, presumably also hidden in the box carried by the 'orderly'. They knew they had to keep off the main roads and avoid villages or habitations. Their worse enemies were the village dogs, who would pick up the scent of any stranger passing by from quite a distance, and would bark furiously. All three men had been weakened by their very poor diet and lack of proper exercise during captivity, so the route march proved additionally difficult.

Finally, to their great relief, they reached the sea. Now their plan was to steal a small boat. In the isolation of Campo 21, this had seemed a viable plan. Sadly, they had not allowed for the effects of the war on the availability of such craft. Having reached the coast on the night of 11 October, they spent the rest of that night and the next searching for a boat that they might steal, with no success at all. On 13 October, as they lay up on a hillside overlooking the coast, they were spotted by a local girl who raised the alarm, and they were shortly afterwards arrested by Italian soldiers. The game was up and they were returned to Campo 21 in handcuffs. They had been free for four and a half days. Once back at Chieti, they were sentenced to 21 days close imprisonment. When finally released all three were, like Farrell, transferred to the Italian Colditz at Gavi, Campo 5.

Whilst Whitby, Holden and Duncan were still on the run, things had improved a little in the camp, despite the irksome extra parades. The day after the escape, on 10 October, a rumour spread through the camp that 4,000 Red Cross parcels were being held at Chieti Scalo station, albeit, as Pelley commented, they wouldn't go far with 1,600 'hungry and smoke mad officers and other ranks'. All sorts of rumours reached the camp through the Italian guards. Most proved to be false, but for once the existence of the Red Cross parcels proved to be true, and on the following day, 11 October, they arrived. Pelley noted in his diary with satisfaction that he had received fifty cigarettes.

Barela could not survive a third escape and was replaced on 12 October by a new Commandant. This one's distinguishing feature is that neither Captain Croce nor any of the prisoners under his control seemed to be able to remember his name. Croce simply said, when questioned about it in January 1946, that the new Commandant was a lieutenant colonel in the infantry. Lett remembered only his nickname – 'the Butcher' – apparently bestowed upon him because he looked far more like a pork butcher than a military man. Lett comments that his most notable feature was a big cruel looking mouth, but adds that 'we had no cause to complain about anything particularly outrageous during his brief regime.' Nonetheless, when the new man arrived, Whitby and his companions were still on the run and various efforts to tighten up security and discourage further escapes were put in train. Firstly, a detailed record was made of the appearance of every prisoner, so that if anyone escaped, accurate descriptions of them could be circulated. Strangely, no photographs were taken, although this was remedied at a later time. Probably, the camp administration were worried about recording the ragamuffin appearance of most of their ill-clad prisoners.

It was getting colder, and still many prisoners were without any proper winter clothing. Apart from the organized games now made possible by possession of a football (a significant improvement on the Bill Bowes home-made variety), the only regular exercise available was within the compound, and every day bedraggled groups of officers could be seen walking backwards and forwards along the road that ran through the centre of the camp. Shortages of cooking and eating utensils continued, for no apparent reason, and incoming post was scarce. Anything that was available for the officers to buy to supplement their rations was ridiculously expensive. Croce, who was the conduit pipe for all things, had a very profitable racket going.

THE CHIETI NEWS AGENCY

On the day after the 'Croce' escape, Sunday, 10 October, the Chieti News Agency was officially born and gave its first talk in the camp. The Chieti News Agency, or CNA as it became known, was the brainchild of Major Gordon Lett. It was not long before the news talks that he gave became known as Lett's Diaries. Gordon Lett was born on 17 November 1910, and was therefore 31 years of age when he arrived in Campo 21. He was a professional soldier who had seen service in Africa and India before the war. He had a love of mountains and considerable experience of climbing them. He was also, through force of circumstance, a very independent man. His very existence was a tribute to his endurance and determination, since he had been born two months prematurely in a primitive hut in the remote village of Domera, Papua New Guinea, where his father had been working as an engineer in one of the early attempts to open up that country. His mother had died from the complications of childbirth, but somehow he had survived. He had been brought up initially by his maternal grandmother in Sydney, Australia, before being sent back to England in 1922 at the age of 11, to complete his education at Claysmore School in Dorset. He was cared for when not at school by members of his father's English family, before eventually taking up a commission in the 2nd Battalion, East Surrey Regiment, at Shorncliffe on 2 March 1933. Posted to India with his regiment, Lett enjoyed climbing in the Himalayas so much that he transferred into the British Indian Army. Despite perhaps giving the outward appearance of a typical public-school educated English officer, Lett had a great understanding of ordinary people from all backgrounds, which served him well in Campo 21 and thereafter. Of medium build and height (though considered tall by the Italians), he was possessed of extraordinary endurance. He was something of a linguist and was able to speak passable Italian. Lett had seen service with the Eighth Army in the North African desert, and with the 4th Indian Division in Eritrea. He had been at Tobruk, North Africa, in June 1942 when it fell to the enemy, and after a week on the run and two attempts to escape out to sea by raft, he had been taken prisoner.

To found the CNA, Lett teamed up with Captain Jack White Abbott, Royal Artillery, who also felt that such an organization could greatly boost the morale of Campo 21. One of the enormous disadvantages of being a prisoner of war was that you knew little of what was going on in the outside world and, in particular, how the war was going. All letters into the camp were subject to censors, so even if post got through it would tell the prisoner little about what was really happening. In Campo 21, only Fascist newspapers were allowed and they simply preached the Fascist gospel, spoke of great Italian and German victories and of Anglo-Saxon (as the Italians termed the Allies) losses.

A rather unusual prisoner in Campo 21 was the American Larry Allen, one of a handful of Allied war correspondents to be held in the Italian camps. Lawrence Edmund Allen was born in Mount Savage, Maryland on 19 October 1908. When war broke out in Europe he became an accredited war correspondent with Associated Press, and was assigned to the North African theatre of war. A few days after the Japanese attacked Pearl Harbor, thereby bringing the United States into the war, Allen was on board the light cruiser HMS *Galatea* when she was sunk off North Africa with the loss of 469 lives. It was the night of 14/15 December 1941, and *Galatea* was returning from a patrol between Alexandria and Tobruk when she was attacked. Allen, who was one of about 100 survivors, reported that after beating off a series of dive-bombing attacks, the *Galatea* was 'struck by three torpedos fired by an Axis submarine, flopped over like a stabbed turtle and went down in three minutes off Egypt...I clung to the starboard rail of the quarterdeck until flung into the sea as the warship heeled

over. I battled through thick oily scum for 45 minutes before being rescued...'
Allen was fortunate that he had been able to get onto the deck shortly before
the first torpedo struck. He wore an inflatable lifebelt that he just had time to
blow into and inflate before he went over the side. He was unable to swim. After
a horrendous time trying to keep afloat and not swallow mouthfuls of the oily
seawater, Allen was hauled aboard the accompanying destroyer HMS *Griffin*.
Despite this experience, Allen continued his work as a war correspondent,
winning the Pulitzer prize for war reporting in 1942. He returned to sea a
number of times and in September 1942 was on board the destroyer HMS
Sikh, covering a commando raid on Tobruk. Sadly, the *Sikh* was bombed and
eventually sank and this time Allen fell into enemy hands. Despite his status
as an accredited war correspondent, Allen was initially treated exactly like any
captured serviceman, being sent off to Italy and eventually to Campo 21. A
feisty individual, his expertise in the world of journalism was no doubt helpful
to the CNA when they were interpreting the Fascist press, though Allen's style
was very American and in the early days there were few Americans in the camp.

A fellow American, Captain Joseph S. Frelinghuysen from New Jersey who
arrived in the camp in January, described Larry Allen as bright, quick, a fast
talker, and, despite the prison camp regime, podgy and 'soft as a bowl of Jello'.
He apparently spoke fast, ungrammatical Italian. As a civilian, he did not
regard himself as fully subject to army discipline, and spoke his mind whenever
he wanted to. This was not popular with either the senior British or senior
American officers. As the US population of the camp grew, Allen established
his own notice board, and covered it with 'sound bite' news flashes.

When in early May 1943 he was transferred for a time to the camp at
Fontanellato, Allen gave a number of news talks himself, in what was apparently
a very different style to that of the CNA. He did not remain at Fontanellato
for long however, and was back in Chieti by September 1943 while the Italians
figured out what to do with him. He was eventually repatriated to the United
States in June 1944.

The CNA had a significant task to perform. In October 1942, amongst
other things, the Fascist press were running a campaign alleging various Allied
atrocities. These included acts by both the United States and the British towards
Japanese internees, Russian atrocities towards Germans on the Eastern Front,
and atrocities by the RAF, who were said to have machine gunned a medical
dressing station in the Western Desert and an Italian Field Hospital. The press
issued a warning that 'reprisals would be taken in future'. A rumour spread

around the camp that the Italians had already taken action against a number of Australian prisoners by tying them up, as the Germans had done towards a number of British and Canadian prisoners following alleged war crimes on the Dieppe raid, and a Commando raid on the island of Sark called Operation Basalt.[2]

Inevitably, all sorts of rumours circulated in the camp, many of them damaging to the men's morale. Lett and White Abbott set out to analyse all the Fascist newspapers with very great care, particularly to read between the lines. They interviewed all new arrivals to the camp to find out as much as they could about how the war was really going, and pumped any of the Italian guards who proved friendly for up-to-date information. They also asked for any snippets of information received in letters from home that might help to complete the wider picture. News items would be posted from time to time on the noticeboards in each bungalow and a team of Italian-speaking helpers were enlisted by Lett and White Abbott to go through every press item that came into the camp, and to listen to Italian radio broadcasts.

As in any country at war, Italy's press had a number of purposes to serve. They had to maintain the party line and, so far as they could, maintain the morale of the citizens. However, they had to be careful that their readership did not catch them out in too obvious a lie, because information was constantly filtering back to Italy from those involved in the fighting. Thus the usual propaganda language was employed, where retreats following defeats become 'strategic withdrawals to pre-prepared positions', and occasionally maps in the press would be gently tweaked to disguise how far the 'withdrawal' had actually been. Lett's interpretation of the Fascist media was often successful, although predicted developments regularly took considerably longer than he had estimated. However, he earned a reputation as a bit of a prophet, and obtained certain mystique as the months went by. Lett was in fact simply a well-educated regular soldier, more intelligent than some, who had served in Africa and India before the war. However, Harold Sell described him as 'a very able journalist and widely travelled in Italy in peace time', and Lance Bombardier Frank Osborne said: 'Major Gordon Lett was the principal morale booster of the camp. He was something of a mystery figure to the other ranks and to most of the officers as well. Rumour had it that he was an important official in the Foreign Office branch of the civil service who was stationed in northern Italy

---

[2] See *The Small Scale Raiding Force*, by Brian Lett.

before pre-war. Some thought that he had secret radio contact with the British consulate.'

At this stage, the CNA talks were given in the afternoon, outside at the well in the northwestern corner of the camp. After the first few public appearances at the well, as the weather became less hospitable and as the Italians became more suspicious about what was going on, the meetings of the CNA moved indoors to the cookhouse. Where appropriate, Lett would invite guest speakers to offer an insight into the news items – usually new arrivals to the camp. Harold Sell explained that in due course these meetings would take place on Sunday mornings so that they could be disguised as meetings for 'devotional reasons'. Lookouts were always posted, ready to warn of Italian snoopers and when necessary the meeting would burst into prayer or hymn singing. Sell commented that the whole business was run like a newspaper and secret service combined.

Lett also gave some training to those who wanted to learn the 'science' of analysing the Italian press and the camp gossip generally. Sell described how it worked:

It is all here for anyone to read, little bits here and there in the Italian and German papers, news from new prisoners, whispers from other camps and in letters from home. The reading of newspapers is a neglected science but we do our best to repair the omissions of earlier years. In our room we are keen students of world affairs from all angles, we debate to the limit the war strategy, economics, racial barriers etc. We undergo a course under the tuition of Lett and I realize at once that the value in a newspaper is in the omissions. The printed word is that which the originator wishes the reader to know about – the gems appear as insignificant bits tucked away in the corners or inspired inferences from between the lines. As in our own reports, so in the Italian press, 'withdrawn to pre-prepared positions' is a phrase covering some horrible local disaster (despite the assurance that the place is of no military importance anyway). The headlines announcing prolific sinkings in the Atlantic cover up a reverse on the Eastern front, while the stuff about the Julia Division writing pages of glory on the Don indicates that Uncle Joe Stalin has turned on the heat, and, when finally the Commander receives the Medaglio D'Oro, we know that the Division has ceased to exist. It is all carefully written, but sometimes it comes unstuck and the battle moves faster than the situation can, with decency, be moved on paper. The final report (and this is a sure winner to the public) is to give an inspired report of the whole happening, illustrated by many maps, the scale of which has been distorted, and slight alterations have been made to river positions. We soon find that these distortions may not be uniform over the whole surface, and we go to great trouble to make master maps...

The text of Lett's first CNA lecture on 11 October has not survived, but others have, and will be dealt with later. The initial 'news summary' went down well, and they became a regular event. Initially at least, a notice would be posted on the bungalow noticeboards, announcing the time and place of the next lecture. This changed when the lectures moved into the cookhouse and became covert. However, it was not long before Croce identified Lett as being a prime contributor to the relatively high morale of the camp and selected him for individual persecution.

Meanwhile, during mid-October, Pelley remained heavily involved in the activities of the Dramatic Society. A large room in the main cookhouse had now been converted into a permanent theatre and concert hall. It was christened The New Theatre, and enabled the society to put on far more ambitious productions. At the same time, they decided to put on a special show for the 21 Club. It was to be a cabaret in a simulated nightclub. Handbills were created and tickets were issued per table of five persons to 'The 21 Club Grill Room'. Guests would have to contribute their own food and were required to come in fancy dress. John Jenkins and one of his friends (who attended on 23 October) added colour by arriving dressed as 'South Sea belles' – featuring skirts made from Red Cross parcels, bosoms stuffed with army socks, necklaces and bright 'halos' (this is the word he used, presumably some sort of garland). They won a prize from the organizers for their costumes. Jenkins noted in his diary: 'Had a thoroughly enjoyable evening despite its false atmosphere (perhaps the vino helped). It says a lot for our self control that we didn't lose our virginity!!!' The room was decorated as a nightclub, and there was a band and cabaret. Actors played the part of nightclub waiters, dressed in shirts with long sleeves and cardboard bow ties. Pelley was of course involved, and describes the cabaret as 'good, with two Beatrice Lily acts by MacFarlane, a Bolero by Scott Atkinson and Plunger Smith, and an apache dance by Johnny Hughes.' The 21 Club ran for a number of nights and half a bungalow was invited on each night.

One of the theatrical parts at the nightclub was that of the 'chocolate girl', an usherette purporting to sell sweets to the customers. At short notice, the actor lined up for the part fell sick and a replacement had to be found. 'Bonzo' Burdon-Taylor was prevailed upon by his friends to take the part. He was not a regular actor, but clearly threw himself into the role. He described his appearance in costume as 'a booby lass', wearing make-up and a frilly skirt, with lines drawn down the back of his legs to represent seamed stockings. There were rehearsals and then five performances. Burdon-Taylor remembers that on one night, one of the officer guests came dressed up as a sheikh, complete with harem. Thoroughly enjoying his role, the sheikh not only pinched Burdon-Taylor's bottom, but offered the Club management a large sum of money to buy 'her' for his harem. It was all slapstick fun and without any real sexual undertones. Burdon-Taylor observed later: 'For that week, I was completely out of camp life – from about 4.30 to 9.30 you were absolutely in another world. I suppose you were free, and therapeutically it was a good thing ... It was the lack of personal freedom that mattered. I don't recall being upset by the absence of women.' He explained that talk about sex would occasionally occur, and would start off a chain of raunchy reminiscences, but this was rare. Burdon-Taylor reported that he knew of no homosexuality in the camp – the absence of tobacco and food were the primary worries. Nonetheless he commented many years later: 'We had some gorgeous boy/girls. One Beatrice Lily type was most convincing, will never be the same again'. George Hervey-Murray also recalls that two young British officers were taken away from their stage duties as glamorous young ladies when it was perceived that the stage roles were affecting their behaviour off stage. Captain Carmichael perhaps summed up the situation most accurately, saying: 'In answer to the question: "Would you prefer a lovely lady or a tin of bully [beef]?" The tin of bully won every time.' Jack Shepherd drew a nice cartoon of a sad-faced prisoner coming from the Red Cross parcels room at Christmas 1942 carrying a parcel containing an attractive young lady, completely naked. The caption read: 'What, no KLIM?'

On 18 October, John Jenkins noted that there were now two footballs in the camp. A second one had arrived, also costing £6. On the 19th, John Pelley noted that the 21 Club, whose performances had now started, was a great success. He enjoyed a lively game of basketball in the afternoon, which 'as good as turned into a game of rugger by the end.' It was at about this time that a particular song appeared as a part of one of the Saturday Night Music Hall shows. Apart from Captain Croce, a regular head of the tunnel-tapping team was a lieutenant of the Alpini. These are an elite mountain regiment in the Italian army, who wear a long feather in their Alpine military hats. Toby Graham recorded that there was a skit presented on a night when the Alpini lieutenant was present in the audience, which included this song, which went (roughly):

Tapping tiles for tunnels,
Tap them Itie tap,
Tapping tiles for tunnels
With a feather in your hat.

On 20 October, it was announced that Chieti's South African contingent was to be moved to a separate camp further north. This was in accordance with Italian policy, which was, so far as possible, to confine each nationality to its own camp. There was also still an underlying hope that this might help to sow dissent within the Allied ranks. Although there had been some initial resentment on the part of the South Africans following the surrender of Tobruk, in the months that they had been in Campo 21 they had rallied round and contributed much, particularly to the education classes. On the evening of 21 October, the South Africans hosted a farewell 'cocktail' party, for which they bought in quite a large quantity of wine at exorbitant prices from the Italians. They concluded the evening by singing the South African national anthem. The Italian guards forbade the singing of the British national anthem (it was banned throughout Italy, though allowed in the German prisoner-of-war camps), but this one they did not recognize, so the South Africans were able to give it full voice. Also on 21 October, snow appeared for the first time on the mountains outside the camp and the temperature fell. The prisoners began to feel the cold. That night, an officer in Pelley's bungalow accidentally dropped a towel out of a bungalow window after lights out. He climbed out to retrieve it and was immediately fired upon by one of the camp guards. Happily he was unhurt and successfully regained the safety of the bungalow. The incident reminded the prisoners that at least some of their guards were happy take any excuse to kill them.

On the morning of 22 October, 346 South Africans were taken away, leaving behind only the Church of England Camp Padre, Major Chutter, since there was no other Church of England Padre available, and 49 other ranks. Amongst the musical instruments now in the camp was a set of bagpipes, and Captain Alan Cameron of the Cameron Highlanders piped the South Africans out of the camp.

On 24 October, news reached Lett and the CNA for the first time of the heavy bombing of Turin and Genoa by the RAF – Lett commented that judging by what the Italian papers did not say, and what the camp guards did, the raids appeared to have been a great success for the RAF. Soon, rumours began to filter in to the camp of a big Allied offensive at El Alamein. The positive news helped to offset the discomfort of cold and hunger. On Sunday, 25 October, there was an orchestral concert in the New Theatre. With the new instruments now included in the orchestra, the programme boasted three soloists: Richard Fletcher (singer), Peter Brewin (clarinet) and Eric Downs (piano), all of the Royal Artillery. The orchestra was conducted by Anthony Baines, who in the camp threw himself back into his old life as a musician and conductor to such an extent that it soon became difficult for his fellow prisoners to think of him as anything else, certainly not as a British Army officer. Pelley records that also on 25 October, the bungalow basketball final was played. Suddenly, on 30 October 1942, his diary finishes. Pelley was clearly a very upbeat young man who was throwing himself into all sorts of camp activities. One hopes that he ceased to write his diary (as many did) only because he was too busy.

It was during this month that two more would-be escapers, both from the Worcestershire Regiment, Lieutenant Charles Napier Cross and Second Lieutenant C. Broad, put forward their plan to the Escape Committee, then under the command of Lieutenant Colonel L. C. Cooper, Sherwood Foresters. Cross and Broad had developed a scheme to escape across the roof of the hospital wing, which would give them access to the Italian guards' compound. The full details of the plan, including what the two prisoners would do once they had entered the guards' compound are no longer available, but it was a plausible enough scheme and gained approval from the committee. The security for the guards' compound was far laxer than in the main camp, since it was believed by the Italians to be 'friendly territory'. The Escape Committee offered their practical support, of which more later. Cross and Broad then set out to get themselves as fit as possible. Their plan involved climbing up the Gran Sasso and escaping north along the mountain range towards Switzerland. They would make their attempt once weather conditions were right in the New Year.

November 1942

NEWS OF OPERATION TORCH

As the new month began, there was no sign of any of the improvements recommended in Captain Trippi's report. The weather was increasingly cold and wet, and the daylight hours were shortening. The latter was particularly significant since the lighting in the huts was so poor that it was impossible to read once darkness had fallen outside. Nonetheless, it was still possible to hold a party. The Durham Light Infantry (DLI) were well represented in the camp. 'Bonzo' Burdon-Taylor was one of their number and recalls how they decided to celebrate the Battle of Inkerman, one of the regiment's great victories in its previous incarnation as the 68th Light Infantry. The battle had taken place during the Crimean War, on 5 November 1854, and as was customary in the regiment it was decided to hold the party on the 5th. The event was planned well in advance and Burdon-Taylor described how they ensured there would be enough to drink. As part of their rations from the Italians, the prisoners were given cans of rough young wine. 'We mortgaged our vino for weeks and weeks and weeks, gave it to somebody else and said: "I want your can of vino on the date."' As a result, there was plenty of the rough wine to go round and Burdon-Taylor commented, 'The next day, the DLI blokes had dreadful hangovers.'

The next day was 6 November and far away in North Africa the war was now going very well, with the Allies turning the tables on Field Marshal Rommel at the end of October and into the first days of November. On the 6th, Lett records that several of the *carabinieri* volunteered the information that there had been 20,000 Italian casualties at the battle of Alamein, which Lett was told had begun on 23 October. The behaviour of Croce became increasingly vicious towards the prisoners, whilst at the same time the morale of the garrison appeared to sink. Lett and his team had ample material for the CNA lecture on Sunday, 8 November, which he gave at the well at 1415hrs. It was the fifth CNA news summary. What he had no way of knowing at the time was that on that very day a major new Allied attack took place. Operation Torch was launched – the joint US and British three-pronged invasion of Vichy French North Africa at Casablanca, Oran and Algiers. The notes for the CNA news summary still exist, and make interesting reading. Lett's opening remarks were as follows:

The news this week continues to give us reason for optimism, in spite of the considerable efforts of the Itie press to hide Allied advantages gained under sensational accounts of mass sinkings of shipping in the Atlantic, and Jap victories in the Far East ... Many listeners, I know, have felt that these new summaries are based on wishful thinking, and that in the words of one critic, we are juggling with extracts from the press in such a manner as to make our arguments appear all the more plausible. I hope that the news which has now come to light concerning obvious successes of our 8th Army will do something to alter that opinion ... The daily bulletins on the fighting in Egypt have been posted on the news boards throughout the week, and therefore it is not necessary to deal with them all in detail ... It is now clear that the large air battles, which were mentioned at some length last Sunday, with their fantastic claims of Allied losses to the various pilots, were curtain raisers to the big attack, and the subsequent land operations were sufficient proof that the Allies had gained control of the air ... until Thursday 5th inclusive, according to the Press, the fighting on the El Alamein line was very bitter, with casualties in tanks and personnel on both sides ... for the first time we had a hint of how the enemy was faring, with the cryptic utterance: 'also our own losses have increased.' On Friday 6th, there came at last the admission that Axis forces had been obliged to 'withdraw to new lines to the West'... The special bulletin published yesterday is worth repeating: 'To the growing preponderance of enemy numbers in armoured vehicles and aviation, the Axis forces have shown fierce resistance since the 23rd [October], often passing to counter attack. The British Command has not ceased to continually increase its forces with fresh reinforcements of infantry and armour, and only after hard fighting, especially in the coastal sector, have the Axis forces been compelled to withdraw further West. The immense forces sent from

England and America at this present moment emphasise once more the importance of the Mediterranean theatre of war. The tactical situation still remains uncertain, in spite of heavy losses in men and vehicles inflicted on the enemy.

Lett had been predicting a big push by the Allies to win the desert war and the news was now suggesting that he was right. He went on to emphasize that, reading between the lines of the Italian press reports, the US was obviously throwing resources into North Africa in support of a major Allied effort.

Lett moved on to deal with the other theatres of war, stressing that it seemed that the Russians were about to commence a major counter-offensive against the Axis troops in Russia. Most educated officers realized the importance of Hitler wasting his strength in battle against the Russians. The general belief (which proved in course of time to be accurate) was that the Allies would only win if many of Hitler's enormous and very well trained and equipped divisions were lost on the Eastern Front. Lett next pointed out inconsistencies in the Japanese claims to air supremacy in the Far East, then moved on to deal with the internal situation in Italy. The only two papers allowed to prisoners in the camp were the *Populo di Roma* and the *Messagero*. Both were enthusiastic supporters of the Fascist state. Looking at how they were reacting to the losses in North Africa, and listening to what the more friendly of the camp guards were saying, Lett drew attention to the existence of a Royalist Party in Italy (they still had a king), and the hope expressed by some guards that the Royalists might bring some influence to bear on Mussolini. The Fascists and Royalists had no love for each other, but Lett noted that Crown Prince Umberto had recently been made a Marshal of Italy – a suggestion that there might be some appeasement between the Fascists and the Royalists, a promising sign for the future. Looking at activity on the Italian Stock Exchange, a good barometer of public confidence, Lett noted that government securities had dropped several points in value before being forcibly underpinned by the State. Further, he noted that for the first time a newspaper article had mentioned an Allied aim of the invasion of Italy, and that restrictions had been imposed on civilian travellers to make all forms of transport, particularly on the railway, available for military purposes. Two things, Lett concluded, were making the Italians particularly anxious – one was the fact that German as well as Italian forces were being driven back, the second was the growing US influence on the areas of battle.

Victory in North Africa, combined with air supremacy, would mean that all Italian towns were in range of Allied bombing – it was already happening. American involvement had a particular effect on the Italians, since the USA had long been the favoured destination for Italian emigrants and they admired its wealth and the size of its production industry. Lett, in summing up, optimistically suggested that the Allies might not wait for the fall of Tripoli and total victory in North Africa, but might invade Italy before that. With Germany's strength already being drained on the Eastern Front and in North Africa, a third front in Italy, Lett argued, would stretch German resources too far. He assumed, probably fairly, that wherever fighting was going on it would be the Germans rather than the Italians who would bear the brunt of it. Lett closed his lecture by predicting an invasion from the sea in North Africa, possibly at Dakar, saying: 'In any case we will all be fully justified in watching events thoughout the coming week with more hope and cheerfulness than we have ever had occasion to feel since becoming prisoners of war.' Thus, on the following day, when news of Operation Torch reached the camp, Lett noted in his diary that he had achieved the status of 'Camp Prophet'.

One of Lett's problems was to find paper on which he could safely record his notes for the lectures, without the danger that they would be confiscated in a snap search by the Italians. He eventually came up with the idea of writing his notes, when possible, on the back of the longer typed letters that he had received, and which had therefore already been approved by the censor. Although he received very few letters, a couple of them seemed suitable. Sometime in late 1942, Lett received a letter from Lieutenant Colonel G. N. Davidson in Cairo. Davidson was taking care of various possessions that Lett had left behind there. It was a typed letter and the reverse of the page was clear. Lett recorded his notes for the CNA 3/1/43 news summary on the back of it, heading it, 'Dear Gordon'. The letter passed the searchers' inspection a number of times. Lett did the same thing with a letter from the Royal Geographical Society (of which he had been elected a fellow in May 1942) received in the summer of 1943, again in a format that suggested it was simply a continuation of the typed letter. Again, this succeeded in fooling the guards.

Although the Chieti News Agency had been criticized for being over-optimistic in the past, the news summary on 8 November was all good news. It was a happy event for Captain Arthur Green of the Honourable Artillery Company, because it was the assigned date for his birthday party. His actual birthday had been on the 5th, but the party was being shared with a friend,

Captain D. R. Burgoyne-Johnson of the Royal Tank Regiment, whose birthday was on 12 November. On a beautifully drawn invitation, guests were informed that the birthday tea would last from after the CNA lecture until roll call and that tea would be: pancakes (lemon), pancakes savoury (cheese), China tea, nuts, apples, dried figs, cigarettes, bread, margarine, jam, condensed milk and sugar – all luxury items carefully hoarded for the party. It was a common practice in Campo 21 for the prisoners to deliberately go without for days or weeks, in order to build up enough for a 'blow out' celebration of some sort or another. Amongst those to enjoy the tea was Captain Kenwyn Walters.

After the CNA news summary, and the birthday tea for those lucky enough to be invited, there were a variety of other entertainments to help stave off the hunger and the cold including a talk in D block by Second Lieutenant W. G. Lockhart, entitled The Monte Carlo Rally 1938, in which he had no doubt taken part. When on the following day the news arrived of Operation Torch and the invasion of French North Africa, the inmates of Campo 21 began to dream of being home by Christmas. One of the results of the Allied successes, however, was that from around 10 November the Italian newspapers were no longer allowed into the camp. Word had got back to Croce that they were being used to boost the prisoners' morale. It was probably around this time that Croce began to target Lett as one of the troublemakers in the camp.

On 11 November, Remembrance Day for the fallen of the First World War (when the Italians had fought on the same side as their current prisoners) there was a special presentation put on in the afternoon, entitled 'Homage'. It was presented by Bungalow C, and comprised a series of readings with musical background. The same day happened to be one of the official dates for the birthday celebrations for King Victor Emmanuel III of Italy, and unusually the Fascist regime allowed him to make a speech to the nation. Although Lett and the CNA were never able to find out exactly what was said, as the week went by, and guards sheltered from the rain under the porticos of the bungalows as some of them were wont to do, Lett and his team noticed that many were whispering to the prisoners that they were in fact staunch Royalists and thought perhaps their king would pull Italy out of the war – they were all sick of it, they said, and wanted to return home to their families. The fact that the Italians were obviously getting tired of the war, now that the Germans were no longer winning it for them, seemed all important. If the Italians were simply to give up, or were beaten, then most prisoners thought that freedom would automatically follow. Get rid of Mussolini and the Fascists, most people thought, and the war would end. Thus Remembrance Day was a good reminder that not so long before, Italy and Britain had been standing *fianco a fianco* (shoulder to shoulder) against Germany and Austria.

THE RED CROSS INSPECTS

On 14 November 1942, a representative of the International Red Cross arrived to inspect Chieti 21 for the first time. This was a Dr de Salis, believed by Lieutenant Eric Newby to have been a count. De Salis was not fooled by the 'whited sepulchre' of modern fittings and smart tiles. He noted that the camp now contained 1,237 prisoners (most of the South Africans had recently gone), of whom 253 were other ranks, and reported that in order to solve the problem of overcrowding, the number of officer prisoners should be reduced to between 600 and 700, and the ORs reduced accordingly – a reduction of more than a third. He listed in his report all of the many complaints presented to him by the SBO and gave his general impressions: 'The Camp is overcrowded, and therefore cannot be considered as an ideal one for the officers. The necessary minimum furniture in the dormitories is lacking: there are no cupboards, no drawers in which to put things, no hooks on which to hang their clothes. The problem with the water supply has not yet been satisfactorily solved. None of the heating system has yet been installed and no steps are being taken to see that it is. There is no form of fire protection.'

In the detail of Dr de Salis' report can be found concerns about the lack of Red Cross food parcels, the lack of adequate blankets for the prisoners, the fact that the prison hospital was 'sketchily installed' and lacked isolation wards, a dental surgery and an oculist's room – also that there was a total lack of dental instruments and the Italian doctors used very few anaesthetics. There was an outbreak of 'camp jaundice' with 50 patients suffering from it in the hospital and others less seriously ill in bed in the bungalows. No medical parcels had arrived at the camp, and there was a shortage of bandages. De Salis commented on the lack of footwear: 'The bad condition in which the prisoners' shoes now are gives rise to frequent wounds on their feet.' There was a particular request for football boots from the Red Cross, so that the prisoners could play football.

De Salis was impressed by the efforts of the prisoners to create music and theatre for themselves: 'A piano for practising, which is on hire, is in a large room in a wing of the officers' building which is not set aside for toilet purposes as are those in other parts of the building. Opposite is a room, used as a wash place previously, which now serves as a barber's and hairdresser's shop. It is here that the officers make, in face of great difficulties (since even the cords, string and other packing materials from Red Cross parcels have to be surrendered to the Command) the costumes and scenery for their splendid theatre. The theatre has a second piano which is also hired.' Included in the list of specific complaints from the prisoners was the suggestion that their letters of complaint to the Red Cross, and general post were being interfered with: 'Letters and requests addressed to the Commandant by the Senior Officer are never replied to. The prisoners want to know whether all their letters are really delivered. The Camp Leader, for instance, sent 15 letters and 4 telegrams to the Committee of the International Red Cross, and has never had any replies.'

The reports by the International Red Cross were, as with the Protecting Power, presented as a matter of course not only to the Holding State (Italy) but also to the State or States from which the prisoners came. Thus, at last, a full and uncensored report of conditions in Campo 21 was to reach London. Unhappily, the British summary of the Red Cross report that was sent to London on 18 December 1942, in advance of the full report, described the camp as 'satisfactory but overcrowded'.

De Salis's visit almost resulted in one bad mishap. Lieutenant Eric Newby was part of a team working on an escape tunnel that was based in a room used for peeling potatoes for the camp cookhouse. Newby, who later became a highly successful travel writer, was a young Special Boat Section (SBS) officer, who had been one of a number of men captured in a raid on a Sicilian airfield in August 1942. Born in December 1919, he was a youngster of 22 when he arrived in Campo 21 with his troop commander, Captain George Duncan MC (Duncan had been part of the 'Croce' escape in October). Newby, like Duncan, had no intention of staying in Campo 21 longer than was absolutely necessary and had involved himself enthusiastically in a tunnel project. The digging team were employing a number of lookouts to warn them of the approach of any guards, but the lookouts failed them when the de Salis entourage unexpectedly swept into the compound. De Salis was accompanied by the Commandant and Captain Croce, as well as a number of other Italians. De Salis decided to pay a visit to the room where Newby was peeling potatoes, catching them by surprise. There was only time for one of the prisoners to sit on the otherwise uncovered hole, where he continued to peel potatoes, whilst de Salis inspected the facility. Newby and the others jumped to their feet, and did their best to screen their sedentary colleague and the tunnel entrance from Italian eyes. Strange though the scene must have been, their ruse seems to have succeeded. De Salis and his entourage moved on without incident. (Sadly, the tunnel was later discovered by Italian guards and duly filled in.)

Thus, Campo 21 had now been inspected both by the Protecting Power, and the International Red Cross. It is worthy of note that the Italians also had their own Inspector General of Prisoners of War. He was General Luigi Jengo, who reported to the Prisoners of War Office in Rome. This office was headed by Colonel Pallotta, and was answerable to the General Army Staff. General Jengo's job, as he later described it after the war, was to visit the camps, interview the Camp Commandant, discover what he needed, and to inspect and note the deficiencies of the camp. Jengo claimed that he had no real power, and could only advise the commandants, he could not order them to do anything. He would also interview the SBO of the camp, but through an interpreter (which in Campo 21 would have been Croce). General Jengo said that he had submitted detailed reports to Rome on the conditions in the camps and that he had thought the food insufficient. He had been informed, however, that the rations given to prisoners had been decided by the Direzione Generale di Sanita (the Italian equivalent of the General Medical Council) upon the basis of their value in calories, and that therefore nothing would be changed. Later, it was accepted that the rations for prisoners were lower than those for Italian base troops – in contravention of the Geneva Convention – but this decision was based on the assumption that prisoners were receiving Red Cross parcels. Colonel Pallotta, the head of the Italian Prisoner of War Office, appeared, when interviewed after the war, to be scared of his superiors. However, he said that whatever reports he had received from General Jengo, only the Supreme Army Command could alter the rations and that he himself was powerless.

On the same day that Dr de Salis visited, 14 November, Gordon Lett wrote yet another in a series of letters to his uncle and family in England. This one seems eventually to have got through, though so many others had not – possibly because of the presence of de Salis in the camp that day's outgoing post was not interfered with in the usual way. The standard Prisoner of War letter form was only one side of paper. Lett's letter read:

14.XI.42

Dear Family,

Here is yet another letter, though it will doubtless never reach you, as none seem to have done so far. A cable arrived from Australia yesterday [where Lett's father was], asking for news of me. It took a day to come from

Australia to the Vatican, and ten weeks to come from the Vatican to me! No news except it is getting colder, and there is now a good deal of snow about; the hills look lovely, especially in the early mornings. A Xmas card reached me from Aunt Dolly the other day, which all the other officers in the same cell as myself enjoyed as much as I did. No other letters have arrived for some time, and I gather you had not heard from me up to October 2nd. I hope you are all well and flourishing. I am much looking forward to news of everybody, *particularly the cousins; they must be very active these days, as the theatre seems to be increasing in activity. I wonder what plays they are taking part in?* [author's italics]. A very merry Xmas to you all, sorry I can't send you appropriate greetings ... I wonder if father's books have been published, and where he is, and what he is doing now. Best wishes, and lots of love to everybody – may we at least spend next Christmas together once again.

Gordon

The section in italics was a basic form of code, which Lett hoped would get past the Italian censor if the letter ever left the camp office, but which his family would be able to understand. The *cousins* were of course the Americans, the *theatre* was the theatre of war, and the *plays* were significant actions or campaigns. Lett, as head of the Chieti News Agency, was hoping that his family would use the same simple code to pass news back to him of what was actually going on in Operation Torch and any other campaigns in which the US was involved. Many other prisoners were trying to achieve the same thing, some with appreciable success. In Lett's case, the continued lack of letters from home meant he learned little from this source.

It should be remembered at all times how very hard it was for any prisoner to be deprived of meaningful contact with his loved ones. Many civilians were themselves under attack from enemy bombing in the United Kingdom and elsewhere. A prisoner would be rightly worried about the well-being of his relatives, particularly if they lived in a city such as London that was regularly subjected to air attacks. The absence of a letter from home might well mean that something had happened to them. The arrival and devastating effect of 'Dear John' letters (a wife or sweetheart writing to announce that she had found someone else and that their relationship was over) has been much written about, but for most prisoners there was the continual, nagging worry about the safety of their families. George Hervey-Murray was at one time the 'postman' for his bungalow and it was his job to collect all the mail from the camp's central post office and distribute it to the lucky inmates of his block. It was always a difficult job to do because of the deep emotions involved. Prisoners would see him returning with mail, their hopes would be raised, and then so often dashed again if there was nothing for them. One immediate result of Dr de Salis's visit was that on 17 November, the Italian papers were again allowed into the camp. It happened to be Lett's 32nd birthday. The next day he received his first letter from home, dated 15 July. The writer only knew that he had been posted as missing. Lett hoped that by now, his family knew that he was a prisoner in Chieti. The prisoners' families, deprived of news and often not knowing if their loved ones were alive or dead, were also suffering grievously.

Tunnels were still a part of daily life in the camp. It was true that all five successful escapes had been made by passing through the main gate, but that did not deter the prisoners from the desire to dig. The author has already dealt in outline with the hierarchy of the Escape Committee. Tunnels caused little risk in their early stages, thus many were approved. At various times there might be as many as a dozen tunnels going at once. Second Lieutenant John Pennycook, Royal Artillery, was one of those bent on escaping by this means. In his memoir, he described his main occupation in Campo 21 as being 'escape'. He recalled first becoming involved in a tunnel scheme during November. He was invited by Lieutenant Hugh Gordon-Brown, a 6ft 6in. officer of the Northumberland Hussars, to join his tunnelling party. Pennycook was a digger, and they worked in pairs on three separate shifts – morning, afternoon and evening. His partner was an officer from the Royal Artillery, Lieutenant Tony Gregson, who shared his overwhelming desire for escape. In addition to the six diggers, the full tunnel group was about forty strong, since there were many secondary roles to be filled, some of the most vital being lookouts. If Italian guards were spotted coming in the direction of the bungalow all work was to stop immediately and the tunnel site had to be rapidly restored to its original condition. Thus the 'watchers' would be positioned at various vantage points that offered a good view of the approaches to the tunnel entrance. If placed outside the huts they would seem to be innocently passing the time, perhaps drawing or reading (if a book was available). In fact they would be watching for any sign of a guard approaching. If one appeared, the watcher would give a previously agreed, unremarkable signal – perhaps scratching his knee or his head. He would then remain exactly where he was and carry on with his harmless pastime. There would be another watcher who would pick up the signal and pass it on, either directly down into the tunnel, or through another intermediary. The tunnel would then be rapidly evacuated and the entrance covered up.

The other aspect of tunnelling that required additional manpower was the disposal of the spoil – the earth and other materials dug out of the tunnel. This was dealt with in all sorts of ways, depending often on the location of the tunnel. A common method, particularly in the spring and summer of the following year, was to distribute the soil outside around the camp. This was done by use of leg bags hung around the neck and worn under trousers. Soil was gradually 'leaked' from these bags around the base of the young trees or in the gardening section of the camp. Gardening was permitted by the Commandant, although the tools were very strictly controlled and always had to be returned after use. Earth was scattered from the tunnels on the gardens, and although the level of the soil became higher and higher, and also changed in colour, the Italians never seemed to realize what was going on. Some tunnels were supported by timber for a part or all of their length. As in many other camps, this timber usually came from the bedboards of the bunks. When the Italians queried where these boards had gone the standard prisoners' response was that they had used them for fuel, either on the cooking fires or later, when a few small stoves finally arrived, in the stoves.

Gordon-Brown's first tunnel ran from the latrines, simply because this was the part of the bungalow closest to the perimeter wall and wire of Campo 21. Both Gregson and Pennycook worked on this with him. The shorter the necessary length of the tunnel, the better. The interior of the latrine room was out of sight of the guards, but there were regular inspections by the tapping teams. To start the tunnel, the tiles on the floor of the latrines had to be removed and solid concrete over a foot in depth had to be dug through. The Italians were fully aware of the need to break through the concrete when beginning a tunnel, and kept close control over all suitable tools in the camp. It meant that the prisoners were usually working with makeshift tools, and it took them a long time to make progress. Pennycook describes using a few pieces of metal scrounged from around the camp, and large granite-type stones as hammers. It was important to obtain undamaged tiles from elsewhere in the bungalow in order to replace those inevitably smashed when they began work. The problem of disposing of waste never really arose with Gordon-Brown's first tunnel, since it was discovered by the Italians within a week of starting. The tunnel team had not yet managed to get underground and were still chipping through the concrete. As we have seen, the Italians checked very regularly for tunnels and it was a simple procedure. Pennycook described it as follows: 'A search party of one officer and two or three soldiers carried long hammers like those used on the railway to sound the rails. With these they tapped the floor, listening for any hollow sound, or hoping to find loose or damaged tiles.' Tony Gregson soon started a second tunnel, again from within the washroom/latrine area, but this too was discovered by the guards within a very short time.

The discovery of a tunnel was of course always depressing for the team digging it. When his first tunnel was found, Pennycook says, they 'were subjected to lengthy roll call which caused inconvenience to the whole camp, and, believe it or not, this caused some ill feeling with some who had no intention of ever trying to escape, and for whom "the war was over".' If identified, the tunnel team would be sent to the cooler for up to a month, but although tunnels were regularly discovered, the guards found identifying the culprits was far more difficult. Toby Graham, another enthusiastic tunneller, says that for a while, if they could not identify those who had dug the tunnel, the Italians would take sample 'hostages' and send them to the cooler instead, hoping to deter others. However, Graham relates how in one room where a tunnel was discovered, all 40 occupants claimed to be responsible, and demanded that they all be sent to the cooler, which was far more than the Italians could cope with. The lieutenant in charge of the search party was said to have pleaded with them, saying: 'Please, Gentlemen! It is such a little hole, I only want two officers.' The officers would not back down and in due course, the 'hostage taking' stopped.

Generally, the news coming from the outside world in November was encouraging and morale had remained good. However, despite Dr de Salis's frank report, conditions did not improve. The camp administration became even more inefficient. Lett says that the new Commandant turned out to be completely apathetic and that in spite of the numerous promises he made, conditions actually deteriorated: 'The water shortage became worse than ever, the food ration decreased, hygiene was atrocious and necessities such as dental treatment simply did not exist at all. The overcrowding was nearly as bad as ever, but it did help us to keep fairly warm in the barrack rooms. Protest after protest was put up by the SBO, and neatly side-tracked by the interpreter [Croce].' An encouraging moment, however, came towards the end of November, when all the Italian sentries were suddenly issued with steel helmets. No official explanation for this was given, but the obvious conclusion was that the Italians were expecting to be attacked from the air. The prisoners who spoke enough

Italian had great fun telling the sentries how dangerous it would be for them, stuck in their sentry boxes on top of the walls, when Allied aircraft came over and machine-gunned them.

It became obvious to Lett and the CNA team that a number of the guards were now in the habit of listening at night to the Voce di Londra radio station, which broadcast in Italian from London at 0200hrs every morning. There were apparently several radio sets in Chieti town that were able to pick up the broadcasts, and on more than one occasion, Lett was brought fairly detailed reports made on Radio Londra by the journalists 'Candidus' and 'Colonel Stevens'. Candidus was the pseudonym for John Marus, an excellent Italian linguist, while Colonel Stevens was Colonel Harold Stevens, another fluent Italian speaker and a pre-war British Military Attaché in Rome. Stevens was nicknamed by his covert Italian audience *Colonnello Buonasera* since he invariably commenced his broadcasts with the words 'Buonasera, qui Radio Londra' (Good evening, this is Radio London). At this time, their job was to broadcast anti-Fascist propaganda to any Italians who might wish to listen. Later, they would take on the vital task of sending coded messages to the Italian resistance – the partisans.

On 25 November, the second Commandant was removed, allegedly on the edge of a nervous breakdown. He had lasted a mere six weeks, which is probably why none of the prisoners seem to recall his name. Lett says he had been full of empty promises and attempts at appeasement and that eventually the prisoners 'got rid of him' by arranging for an abandoned tunnel to be found, as a result of which the Commandant was thought to have lost control. His replacement was Colonel Guiseppe Massi, who arrived on 30 November and was to remain until September 1943. That same day, the first rumours reached the camp (probably from Radio Londra on the previous night's broadcast) of a major speech given by Winston Churchill on the state of the war. The speech had apparently been made on 29 November. On 2 December, Mussolini acknowledged the importance of Churchill's account (and the fact that many of his subjects almost certainly knew of it) by attempting to reply to it in detail. Lett later reconstructed Churchill's speech as he believed it to have been. It was all good news and reflected the Allied successes in North Africa.

Hopes of being home by Christmas were somewhat dented, however, when the prisoners were given the opportunity of writing and sending single-page letters giving Christmas greetings to their loved ones. These were supplied by the Vatican and allowed for a maximum of ten words as the message, which should be 'season's greetings' only. Gordon Lett wrote on 25 November to his uncle, who was in London. His father and step-mother had been evacuated from Papua New Guinea to Melbourne, Australia, and Lett still had no address for them. There was no chance anyway that a Christmas message would reach Australia in time. Lett's message was, not surprisingly, the maximum ten words: 'HAPPY XMAS GREETINGS TO YOU ALL LOVE TO EVERYBODY GORDON'.

As the weather got colder, food remained short, the lack of water and sanitation remained a constant problem, and decent clothing was nowhere to be found, many of the inmates plunged into the depths of despair. They lacked such basic commodities as tooth brushes and razor blades. Proper drinking and eating utensils remained virtually non–existent. The prisoners were thankful for the Canadian KLIM tins, from which they could manufacture makeshift drinking mugs with wire handles.

December 1942

COLD, DISCOMFORT AND CHRISTMAS CELEBRATIONS

The realization soon sank in for the men that any hope of being home for Christmas was in vain. The weather worsened, it grew wetter and colder, and conditions more uncomfortable. However well the Allies were doing, it was obvious that the war was not going to end in the near future and the prisoners would be staying where they were for quite some time. For most, Christmas was a family occasion, and even for those who had been stuck far from home in the desert for the last two Christmases, there had been a party of some sort in the mess with plenty of good food and drink, a feeling of enduring comradeship, and some contact with their family far away. Chieti was very different and the approach of Christmas made many feel more deeply than before how much they were missing home. Mail in early December was sparse. Toby Graham showed understanding for those who surrendered to apathy, saying: 'Picture crowded rooms with double-decked bunks only 12 inches apart, bitter weather with only blankets worn over torn shirts to keep out the cold. Few books to read and an allowance of food so miserable that a mind left in idleness thought only of food. Small wonder that those who did not use their minds in some pursuit soon lost the power to do anything that required concentration.'

Their three main morale-boosting activities – theatre, music and sport – were carried on as best they could. Religion also played a significant part for many. In times of apparent hopelessness, faith for those who had it was a real support. The Church of England was the predominant faith. In the very early days, there had been no C of E padre in the camp, so the SBO had read the morning service on the first Sunday. In due course, Major Chutter arrived, and became the chaplain.

There were also two Roman Catholic priests and a Scottish Presbyterian padre. A Church of England council had been set up, along English lines, with elected members. Lieutenant Colonel Henry Lowry Corry, Royal Artillery, was the chaplain's warden, Lieutenant L. Sackville West, Coldstream Guards, was the people's warden, Lieutenant C. Ackroyd was the lay reader, and also among the council members was a Captain McKenzie, possibly the Red Cross parcel coordinator. Many who had not taken much time to think about religion before now began to do so. Confirmation and bible study classes were available, and a number who first discovered what religion meant to them in Chieti went on later to be confirmed. For some who were already committed Christians, like Pilot Officer Arthur Dodds, an RAF navigator and bomb aimer who had been shot down in the Western Desert, Campo 21 offered an opportunity to begin ordination classes. Major Chutter organized a structured devotional life and a course of lectures for Dodds and a number of others of like mind. Dodds was later to escape from Italy, and after the war ended he returned to theological study and was indeed ordained, rising to become a dean. In the early days of his time in Campo 21, Dodds had suffered from jaundice and acute stomach pains, which one of the Italian doctors in the camp diagnosed as being a stomach ulcer. Dodds was advised by the doctor to change his diet to just two plates of plain rice each day, and he duly followed this harsh regime for two months. During this time, Dodds suffered a lot of pain, and records that one night he came close to suicide, seriously considering plunging a knife into his stomach to bring the pain, and his life, to an end. Only his faith, and his belief in the suffering of Christ on the Cross, persuaded him not to commit suicide. He survived the night, gave up the very strict diet, and in due course with the coming of spring his health improved.

At the beginning of December, the Dramatic Society presented a new play: 'Tomorrow is a Dream', starring Geoffrey Lewis as Captain John Rymington, and the emerging Paul Hardwick as a vicar. The play was described as being 'a dream of reality in three acts', written by Victor Canning and Frederick Towle. George Hervey-Murray tells the story behind it. The real Victor Canning, born in 1911, was a very well-known pre-war writer and novelist. He was commissioned into the Royal Artillery following the outbreak of war, and later served in North Africa and in the Italian campaign. However, he was never captured, and was certainly never a prisoner of war in Campo 21. After the war, Victor Canning continued his career as a leading thriller writer up until his death in the 1980s. As might be tempting in the restricted society of a prisoner-of-war camp, an officer with a similar name to Victor Canning had allowed it to be believed, partly as a result of peer pressure, that he was the famous author. A number of ex-prisoners from Campo 21 remember 'Victor Canning' writing a play, and George Hervey-Murray remembers the result. The false Victor Canning had had his bluff called. Under pressure to write a play for the Dramatic Society, he did so, but Hervey-Murray's recollection is that it was of poor quality and exposed him as a fake.

John Jenkins noted in his diary that the theatre shows were continuing, and he had also seen a lively demonstration by Bill Bowes and Freddie Brown, the England cricketers, on how to bowl the googly and the inswinger. He himself was looking forward to playing a big part in the Christmas pantomime, which was to be Cinderella and was scheduled to be performed at the New Theatre on 22, 23, 28 and 29 December. The inmates of the camp made a significant effort to make Christmas enjoyable, including decorating their barrack rooms with home-made paper chains and other festive materials. On 12 December, Jenkins recorded that all the big Italian towns were being thoroughly bombed.

The tunnel teams kept on working. Gordon-Brown's team, again including Gregson and Pennycook, obtained the permission of the Escape Committee to start another tunnel – Gregson's third attempt. This was again inside their bungalow, from a barrack room opposite the one in which Pennycook himself slept. As before, breaking through the concrete was the initial task. Having constructed a dummy cover from unbroken tiles, the diggers broke through the surface and began chipping away at the concrete beneath. It was long and painstaking work, and one of the important things was to keep those residents of the room who were not a part of the attempt happy. Progress was interrupted by roll calls, mealtimes and by alarms when a guard came near. Each time, the entrance to the tunnel had to be carefully covered up. They laboured for several weeks, but again, the tunnel was discovered by the team of Italian tappers. It was a bad time of year for the tunnel teams. The weather in mid-winter was too poor to consider starting their tunnels from anywhere out in the open, and all the buildings were now checked very thoroughly by Croce and his tapping teams.

Douglas Flowerdew recalled one exciting moment which caused great concern to the Italian garrison. There was an Irish doctor (whose name Flowerdew does not supply) who had decided to try to turn the vinegary wine that the Italians supplied into something more exciting, no doubt with the Christmas celebrations in mind. Drawing perhaps on a knowledge of 'poteen', the spirit often home-made in Ireland, the doctor tried to distil a spirit from the wine, adding potato peelings and other ingredients into a sealed flask. So volatile was the liquid he created that one night the flask exploded with a loud bang. The Italians heard it and concluded that the prisoners must have come into possession of explosives, possibly a hand grenade – not surprisingly they instigated a very thorough search of the bungalow concerned, much to the amusement of its inmates. Of course they found nothing, but continued for some time to worry about the possibility of concealed explosives.

In December, a number of new prisoners arrived in the camp, including a 26-year-old American, Sergeant Pilot William David 'Bill' Wendt. Wendt had applied in February 1941 to join the United States Air Force, but had been rejected as too tall. He then travelled to Canada and applied to join the Royal Canadian Air Force, as many Americans did. He had been accepted by the RAF in March 1941, and received his wings the following November. He was sent to England, where he became a Spitfire pilot, then to Gibraltar, and finally to the beleaguered island of Malta. On 30 November he was in action over Sicily, and bailed out after his engine caught fire. He was captured within a few hours of landing and was eventually taken to Campo 21, arriving there on 18 December. The problem for Wendt's family was an all too familiar one. Nobody knew what had happened to him. He had written to his family on 5 December, telling them that he was all right, but the letter did not reach his home in Westport, Minnesota, until 8 March 1943. Official notification received in February 1943 had simply recorded that he was missing, having failed to return from a flight on 30 November 1942. There was always comfort for a prisoner's family in knowing which camp he was in, so that they could write to him there, and so that, with the help of the Red Cross, they could find it on a map. However, for Wendt's family, his whereabouts remained a mystery until well into 1943. For his own part, Bill Wendt was not to hear anything of his family for many months. Indeed, although the RAF promoted him to the rank of pilot officer shortly after his capture, Wendt never received notification of this throughout his time as a prisoner of war, and continued to share quarters with the other ranks at Campo 21. This was no great disadvantage since conditions in the Sergeants/Warrant Officers' mess were considerably less crowded than in the Officers' Mess.

Also in December, a number of senior officers were moved to other camps, the last ones going on the 21st. The 22nd should have seen the first performance of the Christmas pantomime, Cinderella, but whether intentionally (the hand of Croce) or merely coincidentally, the Italian guards made the performance impossible. Jenkins noted bitterly: 'The Ities Xmas gift was to pinch the bulbs and fittings from the theatre, so our panto had to be postponed...' Things were difficult enough for the prisoners without such a demoralizing setback. In the event, the pantomime could not be put on before Christmas and had to be rescheduled for the period 29 December–2 January, disappointing many people.

On 23 December, the Pope's representative paid a visit to the camp. He distributed calendars to all the inmates, and diaries to those of the Roman Catholic faith, which included religious messages month by month. A little bizarrely, but very much to the pleasure of the prisoners, he also presented them with a gift of two piano accordions from the Vatican. These later became a part of an accordion band. Not to be outdone, there was also a visit from the small Italian Protestant Church and John Speares, the signals officer, recalls an envoy in a Berseglieri hat from the Tirol visiting to show sympathy with the protestant prisoners.

Frank Osborne described life for the other ranks: 'As the year drew to a close, we shivered in our tattered remnants of the battle field. The Italians made little effort to clothe us, though we received a blue and white marine shirt and a coarse green sweater after prolonged agitation ... the enterprising few produced trousers self-tailored from blankets, and many a Joseph sported his coat of many colours. The first next of kin parcels started to come in December and January 1943.' Next-of-kin parcels assumed a very great importance. They were, of course, personal to each prisoner. Most men had been in custody for six months, yet only now did next-of-kin parcels begin to dribble in. The very lucky few got one before Christmas. On Christmas Eve, the Dramatic Society put on two showings of a production called 'Charlie's House', enough replacement lightbulbs having been obtained.

The 21 Club issued an invitation to a Christmas Day celebration. Guests had to pay in rations and turn up in fancy dress. Everybody was trying to save up things for Christmas – Harold Sell commented that his friend Major George Trench, Royal Artillery, was saving vino and marsala, and had got hold of some surgical spirit from the hospital to mix cocktails. Both survived the experience. Despite the efforts of many, John Jenkins wrote in his diary on Christmas Eve: 'We have been trying to raise a Christmas spirit, but it was very hard.' Christmas Day itself was a remarkable effort and for many in the end it was a thoroughly enjoyable occasion, with the usual over-indulgence that the festive season brings. Red Cross Mac had managed the distribution of Red Cross parcels leading up

to Christmas very carefully, so that on the day there were plenty for all. The
Red Cross had created special parcels, including a Christmas cake and a plum
pudding. Frank Osborne recalled:

Christmas Day lacked nothing of its normal glamour at Chieti in 1942,
save for the absence of snow. I remember with wonder strutting back
and forth upon the tarmac on Christmas Day in brilliant sunshine, a Red
Cross parcel tucked under each arm. It was not a good thing to leave such
treasures unattended on one's bedstead. The distant peaks of the Gran
Sasso d'Italia however had a glistening mantle of snow which kindled many
yearnings among us. All the rooms were decorated. My own particular bay
was adjudged the best by a committee of inspection. I have long forgotten
the benefit we reaped. It was probably an extra issue of special Red Cross
parcels with chocolate biscuits and plum puddings of special excellence.
We feasted royally, and the Officers gave us a Christmas dinner which
defied the most voracious. The Eyeties [Italians] too opened their hearts
and were lavish with cheap sticky nougat and vino that tasted of vinegar.

For all there was breakfast, lunch, tea and dinner on a scale never again seen in
Campo 21. Between meals, many were obliged to walk around the compound,
trying to walk off an excess of food to which their stomachs were totally
unaccustomed. All the decorated barrack rooms were open to friends, who
were welcome to come and inspect the home-made decorations. Apart from
the religious services on Christmas Day, there was a carol service, modelled on
that which still continues today at King's College Cambridge. There were two
performances, one at 1630hrs on the south side of the compound for Bungalows
3, 4 and 5, and the other at 1930hrs for Bungalows 1 and 2 on the north side.

Ronald Hill had difficulty coping with the excess of food that accompanied
the celebrations. He nearly gave up on his Christmas dinner, got through tea,
but then had to go for an hour's walk afterwards before he could face an evening
meal. He also fitted in trips to Holy Communion, the morning service and the
carol service, although he admitted to attending the latter full of wine. John
Jenkins commented in his diary: 'Please God we are all home by next Christmas.'
Jenkins was one of many young men who saw their lives just wasting away in the
difficult conditions of Chieti.

Harold Sell recalled that snow was falling on Christmas Day, but that the
camp was just below the snow line. The Italians asked the prisoners to give

their word of parole for twenty-four hours over Christmas (i.e. that they would not try to escape), but the SBO would only agree to a twelve-hour truce. Sell recorded that he remained in bed all day trying to keep warm. The tiled floors seemed like glaciers. Then, promptly at 1800hrs:

> Robby and I present ourselves at the portals of the Club, and are received in grand style by a Flunkey, who passes us to another so that our arrival can be announced to the assembled company ... an orchestra renders soft music. The dinner is a great success ... the Ladies add charm to the gathering – possibly the blue painted 25 watt light bulbs helped matters – but they arrive in exotic creations to the great slaughter of Italian bed clothing. The Belle of the Ball has a cigarette holder 10 inches long in a dashing manner...the orchestra switched to Hot Rhythm...Next morning was not so good, and Robby and I can hardly bear the sight of each other. The bungalow is a shambles...

Also, those who had cut up an Italian issue blanket to make a costume had to pay an exorbitant price for a replacement. The Italians always charged very high prices to replace anything damaged whilst in the possession of the prisoners.

On 30 December, Gordon Lett sent a postcard to his uncle Hugh, more in hope than in expectation that it would arrive. It said: 'Doubt if this will reach you, as none of my letters appear to have left Italy so far. No news at all from Australia [where his father was]. Xmas was cheered by Red Cross parcels, which were excellent, otherwise there was nothing. Still hoping for warm clothes before the Spring. Hope Red Cross authorities at home now realize the state of this camp, and that the government have been informed accordingly. All very optimistic. Best of luck for 1943, Gordon.' Surprisingly, this did eventually reach his uncle in London. By this time, Lett had been in custody for more than six months and had only received one letter, from a military colleague, one Christmas card (in November) from an aunt, and one letter (in December), happily from the girl who was to become his wife, telling him that none of his letters had yet arrived in England.

January 1943

MISERY – AND SOME RELIEF

For most, the New Year of 1943 did not bring great optimism. It did bring some new inmates, as a result of the Tunisian campaign. One was Lieutenant W. M. G. 'Bill' Bompas, Royal Artillery, who had been captured in December and reached Chieti on 3 January. As with many prisoners who had been through transit camps, his arrival at what was to be his permanent home came initially as a relief. He recalled: 'As I walked through the gates for the first time, my feelings were firstly of pleasure at the size of the camp, the air of cleanliness and the permanence of the buildings which were large brick bungalows; secondly of amazement, because everyone was walking round on a cold January morning in shorts or blankets, the latter worn like a cloak, and in some cases like a skirt as well … I, in battle dress trousers, shirt, pullover and vest felt extremely overdressed.'

It is fair to ask why the officers and other ranks in Campo 21 still did not have proper clothing. The camp had now been established for a very long time and the clothing problems were well known. It is difficult to come to any conclusion other than that the camp administration, which effectively meant Croce, enjoyed the suffering that many of the prisoners were enduring. Fascists, like Nazis, believed that they were members of a superior race, so the humiliation of their opponents brought them great satisfaction. There was no need for the prisoners to suffer as they did from the cold, or indeed from many of the indignities that they had to undergo. Events later that month were to prove that, so far as the Italians were concerned, they were in total control of the situation and deliberately profiting from it.

The weather remained generally cold – with occasional appearances by the sun only emphasizing the drop in temperature at night. Kenwyn Walters' diary tells the story: '3 January: Lovely warm morning. Frost at night and very cold wind; 4 January: Very cold ... walked a lot to keep warm; 8 January: Very poor evening meal, still cold; 10 January: Snow in Chieti; 11 January: Freezing. Still in tropical kit. 13 January: Frost bitten – very wet and miserable ...'

It is probable that the first few weeks of January were the worst period of captivity in Campo 21 for all the prisoners. It is worth summarizing what some of them had to say about the conditions, when interviewed as part of a British War Crimes investigation into Campo 21 after the war had ended. All made sworn affidavits. Charles Napier Cross reported: 'The management and conditions were shocking. The accommodation was very bad: terribly overcrowded. In the bungalow in which I was living the sanitary conditions were utterly inadequate: the latrine of a sort had no flushing and the stench was appalling. We had to take it in turns to live in the room which was nearest to it. Water was extremely short. Food was very scarce ... As to clothing, it was a case of human neglect.'

Lieutenant Thomas Joseph 'Pat' O'Brien, Royal Engineers, commented: 'Conditions were very bad indeed ... the issue of Red Cross parcels was irregular, many were left without clothing except the rags which they had on, which were merely the remains of desert kit, consisting of a shirt and shorts. No winter clothing was issued until 24 January 1943. Meanwhile the resulting diseases were very numerous, and there was a great deal of jaundice and illnesses resulting from chills and exposure. So far as medical arrangements were concerned, the Italian command was entirely non co-operative ... a very bad influence was a Captain Croce who was the interpreter. He was a violent Fascist, and did his best to add to our discomfort.'

Captain William Magson, Royal Engineers, concurred: 'One Italian officer who stands out in my mind is an officer who was Adjutant and Interpreter named Croce. This officer appeared to be the power behind the Commandant Colonello Massi. Croce was particularly nasty to POWs. He would order parades five or six times a day for no reason at all, and conduct extensive searches leaving the rooms in complete disorder, and in many cases cutting open mattresses, haversacks, and other private possessions ... He was a keen Fascist and violently anti-British ... the water supply was inadequate and was less than three pints a day for all purposes.' All purposes would include drinking, washing one's body and clothes, and flushing the latrines after use.

Ronald Hill's recollections were similar: 'The sanitation at the camp was disgraceful. The water supply was inadequate and the latrines were not flushed the whole time that I was there. The smell was appalling. In the bungalow I was in ... we had water for about half an hour only morning and evening for washing. The bungalow next to ours was sometimes without water altogether and had to share ours. This would mean 400 officers [sharing half an hour's water] ... As a result of the neglect there were many cases of disease – gastric trouble, jaundice, sores, impetigo and other skin troubles ... the camp had little or no medical equipment or stores ... the camp was run mainly by Captain Interpreter Croce who was a Fascist and very anti-British. He would do nothing for us nor attend to any complaints and he would not pass on requests or complaints.'

On the latter topic, Lieutenant Roy Wiggins, Somerset Light Infantry, attested: 'We used to address telegrams from time to time to the Red Cross authorities requesting Red Cross parcels etc. These telegrams were entrusted to Captain Interpreter Croce for despatch ... we were told that none had been received. Our SBO took the matter up with the Camp Commandant and demanded an explanation. It was found on investigation that the telegrams had not been sent out, but had been filed in Croce's office.'

Lieutenant Michael Murray, Essex Regiment, wrote: 'For myself, I only had desert kit consisting of shorts, shirt, socks and boots (the latter very much worn) and a pullover. As a result I wore my blanket most of the winter ... the worst point of the camp was the lack of water ... there were showers in the camp, but as far as I can remember they were only in use twice. I had one shower only. Apart from this there was one tap in the wash room above a tiled floor and two feet from the floor to serve 150.'

Lieutenant Hugh Haldane Thomson, Royal Artillery, recorded: 'We were very hungry indeed up to about February 1943 ... The slightest damage was exorbitantly charged against the prisoner who happened to have the particular article in his possession at the time. A small hole in a sheet would be charged at 120 lire ... This was deducted from a prisoner's pay ... Two stoves per bungalow were [eventually] provided – one in the open part of the bungalow which contained 180 men, and one in the other room which contained 20 men. There were no stoves provided during the winter at all, and in any case no fuel was ever provided so that they were not of much use.' Even if the prisoners had found something to burn, the picture of 180 men trying to huddle around one small stove is a pathetic one.

Captain Adrian Collingwood, East Yorkshire Regiment, recalled: 'The clothing position was extremely bad ... there was no heating during the winter, and I and a fair proportion of the other POWs were walking about in bare feet. Our clothing was worn to shreds ... Few, if any, had greatcoats, and we used to drape ourselves in blankets to try and keep warm.' Eric Newby was to say that it was a 'truly fearful winter in which the camp was swept by infective jaundice.'

Hunger was at its most acute once the Christmas festivities had died down. Some became mentally as well as physically affected by the lack of food. Stuart Hood spoke of one prisoner who grew so obsessed by hunger that he refused to eat his daily ration of bread (a single small roll). He was suffering from a starvation neurosis and stored all his rolls of bread in a box, fearful that if he didn't keep them he would not be able to survive. As he grew hungrier and hungrier, the obsession only became worse. Smoking, which could alleviate hunger to a small degree, became a more desperate affair, with heavy smokers hunting for old cigarette ends and any waste tobacco that they could possibly find.

The saddest moment of the month came on 10 January, when one of the prisoners, a roommate of John Jenkins in Bungalow 2 called Ronnie Dunlop, died of heart failure. Although a death from natural causes, the harsh regime of the previous few months must inevitably have taken its toll. Campo 21 was a thoroughly miserable place to die.

Croce undoubtedly made matters worse for the prisoners during the cold winter months. He would summon a roll call at 0200hrs, and keep the prisoners standing out in the freezing cold for up to two hours, with snow or frost on the ground and totally inadequate clothing. During the daytime, he would summon a roll call just as food was being served from the cookhouse, so that when the prisoners returned to such food as they had been given, it had gone cold. The prisoners responded in their misery by baiting their guards whenever they could. In Stuart Hood's barrack room, they invented a game to play after lights out, when all was meant to be quiet. It was a game modelled on a journey around the London Underground on the Circle Line. The whole barrack room would chant at the tops of their voices: 'Doors closing ... Stand clear of the doors ... Doors opening ... Mind the Gap!' as they travelled from station to station all the way round the line. It was, of course, a form of escapism, but the noise inevitably led to a visit by the guards. A similar game was to make farmyard noises at a earsplitting volume.

The theatre battled on, still producing a cross-section of plays and entertainments. Bill Bowes starred in a production of Bernard Shaw's 'Mice and Men'. George Hervey-Murray describes him as a very good actor. He went on to take a variety of other parts.

On 4 January, Lett finally received a letter from his uncle Hugh, dated 1 October 1942. It had been sent to the camp at Bari, since the Vatican had announced that Lett was there (he had been moved to Chieti in late August). Hugh's letter finally informed Lett of his father's address in Australia. He included also a promise to send a next-of-kin parcel every three months through the Red Cross (which was the maximum allowed), and asked his nephew to write and tell them what, in particular, he needed. The letter included the following words, that undoubtedly brought Lett great comfort: 'Well my dear lad, I am immensely sorry that your military career is cut short so far as this war is concerned, but you have done jolly good work and can look back on it with satisfaction – we are very proud of it. Now see what you do to make the best of your time. I know full well your disappointment, and time will hang heavily on your hands, but of one thing I am certain: that you will keep up your fine record and help those with you to keep their chins up.'

In January, a more regular supply of next-of-kin parcels finally began to arrive in the camp; Ronald Hill was one of the lucky recipients. Next-of-kin parcels came directly from a prisoner's family and friends, and might contain much-needed clothing, or other items that a prisoner had asked for (if his letters had reached home of course). It may well be that the parcels suddenly started to arrive because Croce knew of the impending arrival of another inspector. There certainly seems to be a marked coincidence between the arrival of much wanted items in the camp and the arrival of a representative of the Protecting Power. However, the Italians were careful to inspect the contents of all parcels. Parcels were opened on an inspection table. Clothing was searched in front of the recipient before he was allowed to receive it. Cigarettes were emptied out of their packets or tins into boxes brought for that purpose, lest the packaging concealed forbidden items. The guards were always on the lookout for hidden maps, money or tools. Bearing in mind what MI9 were trying to do, it was a sensible precaution. Hardback books would be signed by their owners and then sent off to Rome, in order for the covers to be stripped off in case anything had been secreted within them. They were returned damaged and without their covers, but with a censor's stamp of approval. However, as the months went by, the prisoners found means of slipping items away from under the noses of their hosts, so that no inspection actually took place. One of the trophies that Arthur Green kept from Chieti was the flyleaf of a book, bearing the endorsement:

'This book was smuggled away from the parcel unpacking table under the noses of the Carabinieri. After signature by me, it should have been sent to Rome for censorship, and the cover torn off before return in a month or six weeks. However, smuggled and then stamped with our home made censor's stamp, which fooled Italians in subsequent searches.' The flyleaf contains two convincing censor's stamps, and is signed not only by Green, but by other officers who had read it.

Food and clothing were constant problems. On 6 January, John Jenkins noted: 'The Ities have put up [the cost of] our daily ration, because they say that the Italian prisoners are being charged more [by Great Britain]. I fail to see how we could possibly get less food for the amount of money.' On the same day, Hill recorded that his clothes were now in such a bad state that they could not be washed for fear that they would dissolve away.

On about 7 January, there was a second inspection on behalf of the Protecting Power, this time not by the elderly Captain Trippi but by a rather more 'on the ball' inspector, Rudolf I. Iselin. There is a little confusion as to the exact date of his visit as Kenwyn Walters records it in his diary as being 6 January and Lett as being on the 9th. Prisoners of war seem to have been particularly inaccurate as to dates, no doubt a result of their tedious existence. The report itself is dated 7 January. Iselin found and reported that the overcrowding had not changed, there were still in excess of 1,200 prisoners in the camp, including 18 US airmen. Further, now in midwinter, there was still no heating. The Swiss report notes, however, that the promised stoves had arrived and the inspector was told that it would be only a few days before they would be installed. A cynic might have wondered how long the stoves had actually been at the camp and whether they could not have been installed long before, had Croce so wished. Most of the men still had just two thin blankets to use at night. Iselin's report was blunt about the water situation, saying: 'The great misfortune is the shortage of water in this camp. The washing facilities as well as the toilets are quite modern and look like a luxury never seen before in a prisoners' camp. But the trouble is that all these installations do not function at all, due to a shortage of water. The water is running in 24 hours for about one half hour altogether. The prisoners of war since they were transferred to this camp on August 3rd, have not had one drop of hot water. No showers, no bath whatever. This matter has been taken up with Italian High Command after the last visit, but nothing has been done so far. Strong representations will be made again, and the Italian High Command will be asked to remove the camp unless a sufficient water supply can be arranged in a very short time.' In other words, the Swiss were now saying that unless the water situation was sorted out rapidly, the camp should be closed down.

The hospital contained 32 patients, the majority of whom were suffering from jaundice. The medical opinion received by the Inspector was that this was a result of the change of climate from Africa to Italy, most of the men having hardly any clothes. There were three Italian doctors who attended the camp hospital: Major Cranzo Petito, Captain Pecoraro and Dr Caruzi. A dental service still did not exist there, despite the presence of an excellent British dentist, Captain I. S. Goodall. There being no dental instruments, he was of no use. It was said that an Italian dentist from Chieti town visited every so often, but only to perform extractions. No fillings or other dental work were done by him. In other words, the prisoners had to suffer pain until the tooth was a lost cause and then, if they were lucky, it might be removed by the Italian dentist. Failing that, one of the Italian doctors might extract the tooth. Rather as with the issue of heating and stoves, the Inspector was told that a few days before, the demand for dental instruments had been granted, and that as soon as these arrived the British dentist would be able to start work.

There was a similar problem with eye care. There was a system whereby the prisoners could apply through the Red Cross for spectacles and a number had done so, but nothing had arrived. There was no proper oculist or optician's service, although again one of the Italian doctors was an eye specialist, and had apparently just received permission to bring his instruments into camp. Of course, amongst the prisoners was a trained optometrist, Geoffrey Bateman. In his civilian life he would carry out refractions (sight testing). Bateman was one of those with experience of the hospital both as a patient and a carer, since he suffered from desert sores that took months to heal under rudimentary treatment, but once instruments were available, he worked as the camp's optician. He also recounted that once provided with proper instruments, the British dentist, Captain Goodall, did a very good job. Before that, the prisoners were in the care of the Italian doctors for all their medical and dental needs (unless the dentist from Chieti town turned up). One of the doctors, Cranzo Petito, was an older man with the rank of major. It was he who carried out the tooth extractions for all the Italian soldiery in the camp, always without anaesthetic, and with shouts of 'Bravo, Bravo!' as they cried out in pain. He was, however, a genial and well-meaning doctor. It was not his fault that Italy had, from the start, been too poorly equipped to join a world war, and was now suffering desperate shortages of medical supplies. Bateman described a second doctor, presumably Captain Pecoraro, as a younger man, said to be an ophthalmic surgeon. However, Bateman was scathing about his abilities when doing refractions, which Bateman commented that he did very badly. The younger doctor was possessed of a tenor voice which he used often, and he loved to boast about his affairs of the heart with the ladies of Chieti town.

It was one of these two doctors who treated Lieutenant John H. 'Solly' Joel, Green Howards. Not long after arriving in Chieti, he developed a boil on the back of his neck, a form of desert sore. He was not keen to report sick, but as the boil matured and became extremely painful, it reached the stage where he could stand it no longer, and off to the Italian doctor he went. 'He looked at it, and rubbed his hands in what I thought was quite unwarranted glee,' recorded Joel. 'With my back to him I felt a pretty sharp pain in my neck and he said finished. The PoW behind me was feeling sick. He told me the Doctor had picked up a blunt ended pair of scissors, stuck them at the base of the boil and scissored up catching the resulting mess in a not too clean cloth. Drastic but it cured the boil.'

Bateman recalled that he treated over 300 patients at Chieti. At first, he was allowed to buy spectacles (no doubt at a much inflated price) from a local optician, but the local man soon ran out of lenses. He also supplied a number of pairs of sunglasses. The Italians refused to allow prescriptions for spectacles to be sent back to Britain, apparently fearing that they might contain some secret code, so Bateman did such ordering as he could through the International Red Cross. The Red Cross filled these prescriptions by dismantling and re-assembling parts from collections of old unwanted spectacles. They were sometimes, therefore, strange in appearance, but Bateman found the prescriptions were invariably as close to those that he had requested as had proved possible, and they sufficed for the time being for his patients.

In relation to sport, the Representative noted that there was only one football in the camp amongst 1,200 men (the second one had apparently gone, probably kicked over the wall and not returned). Captain Croce claimed that some sporting equipment had arrived in Rome, but had been held back by the censor. When pressed, Croce could not explain how that had happened. He claimed the same was true in relation to a number of chess sets and of indoor games. It was also noted that no books had yet arrived in Campo 21 from the Red Cross. There were numerous complaints about the non-arrival of mail, and yet again the SBO made clear that he had written a number of times to the Swiss Legation, yet none of those letters had apparently arrived. Iselin recorded his general impression as: 'Despite the fact that quite a few things need improvement, the camp, if it was not for the question of water supply, cannot be called a bad camp.' However, in the continuing absence of enough water, that was exactly what it was. A summary of this report reached London on 22 January 1943, and is endorsed: 'Very unsatisfactory report.' At last, London was beginning to realize how bad conditions were in Campo 21, though in reality there was little they could do.

Some private letters did manage to beat both Croce and the censor, and get through to England. On 9 January 1943, Lieutenant H. L. Sherbrooke, the Bays, wrote his 23rd letter to his father. Just 6 of his previous 22 letters had arrived at their destination. Perhaps if 9 January was the date of the visit by Dr de Salis, that may be the reason why letter 23 got through, without interference from the censor (or Croce). Sherbrooke spoke of the fact that next-of-kin parcels had finally started to arrive in the camp, and he hoped to receive his:

They must be somewhere near now, so I live in hope that my time of discomfort must nearly be at an end now. Incidentally, my feet have at last given up the unequal struggle of being permanently wet and I have got an attack of what I suppose is trench foot. Nothing serious, but it means that I can only just hobble around. If there is a pair of shoes in the next of kin parcel, I shall be OK again in a short time. Otherwise I am quite fit. It really has surprised all of us what remarkably little food it takes to keep body and soul together, and how one can resist the cold attired in clothes intended for the desert in June! ... We have shortened our day for the winter, by not getting up until 9 o'clock so as to give us less time to exist on the food provided ... most people spend the afternoon in bed too, for the same reason, as well as to keep warm.

Sherbrooke's father was Lieutenant Colonel R. L. Sherbrooke DSO, then stationed in the United Kingdom on Aerodrome Defence with the RAF Regiment. He was understandably upset and shocked by his son's uncensored account and wrote including a copy of the letter, to the headquarters of the British Red Cross at St James's Palace, London. From there the letter was passed on to the Director of Prisoners of War at the War Office, where a file of information on conditions in Campo 21 was gradually being compiled.

It is probable that after the visit of the Protecting Power on 7 January, Croce decided that he had played his hand as far as he could and that he must now comply with some of the demands being made. Should the Swiss go so far as to order the camp to be closed, then Croce and Commandant Massi would be in real trouble with Rome. Clothing was the greatest need in Chieti, and when the Protecting Power's report reached London later in the month, a question was asked in the House of Commons as to why British prisoners were not being properly clothed by the Italians. Later on, an explanation came through to London from the Red Cross as to why they had not been able to supply clothing to Campo 21. On 16 February, Major General Sir Richard Howard-Vyse, chairman of the prisoners of war department of the British Red Cross, wrote to Major W. J. N. Little at the Office of Prisoners of War, explaining that in the summer, as soon as events in Libya made it clear that the Red Cross would have to deal with a large increase in the number of prisoners, they had sent a considerable consignment of clothing to Geneva in order to supplement their clothing reserves there. Thereafter, the problems had been a) that the prisoners in Italy apparently took a long time to reach their permanent camps; b) that the Italians had then not notified the Red Cross of their whereabouts for an indefensible period of time, aggravated by the fact that Chieti was a new camp of whose existence the Red Cross had not previously known; and c) when the Italians did finally notify the Red Cross, in mid-October 1942 (four months after the surrender of Tobruk), all rail transport between Geneva and Italy ceased – due, the Italians said, to 'dislocation', which may have been partly down to action by the RAF. Parcels of uniform clothing had not been able to leave Geneva until just after Christmas on December 26. Howard-Vyse accepted that the clothing situation in Campo 21 had been appalling.

Geneva to Chieti was not a very difficult journey. When those uniforms actually arrived is open to question. The later suspicion of the prisoners was that they arrived in the first half of January, but Croce still looked to exploit the prisoners' discomfort for profit. On 20 January 1943, before the arrival of proper uniforms was announced, and at a time when the Allied prisoners were still desperate for warm clothing, a particularly mean trick was played. The canteen run by Croce in Campo 21 finally told the men that some Italian clothing was available for sale, albeit at quite unjustifiable prices. According to Bateman this comprised thin fleecy lined vests, artificial silk pants, cotton socks and ties. Despite the prices, the desperate prisoners, not knowing that free issues of British uniform were just around the corner (or more probably already in the stores at the Chieti camp), were prepared to pay whatever the cost. The poor-quality clothing sold well to those most in want. Three days later, it was announced by the Campo 21 authorities that the Red Cross clothing had arrived – battledress, greatcoats, vests, pants, shirts and boots. These of course were free. But Croce had taken his opportunity to profiteer before the British clothing was made available. At any rate, the life of the prisoners of war changed overnight. Miraculously, the stoves then appeared in the huts and, despite what Hugh Haldane Thomson was to say later, a very limited allowance of fuel was made available. Although the stoves were small and there were far too few of them, many of the prisoners felt warm for the first time in three months. Jenkins commented: 'It was wonderful to see everyone looking human again, after changing from ragged and tattered shirts.'

Also within days of the inspection visit, the showers began to work for the first time. However, this did not prove quite so satisfactory as the warm clothing. Hill noted on 15 January: 'First showers in use, not a great success, water only lasted for the first few.' Kenwyn Walters noted on the following day: 'Had a hot shower – first since first day at Bari!' Hill explained that later British officers from the Royal Engineers managed to improve the flow a bit, so that the showers could work for a little longer during the period that the water was switched on. John Jenkins described the arrival of the stoves in his diary. There were only two per bungalow. One small stove was expected to warm six large barrack rooms, each containing up to 40 officers. Jenkins, one of the lucky ones, recorded that they had a stove installed in his room but that the fuel supplied lasted for only about an hour, and because of the lack of space, only four people at a time could get near it. Thus the lack of heating was not much improved. However, at least the Swiss ultimatum following the 7 January visit had had some effect. Conditions in Campo 21 did improve, and quite swiftly. An obvious inference is that all along, encouraged by Croce, the Italian authorities had deliberately done nothing about the prisoners' dreadful conditions, and if Croce was responsible for that neglect, it is difficult to regard as anything other than deliberate torture.

The arrival of the stoves and the lack of adequate fuel for them gave rise to another form of sport for the more adventurous prisoners. Toby Graham recalls how it was very speedily realized that the numerous warning boards around the tripwire inside the wall, forbidding 'demurrage' or trespass beyond the wire, made ideal fuel. A game developed known as 'Demurrage board hunting', to steal as many of the boards as possible and burn them in the stoves for extra warmth. Gradually the boards disappeared, until only the most exposed, the ones directly beneath the sentry boxes, were left in position. Toby Graham explained the technique – the prisoners would work in pairs. They were armed with a rope made of Red Cross plaited string. The first man would sidle up to a demurrage board and covertly slip a noose over the board and its stake. He would then wander innocently away. The second member of the team would be holding the other end of the rope, out of sight behind, or inside, one of the bungalows. He would reel in the board, pulling it out of the ground and across to his position. It would then immediately be broken down and fed into a stove. Thus, even if a sentry spotted the sign disappearing across the ground and raised the alarm, the guards would be unable to reach an offending bungalow before the board had become firewood.

It is perhaps appropriate at this moment in the story to draw the contrast between what happened to the Allied prisoners in Campo 21, and what happened to very many Italian prisoners in British hands. The hearts of most ordinary Italians were never in the war. They were, by and large, ill equipped, and they had no hatred of their enemy in the early days in North Africa, the British. Italy had been under the control of the dictator, Benito Mussolini for nearly twenty years when he first declared war in June 1940, and many youngsters had never known anything other than Fascist rule – for them it was the necessary way of life. As always in a dictatorship, as in any political party, there were some dedicated followers and some who chose Fascism in order to profiteer, but most ordinary people simply wanted to get on with their daily lives without trouble. When faced by well-trained British troops in the desert, the Italians surrendered in their thousands. They just wanted to get out of the war. Some were sent to India and other parts of the British Empire, but many came to Britain, where by and large they settled happily into their prisoner-of-war camps, and got on well with the local population. There are many examples of this, one of which is a camp just outside Wells in Somerset. Many Italian prisoners spent a proportion of their war there and were allowed out of the camp to work in the surrounding area, usually on farms. So much did they appreciate their time in the camp that they built a memorial on the site, known as the Romulus and Remus Memorial, as a gesture of thanks to the local population. Many never went home at all and there is to this day a large Italian population in the vicinity of the city of Wells. Once a year, the local Italian community meets for a *festa* at the site of the old camp.

January also saw the beginning of an influx into Campo 21 of American servicemen. This was mainly as a result of the Tunisian campaign, but also because air activity over Italy was increasing. Lett commented that the arrival of the Americans added life to the camp, and certainly they brought with them a new approach to many things, in particular sport. Amongst the arrivals was a batch of ten US officers who entered the camp on 12 January 1943, before the decent clothing arrived. They included Joseph S. Frelinghuysen, a gunnery captain from New Jersey who had been captured on Operation Torch. Frelinghuysen quickly realized the importance of speaking Italian and, with a view to escape, took lessons from a fellow American, a medical officer called Frank Gallo, from Winsted, Connecticut, who, as his name might suggest, spoke several Italian dialects, including pure Florentine Italian. Under Gallo's tutelage, Frelinghuysen was soon able to speak a passable Italian, and therefore to understand much more of what was going on both inside and outside the camp.

February 1943

THE BEGINNING OF SPRING

Toby Graham's feet had finally healed up around Christmas time and he was now fit to make an escape attempt. He teamed up with an American in the next room to his, Peter Glen, from Clarksdale, Mississippi. Glen was an ambulance man, and therefore a non–combatant. He had volunteered before the US entered the war, and had been in the desert attached to the 8th Army since 1941. As an ambulance man, after capture, Glen had initially hoped for repatriation, but he was still in Campo 21. It had apparently been decided that since he had volunteered, he should serve his time like everybody else. Therefore, Glen was as determined as Graham to escape. The geography of the camp was such that, apart from going over or under the walls, or through the gate by some sort of bluff, there was also the possibility of going through the wire fence separating the guards' area of the camp from that of the prisoners. The hope was that it would be much easier to get out of the camp from there, whether over the wall of the guards' compound or through the main gate. Very careful planning had also to go into how they would make their way out of Italy. Graham and Glen knew that their Italian was not nearly good enough for them to pass as natives, nor could they fake passes good enough to travel as foreign workmen. Therefore, they planned to walk north to Switzerland, travelling only at night. Once up in the mountains, away from the cities and the Fascist strongholds, they might be able to pay for help from some of the local people. However, this plan meant that they had to get as fit as possible, after months of poor diet and cold. Thus Graham and Glen joined the many prisoners who pounded around the compound each day for their exercise. Monotonous though it was, they began by doing an estimated 7 miles each afternoon at a slow pace, and after a month found they were able to do 12 miles a day, up and down the central path of the camp, moving at the fast pace of 5 miles an hour. They estimated that this equated to 110 lengths of the path each afternoon.

The other thing that they needed, apart from courage and good luck, was food. One of the greatest difficulties for would-be escapers was that they had to save up food from their limited rations. This involved going without certain necessities for perhaps weeks at a time, at a cost of losing strength and with the danger that everything saved might be discovered and confiscated in one of the guards' random searches. Graham and Glen started to trade vigorously for chocolate, but also general goods, in order to build up a profit which they could then invest in food for their escape. By the end of January, they believed that they were fit enough and had accumulated enough food to make the attempt.

Their final plan for the escape itself evolved during the time of their preparation. They eventually agreed that they would attempt to wriggle under the wire that divided the guards' compound from the rest of the camp, using a shallow gutter at the end of the regular sentry's beat along the wire. That point would only be in the view of that particular sentry, and only so long as he was facing in the right direction. There was a window of opportunity just after darkness had fallen before an extra sentry was posted close to the gutter – after that, their chances would be slim. Once through the wire, hopefully on a very dark night, they would cross the guards' compound and use a fire-escape ladder that always leant against the rear wall of the guardroom to climb over the wall. The attention of the sentries in the guard towers should be on the prisoners' compound, not on what they would regard as 'friendly' territory.

When requesting approval of their plan, however, Graham and Glen discovered that there was another team with an identical scheme, so they were second in the queue. But they were now ready to go. On the afternoon of 2 February, the head of the Escape Committee called Graham and Glen to his room. He told them that their competitors who had been first in the queue were not yet ready, that the nights were getting shorter, and that since they were all set, Graham and Glen could go that night. The two men requested Italian forage caps and tunics as a disguise for when they were in the guards' compound, and were promised that they could have them from the Escape Committee's reserves. They were also promised there would be some sort of distraction to occupy the attention of the sentry. A distraction of this kind was known in the camp as a 'rammy'. Graham and Glen now rushed to gather their supplies together, which were hidden in various obscure parts of the prisoners' compound, and the articles of Italian uniform duly arrived.

As soon as darkness began to fall, Graham and Glen positioned themselves as near to the gutter under the wire as they could properly be. Glen went first, and successfully wriggled through the wire whilst the sentry was at the other end of his beat. His rucksack caught on the wire as he went through, causing what seemed to Graham like a very loud clanging sound, but the Escape Committee stooges had begun their 'rammy', and the clang was swallowed up in an outburst of raucous laughter. Glen then disappeared into a potato patch, where they had agreed to meet. It was now Graham's turn. He chose his moment, but was only halfway through the gutter when he heard the tread of the returning sentry. Graham froze. The sentry slowly approached him and stopped at the end of his beat, so close that Graham could both hear his breathing and smell the garlic on his breath. Then, maddeningly slowly, the sentry turned round and set off on his beat again. Graham pulled himself through to the other side of the wire as quickly as he could, then paused still in the gutter on the guards' side of the wire to check that the coast was clear. Almost immediately he heard the sound of marching feet, as the second guard was posted. Happily, having stood only inches away from the prone and silent Graham for about five minutes, the sentry went to have a chat with his colleague a little distance away, and Graham was able to move out of the gutter. According to Graham's account, it was at this moment that a loud English voice called from within the prisoners' compound: 'Get up and walk!' Presuming that it was one of the Escape Committee, and that therefore the coast was clear, both Graham and Glen did just that, hoping that their Italian caps and tunics would provide sufficient disguise. This was not a move one that either man had originally intended to take – their plan had been to lie low in the potato field until they themselves judged that the coast was clear. And it turned out to be the wrong move. As both men stood up and walked, a guard emerged from the guardhouse and walked directly towards them. Graham and Glen split up but both were very shortly afterwards challenged and apprehended. Graham's bitterness at the way their plan had been spoiled by the action of some member of the Escape Committee rings through in the account that he wrote many years later in his book, *The Escapes and Evasion of an Obstinate Bastard*. Left to their own devices, he clearly thought that their plan would have succeeded, and that they would have got out of the camp.

The pair were taken to the guard house, where a gloating and abusive Croce soon appeared and began asking questions. As with the previous escapes, Croce

Drawing of Campo 21, from the collection of Lieutenant D. A. Roberts MC. *(Courtesy of his family)*

Campo 21 looking towards the town of Chieti, drawn by Lieutenant Jack Hodgson Shepherd. *(Courtesy of Mrs Barbara Shepherd)*

Campo 21, looking towards the Gran Sasso, drawn by Lieutenant Jack Hodgson Shepherd. *(Courtesy of Mrs Barbara Shepherd)*

1953 photo of camp – looking towards gate. *(Courtesy of the family of the late Major Tony Gregson)*

1953 photo of camp – looking towards cook house. *(Courtesy of the family of the late Major Tony Gregson)*

CHIETI   April 1953

Well (The 'hut' was new since 1943)

1953 photo behind D block.
(Courtesy of the family of the late Major Tony Gregson)

CHIETI   11

1953, Mrs Margaret Gregson at the entrance to Tunnel 2. *(Courtesy of the family of the late Major Tony Gregson)*

C, B and A Blocks in 1953. *(Courtesy of the family of the late Major Tony Gregson)*

The bathing place in the Fiume Pescara, 1953. *(Courtesy of the family of the late Major Tony Gregson)*

Major Gordon Lett DSO.

Captain Dominic Toby Graham MC.

Captain Arthur Green MBE and the bride that he had to leave behind. *(Courtesy of their family)*

Lieutenant Jack Hodgson Shepherd. *(Courtesy Mrs Barbara Shepherd)*

The Sportsmen

Lieutenant Bill Bowes.

Captain Freddie Brown.

Lieutenant A. D. S. Roncoroni, second from left, back row, winning his first England cap in 1933.
(Courtesy of the Rugby Museum, Twickenham)

Flying Officer Claude Weaver III DFC receiving his wings on 10 October 1941. *(Courtesy of acesofww2.com)*

Flying Officer Bill Wendt. *(Courtesy of his family)*

First Lieutenant Samuel Redden Webster Junior, and his wife Mary. *(Courtesy of their family)*

Flight Officer James E. Beck. *(Courtesy of the family of Bill Wendt)*

Flying Officer James Outerbridge.
*(Courtesy of the National Museum
of Bermuda)*

Papantonio. *(Courtesy
National Archives)*

Group photo. Back Row L to R: Richard Edmunston Low, 157 Fd Regt RA, Gordon A. Hick, 107 RHA?, R. C. U. Haddon, 121 A Fd Regt. 3rd row: Jack Hay, 157 Fd Regt, W. E. Lamaison, 68 Hy AA Regt RA, Lieut ? A. Taylor, 4th Royal ? Fusiliers, Capt J. S. Alpherstone, RASC, 68 HAA Regt, W. Durstall, 68 Med Regt, T. J. Miller, 72 Fd Regt RA, (?). 2nd Row: Ronald E. Buxton, 44 Batn RTR, C. G. Topping, 277 HAA, RA, R. F. Cottrell, 68 Med Regt RA, (?), K. A. Bogod, 74 Fd Regt RA, John Lepine, 64 Med Regt RA, Peter L. Foulsham, 157? Regt RA. Front Row: Gordon McFall, L Battery 2 RHA, K. D. Bangham, 11th HAC Regt RHA, Guy C. Tills, 11th HAC Regt RHA, Arthur E. C. Green, 11th HAC Regt RHA, M. M. Crocker, 11th HAC Regt RHA, J. Kemp, 11th HAC Regt RHA, S. Haywood Smith, I Armoured Div Sigs. *(Courtesy of the family of the late Captain Arthur Green MBE)*

CAMERA C.,   SEZIONE 5.,   SETTORE II.

CAMPO CONCENTRAMENTO PRIGIONIERI DI GUERRA № 21.

POSTA MILITARE 3300. CHIETI. ITALIA.

Group photo. Back row: Derek Cotton, Intelligence, Arthur E. C. Green, Jock Hubbard, 72 Punjabs, P. B. Lable, Essex Regt, B. A. Gown, Royal Corps of Sigs, David R. Burgoyne, 7 RTR, Peter K. Pack, VIII KRI Hussars. Front Row: Digby A. Trout, 2 Punjab Regt, Edward J. Lane, RAOC, Allan J. F. Johnstone, Mahratta Light Infantry, Stanley Davis, 2nd Punjab Regt, John S. Sinkins, 68 Med Regt RA, TA. *(Courtesy of the family of the late Captain Arthur Green MBE)*

Group photo. Back Row: M. I. Ardizzone, 4 RTR, ? Roberts, 1 LAA, RA, P. Montague, 2 Indian Field Artillery, ?M Ebbay, 1st 24 Regt. Middle row: ? Chapman, A. E. Willis, ? Johnson Lt, RA, R. J.? Heslop, RA, D. E. Russett. Front Row: ? Bolton, T. L. Hutchinson, 1 Worcs, ? Rawlinson, RAOC, W. Ogden-Smith, Capt, 7 Green Howards, J. H. Simpson, 4/6 Rajputana Rifles. *(Courtesy of the family of the late Captain Arthur Green MBE)*

Group photo. Back Row: Lt W. C. Smith, Lt D. A. Roberts, Lt Haydn Stokes, Lt H. J. Owen, Lt J. H. Jackson, Capt Lee Morgan. Second Row: Lt J. B. Evans, Lt J. Tegid Jones, Lt C. Carr, Lt Wilson Lloyd, Lt Ferrigan, Lt J. C. Morgan. Third Row: Capt P. R. Evans, Lt I. Banner-Mendus, Lt E. Bowen, Capt B. Egerton, Capt J. Bedford, Capt J. E. K. Walters. *(Courtesy of the family of the late David Roberts MBE)*

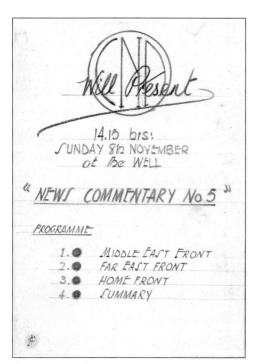

CNA poster. *(Courtesy of the family of the late Captain Arthur Green MBE)*

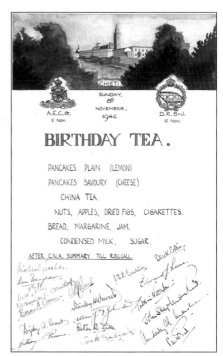

Tea party invitation, 8 November. *(Courtesy of the family of the late Captain Arthur Green MBE)*

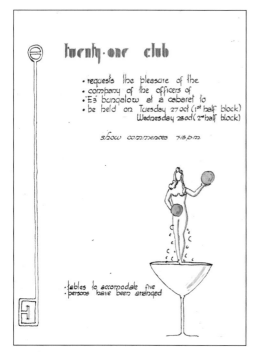

21 Club invitation. *(Courtesy of the family of the late Captain Arthur Green MBE)*

'No Klim' cartoon. *(Courtesy of the family of the late Captain Arthur Green MBE)*

Menu Welsh dinner. *(From the collection of the late Major Gordon Lett DSO)*

Menu Cheren dinner. *(From the collection of the late Major Gordon Lett DSO)*

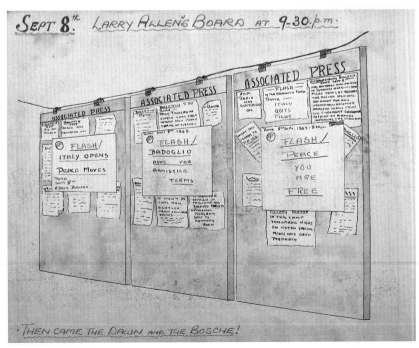

Larry Allen's noticeboard after the Armistice is announced. *(Courtesy of the late Lieutenant David Roberts, MC)*

Italian guard, drawn by Lieutenant Jack Hodgson Shepherd. *(Courtesy of Mrs Barbara Shepherd)*

Captain Croce, drawn by Lieutenant Jack Hodgson Shepherd. *(Courtesy of Mrs Barbara Shepherd)*

Officers' living quarters, drawn by Lieutenant Jack Hodgson Shepherd. *(Courtesy of Mrs Barbara Shepherd)*

A class at the water tower, drawn by Major Gordon Lett DSO.

Plan of Tunnel 3, as in September 1943 – the date on the drawing is wrong. *(Courtesy of the family of the late Captain Arthur Green MBE)*

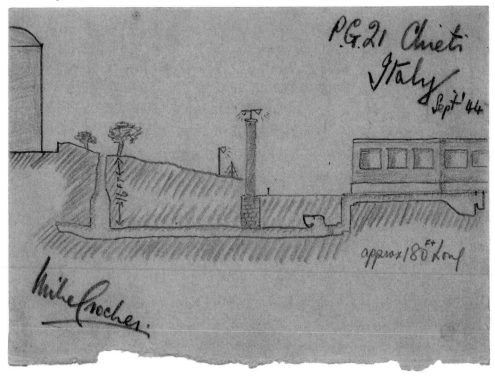

P.G.21 Chieti
Italy
Sept 44

approx 180 ft long

Mike Crocker.

Wall of Campo 21 in November 2013. *(Author's collection)*

The author with the current Commandant of Campo 21, Colonel Marco Mochi, in November 2013. *(Author's collection)*

was keen to find out how the two men had arrived in the guards' part of the camp. Graham and Glen replied with facetious remarks. Croce reacted by demanding to know from his guards why these men had not been shot whilst attempting to escape. He told the two prisoners that if he had had his way, they would have been spending the night, and all the other nights, in the cemetery, rather than just being condemned to solitary confinement. He was desperate to know how they had arrived on the guards' side of the wire, but of course Graham and Glen would not tell him. The prisoners were searched and their hoard of food and maps was found. Croce continued to question them for some time without result, while the two men looked sadly at the pile of their escape possessions as it mounted on the table in front of them, realizing that it would take a very long time to assemble the same again. Happily, one thing was not found. Each had taped the money that he was taking with him to the soles of his feet, one place that the Italians never looked.

Graham and Glen were led off to the cooler. Graham comments that the first three nights were very hard, because they were given no blankets. They were joined in their confinement by the two men who had answered Graham and Glen's names on roll call after they went through the wire. The Escape Committee, hoping the two men had got away, had provided cover for them. This caused great confusion to the Italians at first, because it seemed as if they had two more prisoners than they were meant to. Graham says that it was not until the fifteenth count that the two stand-ins were detected and sent off to the cooler. Whilst there, both Graham and Glen received messages sent in by the Escape Committee through the orderly who brought them their food. Any information that they could supply about conditions in the guards' compound would help with future escape attempts. After three days, Graham and Glen's complaints that they were being held in conditions which breached the Geneva Convention prevailed, and they were allowed palliasses for their beds, an hour's exercise each day, and their full personal kit. In fact, Graham comments that life in the cooler was not so bad. After living cheek by jowl for so long with too many roommates, a degree of privacy was a relief. They served an initial 14 days and then had to occupy a room with three others who were regarded as troublesome – the rugby international, Tony Roncoroni, Captain Denis Duke, Royal Artillery, and another American called Claude Weaver, of the Royal Canadian Air Force. For a further week, they had to parade six times a day. Then the Italians relaxed the punishment, and Graham and Glen felt delighted to have been moved into a smaller, much less crowded room, with only four other men. They were told that the authorities (i.e. Croce) would have liked to send them to Campo 5 at Gavi, the Italian Colditz to which other escapers had been sent, but that it was now full.

One of the good things about February was that the weather improved. Osborne recorded that there was splendid weather throughout the month. Two days after Graham and Glen's attempted escape, on 4 February 1943, there was an incident in the camp which most inmates remember. Pip Gardner VC, Frank Osborne, Gordon Horner and Toby Graham are amongst those to have given accounts of it, but the accounts all seem to vary in one way or another. A fair summary seems to be this: a workman's hammer, 'a beautiful lead hammer, an instrument that we had been wanting for a long time, for getting through obstinate foundations' according to Graham, was stolen from an Italian workman in the camp. The suspected culprit was apparently pursued across the camp to the main well, where he was finally apprehended. He was found to be empty-handed. Asked where the hammer was, he pointed down the well. The truth was that it had already been passed on and carefully hidden away for future use. Commandant Massi may or may not have believed that the hammer was down the well. However, he was not prepared to leave the matter uninvestigated. He sent for the Chieti town fire brigade, and ordered them to pump the well dry, so that it could be searched. The firemen got down to work surrounded, at a distance, by the prisoners, who were very much enjoying the diversion. The well was duly drained, but most prisoners recollect that the hammer was not found – obviously, since it had been carefully secreted away elsewhere. However, what was discovered was that the well had been in use as a dumping ground for spoil from various tunnels. Whilst the well was being drained, quite a lot of damage was done to the fire engine and equipment – it is variously said that the hose sprang a number of leaks where it had been covertly slashed by prisoners with razor blades, the tyres of the fire engine were punctured, and the fire engine's toolkit was stolen. Clearly, the prisoners hugely enjoyed the incident and felt that it was a victory for them.

However, what had provided entertainment and a valuable tool for some, caused heartache for others. The finding of the spoil in the wellshaft led to the stepping up of searches for tunnels by the Italian guards and one was duly found, although it was believed by its owners that it may only have been identified because the Italians had a spy operating within the prisoners' own ranks, a theory that would surface again in April. One of the team whose tunnel was discovered was Pip Gardner. Captain Philip Gardner VC, MC, was 27 years of age when he arrived in Chieti, born in South London on 25 December 1914, the first Christmas Day of the First World War. He was schooled at Dulwich College, where he was a keen rugby player. He had left school in 1932 and joined the family engineering business, then worked for a year in Hong Kong, where he joined the Hong Kong Volunteer Defence Force (Armoured Cars). Following his return to London in 1938, with war looming, Gardner joined the Westminster Dragoons, a territorial unit, apparently commenting to a friend: 'I must do my duty, but I'm no soldier.' Once the war began he was commissioned into the 4th Royal Tank Regiment in March 1940, was posted to North Africa and won his MC for heroism under fire in Libya in June 1941. The morning of 23 November 1941 found him again in battle, southeast of Tobruk. He was ordered to take two tanks to the rescue of two armoured cars from the King's Dragoon Guards which were out of action and under heavy attack. Whilst the other tank gave covering fire, Gardner dismounted from his own tank, thereby exposing himself to enemy fire, and hitched a tow rope to one of the armoured cars. He discovered Lieutenant Beame, Dragoon Guards, lying with both legs shattered outside the armoured vehicle, and lifted the wounded officer back into its relative safety before returning to his tank to begin the tow. While towing the armoured car to safety the rope broke, so Gardner again exposed himself to enemy fire by leaving his tank to return to help the injured officer. He himself was at this point hit and wounded in both an arm and a leg, but despite his injuries, he managed to carry the injured man to his companion tank. He then returned through intense shellfire to British lines. He was awarded the VC, the citation reading: 'The courage, determination and complete disregard for his own safety displayed by Captain Gardner enabled him, despite his wounds and in the face of intense fire at close range, to save the life of his fellow officer in circumstances fraught with great difficulty.' Pip Gardner continued to serve with the Royal Tank Regiment until the fall of Tobruk, when he 'went into the bag' with many others of his regiment.

The tunnel Gardner had been working on in Campo 21, and that had now been discovered, was sited in the camp cookhouse store, under a giant pile of carrots and potatoes. It appears to have been the same one that Eric Newby had been engaged on the previous November, when the tunnel team had been surprised by a visit from the Red Cross inspector, de Salis. The heap of vegetables made a very convenient cover for the hatch to the tunnel when work was not going on. The method for soil disposal that Gardner and others in his team had used was a simple one. They would fill old Red Cross cardboard boxes (the parcels arrived either in cardboard or plywood boxes) with soil, and a volunteer on the team's strength would then wander across the camp with the cardboard box on his hip, not an uncommon sight in the camp. At a suitable moment, he would approach the main well, pause to see if any guard or sentry was watching him, and if the coast was clear, he would quickly tip the contents of the box down the well. This system of disposal proved very successful and hence the soil at the bottom of the well began to build up. Before the incident with the hammer there had already been complaints amongst the prisoners that the quality of the water, used for washing clothes and indeed for everything except drinking, was being affected. The tunnel, however, was progressing far better than many when the incident occurred.

As stated, Gardner and his team feared that the existence of their tunnel had been betrayed. In a camp as large and as mixed as Chieti, it was always possible that one of the inmates might have been 'turned' and persuaded to spy for the Italians. Sometimes, an enemy spy was deliberately introduced into a prison camp, disguised as a captured Allied soldier or airman. This was very difficult to do and when attempted was usually only short term. The greater danger was from a genuine prisoner who decided to change sides, generally due to a promise of rewards of some kind. However, that February there was no hard evidence that there was a spy at work and the matter went no further.

A letter from Second Lieutenant Neil Robertson Glasgow got through to his sister-in-law, Mrs Helen Robertson Glasgow, at about this time. He complained of lack of food, saying that he had written a number of times to his wife and mother, always asking them to send food items. His letter to his sister-in-law had somehow slipped through the censor's net. Mrs Robertson Glasgow passed it on to his commanding officer, who in turn sent it on to the War Office, suggesting that an official enquiry be made through the Protecting Power as to the food situation in Campo 21.

The arrival of next-of-kin parcels had increased the number of books available in the camp. The reading list was very varied and the men would read virtually anything. Frank Osborne kept a note in his papal diary of the books that he read each month and of the theatrical productions that he saw. In February he read two books, *No Walls of Jasper* by Joanna Cannan, and *Orphan Island* by Rose Macaulay, and saw shows called 'Anything Goes', a Macdonald production, and 'Down to Earth' from Shaw's Geneva.

With the war in North Africa now going entirely against them, Fascist radio propaganda was deliberately intensified. Within the camp, Croce decided to erect a number of loudspeakers. These were nominally for the inmates' entertainment, so that the cost of the system could be charged to the prisoners' accounts, but in reality it was so that the Fascist broadcasts could boom out across the compound throughout the day, intermingled with grand opera. Day after day, the prisoners and their guards would go about their lives to cries of 'Vinceremo!' ('We will win') and 'Non molleremo mai!' ('We will never let go' or 'give up') from the radio. It was another obvious sign to the prisoners that things were not going well for their captors.

Meanwhile, the weather became so warm that on 24 February, Kenwyn Walters commented in his diary: 'Many people sunbathing. Reports say that crops may be ruined if this weather continues, as it is too soon by a month. Blossom on trees outside on hill.' Sadly, the hot weather, although welcomed by the prisoners, exacerbated the water shortage. Also, food supplies were reduced. Red Cross parcels were running out and in any event, with the exception of Christmas, the parcels had never extended to more than half a parcel per man per week, though the Red Cross intended that each man should receive one whole parcel each week as a necessary supplement to the sparse Italian rations. One February 26, Ronald Hill listed the food that they were now receiving from the Italians each day as: 'One cup of ersatz coffee, two large plates of watery soup, one onion, two small oranges, 200 grammes of bread, two spoonfuls of grated cheese, one spoonful of ersatz jam.' The term 'ersatz' meant that it was not the real thing, but some form of substitute. Ersatz coffee was commonly made from acorns.

Amongst the US officers who arrived in the camp at about this time was First Lieutenant Samuel Redden Webster Junior. Sam Webster had been captured in Tunisia in early December 1942, fighting with the US 1st Armoured Division as part of Operation Torch. Born on 12 February 1919, Webster had spent his 23rd birthday in the transit camp at Bari. He had married his sweetheart, Mary Elizabeth Pitt, on 11 April 1942, a month before being posted overseas. While travelling to Ireland, England and finally to Tunisia, Webster had discovered that the young wife he left behind was pregnant. Following his capture in December, she and his family had heard nothing of him until 24 December, when his mother received a telegram simply informing her that he was missing. As the arrival of her child, due in February, approached, young Mary Webster did not know whether her husband was dead or alive. Sam Webster wrote the customary Red Cross postcard from Bari, after he reached there on 30 December, but that did not arrive for many months. Still in Bari on 11 February, the day before his birthday, Webster wrote a postcard to his parents saying: 'It won't be long before I'm a papa (makes you feel old, don't it).' Unknown to him, his daughter Mary Ray Webster, had been born eight days earlier on 3 February.

Frelinghuysen remembered that in early spring, dysentry was rampant in the camp. He himself suffered from it, and recalled: 'It was a miserable, bone-chilling business, going into the stinking pit-in-the-floor latrines, where I didn't know which end to let go first.' Frelinghuysen described the US Senior Officer, Colonel Max Gooler, as a slim man in his mid forties, with close cropped grey hair and thick steel-rimmed glasses. He explains that Gooler had difficulty in dealing with a rather undisciplined collection of American officers. The British did their best to maintain military standards, and Gooler tried to introduce proper military discipline to those under his command, ordering that they smarten up on parade, dress neatly and keep their rooms in decent order. Frelinghuysen backed him on this, appreciating the importance of maintaining proper standards. Many of the American prisoners seemed not to appreciate the importance of keeping busy, and Frelinghuysen, who was a fitness fanatic, commented that 'many of the Americans fell into a minimum routine, get up two minutes before roll call; after it, back on the sack till time for soup; avoid PT [physical training] as if it would poison them...' There were, of course, notable exceptions, and the Americans had their fair share of tunnellers and would be escapers.

The CNA, meanwhile, were now suggesting that release might come as early as mid–April.

March 1943

DINNERS AND TUNNELS

St David's Day fell, as always, on the first day of March, and a group of Welsh officers in the camp decided to give a St David's Day dinner. With the improvement in conditions and the weather morale was good and the hosts of this dinner did their very best to make it a success. It took a lot of hard work and considerable self-sacrifice to put on. The chairman of the Welsh organizing committee was Second Lieutenant J. Tegid Jones, Royal Artillery, and the secretary was Second Lieutenant J. B. Evans, Royal Army Service Corps. Invitations were carefully written out and presented to the chosen guests. Gordon Lett was one of them and his invitation, in Gothic script, read: *Gwyl Dewi Sant, Mawrath 1st 1943. The Welsh Officers in the Camp request the Pleasure of the Attendance of Major G. E. Lett, RIASC, at Dinner, at 7pm, on Monday 1st March 1943, in the Tunnel Room, Block C, on the Occasion of the Commemoration of their Patron Saint, St David.*

The dinner had to start early, since all the prisoners faced a curfew of 10.00 pm, after which time they had to be in their own rooms. The venue of 'The Tunnel Room' was of course a joke, but there were at the time a number of tunnels under construction in various parts of the camp, including Block C. Kenwyn Walters, who proposed the toast to St David in Welsh, recalled that about twenty people attended. Rations had to be saved and extra wine bought in to ensure that everyone dined well. Menus were prepared, written by hand, with a Red Welsh Dragon prominent on the front cover. The fare was flatteringly described: *Hors d'oeuvres variés*, was followed by *Galatine de Boeuf Oignons, Goulash Hongroise, Trifle,* and *Welsh Rarebit.* Galatine was simply cooked meat supplied in tins by the Red Cross. One of the guests, the SBO Lieutenant Colonel Gray, proposed the loyal toast and amongst the speeches Major Gordon Lett replied on behalf of the guests. Many of the guests signed the menu as a souvenir, as they might have done in peacetime. One of those present was Lieutenant David Alwyn Roberts, 68 Anti-Tank Battery, Royal Artillery, 18 Indian Brigade. Roberts was 27 when wounded and taken prisoner at the Quattara Depression in North Africa on 2 July 1942. Roberts, like Arthur Green, compiled a fine collection of pictures and mementos from Campo 21, of which the author is fortunate to have been given a copy. It includes Roberts's signed copy of the St David's Day menu.

Despite this fine sounding dinner menu, and the efforts of the prisoners to lay on such occasions (more dinners were held over later months), the inmates of Campo 21 constantly lacked adequate food. John Speares speaks of powerful men being reduced to a bag of bones. Both of the England cricketers in the camp, Bowes and Brown, each lost over four stone in weight whilst in captivity. Sam Webster, now arrived in camp, was another large man, 6ft 2in. tall. When he eventually got home in late 1943 his weight was below 100 lbs. Poor Webster still knew nothing of the birth of his daughter, and his wife and family did not learn until 25 March that Sam was alive and a prisoner of war. The US population of the camp was gradually increasing, mainly as a result of US aircraft shot down over Italy. Eventually there were 178 Americans in the camp. One of them was Claude Weaver III, who for the past few weeks had been one of Toby Graham's roommates. Warrant Officer 'Weavy' Weaver DFM, was a US citizen from Oklahoma City who, like Bill Wendt and a number of other Americans, had travelled to Canada to join the Royal Canadian Air Force. Weaver had signed up on 13 February 1941, shortly before Wendt, and before the United States entered the war in December 1941. Born on 18 August 1923 and still only 17, Weaver was under age when he joined up (no doubt he lied about his age as many did), but proved to be an excellent fighter pilot. Flying Spitfires off the island of Malta, Weaver shot down a series of enemy planes, winning himself a Distinguished Flying Medal (DFM) in early August 1942. On 9 September, he was shot down piloting a Spitfire over Sicily. He was hit by anti-aircraft fire, force landed on the beach near Comiso and was immediately arrested by Italian *carabinieri*, before he was able to destroy his plane. He ended up in Chieti on 29 September 1942, still aged only 18. He, like Wendt, lived in the other ranks section of the camp.

Weaver suffered like all the others throughout the winter of 1942/3. One of his friends was Lieutenant Ernest Lodge, Royal Armoured Corps, a rubber planter from Sumatra, who had travelled back to England in 1940 to sign up. Lodge described Weaver as a forceful but likeable young man. When he arrived in the camp, the first issue of toilet rolls had just arrived and being the oldest in the room, they were given to Lodge to distribute. He offered Weaver one, but 'Claude pulled a slim roll out of his pocket and retorted: 'I won't need it, I'll be out of here before I've finished this.' Lodge described Weaver as being full of fun, loving to wrestle and to box – he was apparently a Golden Gloves boxing champion.

Weaver and another American got approval for an escape plan in early 1943. The method was similar to Graham and Glen's – they intended to crawl under the wire that divided the main camp from the Italian garrison's quarters, and then to go out of the gate or over the outer wall. They made their attempt in March. However, Weaver got hung up on the wire as he tried to pass under it, and after half an hour in which he was unable to go forwards or backwards, was spotted and arrested. What happened to him then perhaps reflects the increasing frustration felt by Croce and his team of guards. Accounts vary as to the detail, and sadly Weaver himself did not survive the war to tell the tale in full, but there is no doubt that he was beaten unconscious by the camp guards. Weaver himself later told a Major McKee of the Judge Advocate General's staff that after he was discovered caught up in the wire, he had been interrogated by Captain Croce, and on the latter's orders he had then been assaulted by an Italian sentry, who knocked his front teeth out. In his escape report (he did successfully escape from Chieti in September 1943 and crossed Allied lines), he says that he was severely beaten by the sentries, one of them breaking his rifle over him. Graham says that when Weaver was caught, the guard who held him called out his pals from the guard room. They had been imbibing Chianti wine freely, and about ten of them set about him with rifles and belts: 'Fortunately, Claude was a tough customer, and his head, which received a direct hit, stood up to the treatment. They finally knocked him unconscious, and he was carried off to the cooler badly bruised. He remained for a few days but was released because of the huge outcry his treatment aroused in the camp.'

On 10 March, a hammer and ruler were stolen from Italian workmen in the camp. Hill believed that the culprits were amongst the US prisoners. Over the new loudspeakers, demands were made for the return of the tools, not surprisingly without any result, and a very thorough search took place. The missing items still not found, all prisoners were confined to their bungalows at 1130hrs and forced to remain inside until 1930hrs. Thus, they missed what passed for both lunch and supper and had not eaten since 1800hrs the previous day. Hill records that except for the morning cup of ersatz coffee, he had gone without any issue of food for 26 hours. The following day, 11 March, Kenwyn Walters felt weak from hunger. For Frank Osborne, however, things were better. It was his birthday and he recorded: 'Birthday celebrated with apple pie and creamed rice.' On 12 March, the Dramatic Society put on a variety show entitled, Anything Goes. The Italian officers were invited, and a number attended and apparently enjoyed themselves, since they sent a gift of six bottles of wine afterwards.

On the evening of 15 March, another dinner was held. This one was given by the many Indian Army officers in the camp who had taken part in the battle for Cheren (or Keren) in Eritrea in 1941. The third and decisive battle of Cheren had started on 15 March 1941, the Ides of March. The 4th and 5th Indian Division, together with a number of other units including the Highland Light Infantry, had defeated the Italians, effectively thereby bringing the Eritrean campaign to a successful end. The Cheren Dinner was another method of boosting morale for the prisoners – it was celebrating a significant victory over their captors. At the time of the battle there had been much talk of the Ides of March leading to the fall of the modern Caesar (Mussolini), Julius Caesar having, of course, met his end at the hands of Brutus and others on that date. Sadly, Mussolini was still in power two years later on 15 March 1943, but with the North African campaign going so well, Lett and the CNA were hoping for significant developments on this Ides of March. Lett himself had been involved in the battle for Cheren.

Again there was a sophisticated sounding menu: 'Crème de Tomate, Croquettes de Poisson, Sauté de Boeuf, Oignon frites, Carrottes Vichy, Trifle, Canapés de Fromage et Oignons, Café.' On his copy of the menu, Gordon Lett wrote: 'Not, of course, as sumptuous as it looks! Made out of Red Cross parcels.' In English the food could be less glamorously described as tomato soup, fishcakes, beef, fried onions and carrots, trifle, cheese and onion savouries. However, it was filling and sustaining, and a lot of effort had gone into gathering a decent meal together. Lett's menu card is signed by many of those present and shows that a variety of tunnellers were having an evening off: Tony Roncoroni was there, as were Bob Walker Brown and Mac MacLucas.

Hot showers were still a rare event and Walters happily noted in his diary on 16 March that he had had his second one. It seems that the ration at this stage was meant to be one hot shower a month. Fuel for the inadequate stoves was stopped at the beginning of March.

A cinema projector was ordered by the prisoners and bought at an exorbitant price from the Italians, in the hope that they could show films (which might come through the Red Cross), using the side of the water tower as their screen. The projector and sound amplifier duly arrived, but never worked. Secretly, valves and other parts had been removed to help in the construction of a radio receiver. George Hervey-Murray recalls that those who enquired as to why the projector was not working were told not to ask awkward questions, and were tipped the wink that there was another purpose for it. John Speares, who was a signals officer, remembers working on this project, but says that it was not, in the end, successful. Speares said that although he built a radio frequency stage to go in front of the amplifier, they never succeeded in making a workable radio receiver, as they were still short of essential parts. Even bribing the camp guards did not work in this case. The bribing of guards was a centralized affair, under the control of the SBO's cabinet, but the real problem was that the camp was in a very poor part of Italy where the sort of parts they needed were not readily available even to the guards. However, the second SBO, Lieutenant Colonel Marshall, recorded that eventually a working secret radio had been constructed, on which he had received orders from London, as Gordon Norbrook confirms.

Rumours now began to circulate that walks outside the camp might be allowed again, and on 24 March, John Jenkins was delighted to take his first walk outside for seven months. The walks offered an opportunity for another way of baiting the guards. The prisoners gave their parole not to escape, but that did not mean that they could not have fun with their escort. The Italians, mainly from the south, were very short in stature, while some of the prisoners were tall. On their walks, the prisoners used to put six of their taller guardsmen at the front of the ranks, who would march off at an increasingly fast pace, wearing light clothing and with nothing to carry. Their guards, with much shorter legs, carrying their weapons and wearing full kit, would end up having to run to keep up, screaming at their prisoners to stop. However, despite the fun, Jenkins found the first walk of 4 miles very tiring and was 'pretty done in' by the time he got back. Fitness was a very real problem within the camp, particularly after the discomforts of the winter. Taking exercise by walking up and down the asphalt road was very boring and the diet defied energy. Happily, on the same day as his first walk

Jenkins won the draw for one of the few real eggs coming into the camp, the first that he had eaten for ten months. He needed energy, because he had a part as a kitchen maid in that week's theatrical production, Hullabaloo, which had an all-female cast.

With the improved weather and warmer conditions, the tunnel season restarted in earnest in March and April. Four of the tunnels which were begun at around this time were to survive until September 1943 and prove to be of real value. What we will call tunnel 1 involved Toby Graham, who having completed his term in the cooler after his failed 'under the wire' escape attempt, joined a syndicate that was headed by Dennis Duke and included Tony Roncoroni, Captain Hugh Holmes, Captain Gordon McFall, Royal Artillery, Captain Peter Joscelyne, Royal Tank Regiment, Peter Glen (also now out of the cooler), John Meares (who Toby Graham names as the escaper who had got out of the camp under a vegetable cart), 'Pip' Gardner (now out of the cooler), Claude Weaver (released and recovered from his beating), Bill Wendt and Captain A. R. 'Colly' Collingwood of the East Yorkshire Regiment. The story of tunnel 1 is perhaps most remarkable as an example of the appalling conditions in which some of those involved worked and the fortitude that they displayed, as we will see. Before his earlier escape attempt with Peter Glen, Tony Roncoroni had invited Graham to join a tunnel team and after his release the invitation was renewed, and Graham accepted. The site of the tunnel was perhaps the most ingenious yet. There was a British other ranks' cookhouse between the hospital and Block B. This had three large circular ovens containing the fires on to which the huge cauldrons containing the watery soup supplied each day as the ORs' main meal, were lowered in order to heat up. It was customary at any one time for at least one of the three ovens to be allowed to cool, so it could be cleaned out. The ovens themselves were simply concrete 'fireboxes', sitting on a concrete bed that formed the floor of the building. The plan was to tunnel through the fire grate at the bottom of an oven, right through the concrete and into the clay beneath. There would be a lid for the tunnel, as usual, and when this was replaced the fire in the oven could be relit on top of it. Should there be a spot search by the guards, the fire could be relit within minutes of a warning, and a cauldron of soup placed on top of the fire. In these circumstances it was highly unlikely that any searchers would be suspicious, or would insist on having the cauldron removed and the fire put out. The most stalwart member of the team was Sergeant Andy Spowatt of the Northumberland Fusiliers, who in civilian life had been a Northumbrian miner. He was put in charge of the digging. All went well and over a number of hard weeks' labour, Spowatt worked his way down through the concrete and into the clay soil.

It is worth emphasizing at this point that each tunnel team worked entirely independently of the others and, for reasons of security, outside the team members only the Escape Committee was meant to know the details of any individual plan. However, for those whose tunnels began outside the bungalows, total secrecy within the prisoner community was extremely difficult. Bored men had nothing better to do than watch their fellow prisoners and gossip about everything, so the posting of lookouts and the creation of diversionary activity was inevitably noticed and talked about. It is perhaps no surprise that three of the tunnel teams came up with very similar plans.

Hugh Gordon-Brown's spring tunnel will be referred to here as tunnel 2. For his syndicate members, it was Tony Gregson's fourth attempt and John Pennycook's third. This one started from outside their bungalow. Each bungalow had a concrete surround, supporting a pavement which followed the line of the building around its courtyard. There were ground drains to catch the water that ran off the roof and down drainpipes. Tony Gregson noticed a small square drain inspection lid set into the pavement at a spot close to one of the bungalow windows. The lid measured just under 14in. square. Gregson investigated and found that the lid sat on a rim of about an inch of concrete, which he chipped away on two of the four sides, leaving an entrance of about 14×12 in. Beneath this was a sump into which a man could just fit with the lid closed on top of him. It was decided that this should be the start of their next tunnel. They believed that their tunnel entrance would be outside the direct line of vision of the sentry boxes, although there were also guards patrolling beside the wall who as they passed would have a grandstand view. Gregson was the first to begin the tunnel, working in a horribly crouched position beneath the closed lid. By now, the team had a stolen workman's hammer and were using steel bolts taken from the structure of their bunk beds for chisels. Happily, there was a duct that ran out of one side of the sump which provided air and some light. Gregson chiselled his way through the side of the sump drain facing the perimeter wall, preserving the lower portion of the sump so that it could still drain off any rainwater from the gutter as before, then started digging for the main wall. As soon as Gregson had got this far, the team could get started in earnest. They began by dumping their spoil down the nearby well in their bungalow courtyard, but after a month or so the water not surprisingly became a cloudy brown and the well noticeably shallower, and they were ordered by the senior officer in their block to dispose of the soil elsewhere. They then began to use trouser bags for disposing of soil on the vegetable patch used by the Chieti Gardening Club. The bags were long sacks, joined by braces and hung around the neck of the prisoner, down into his trouser legs. There was a string at the bottom of the bag to open it, so when the prisoner had reached one of the garden plots he would pull the string and allow the earth to cascade over his feet to the ground, whereupon the gardener would rapidly mix it up with the ordinary soil. A similar technique was portrayed in a German camp in the Steve McQueen film, *The Great Escape*.

The vegetable garden was in the top left corner of the camp, where the Chieti Gardening Club were planting seeds provided by the Red Cross. However, there was a lot of soil to be disposed of when excavating a tunnel, and there were other tunnels being dug in the camp. The level of earth in the garden began to rise noticeably. Captain F. W. 'Frank' Stone, 7 Gurkha Rifles, a 27-year-old captured in North Africa, recalled that the height of the beds rose as much as three or four inches a week, yet apparently the Italians paid no attention. Stone's job on his tunnel team (probably for tunnel 4) was soil disposal, and he recalled that because of the rapidly rising beds in the vegetable garden: 'We broke up some earth around some miserable half dead young trees and heaped more earth on top. When the Italians asked what we were doing, we said we were trying to nurse the trees back to life.' Stone also commented that with the coming of spring, the return of leaves to the trees and crops in the fields would give better cover for escapees once they were out.

Tunnel 2 was relatively spacious compared to some, which meant more spoil. There was a chamber some way along it, where two people could partially stand and turn around. Parts of the tunnel were shored up with bed boards, but most of it was unsecured. Penycook describes one collapse, when a digger was trapped on the far side of the fall, but happily there were others to hand in the tunnel who were able to dig him out.

Tunnel 3 was started by another young officer, Bob Walker Brown of the Highland Light Infantry. Captain Robert 'Bob' Walker Brown was an only child, the son of a doctor, born in Sutton Coldfield on 9 April 1919. He was 23 when he arrived in Chieti. Walker Brown had been captured in North Africa on 10 June 1942, having been badly wounded in action by a piece of German shrapnel in his lower back. The days had long gone when a wound in the back was an indicator of cowardice. Walker Brown was the victim of a German airburst 50ft in the air. Lying injured, he was found and taken prisoner by the Germans, then transported from the battlefield lying on the outside of an armoured German vehicle. That vehicle came under attack from British fire and Walker Brown suffered a second injury, this time from his own side. He became one of an unhappy few who had been wounded both by his enemies and his friends. Walker Brown was treated initially by German doctors and then handed over to the Italians. He was transported to Italy and to a hospital in a convent at Lucca. Walker Brown was a tough character. Conditions in the hospital were of the most basic and there were no antibiotics at all. He survived, though many others did not. An Italian doctor operated on him and found that pieces of his clothing were still embedded in the festering wound in his back. Once these were removed, Walker Brown's condition improved. When sufficiently recovered, he was transferred to Campo 21 at Chieti – hardly the ideal environment for a convalescence. He arrived in the late autumn of 1942, with nothing to wear except his bloodstained and damaged shorts, and a blanket that he wore as a poncho. Nonetheless, on the walk from Chieti Scalo station to the camp, Walker Brown did his best to take mental note of the features of the surrounding countryside, and file them away for future reference. He had no intention of staying in Campo 21 for very long and would need them when he escaped.

Like many others, throughout the winter of 1942/3 Walker Brown investigated the possibilities of tunnelling out of the camp from within his bungalow, but all the attempts to dig were short-lived. Croce and the team of tappers were too efficient for them. Come the early spring, the possibilities of digging an escape tunnel outside the bungalow increased, and in March or early April Bob Walker Brown made a discovery similar to Tony Gregson's. In the concrete pavement surrounding his bungalow, Walker Brown spotted a metal plate in the path that looked like a drain cover. Like tunnel 2, the significant feature of this plate was that it was at a spot where no sentry box had a direct line of vision to it. Crouching down, Walker Brown quickly wiped away some of the dirt and muck that partially covered it and managed to prise it open. What he saw below was a 3ft deep and 18in. square brick sump – that is, a slightly bigger area than the one used for tunnel 2. He quickly replaced the metal plate and moved away, excitement rising within him. He began to consider the possibilities of using the chamber to start on a tunnel, weighing up many of the same considerations as the tunnel 2 team. The sump had the major advantage that it was out of sight of the sentry boxes, but the disadvantage of being outside the bungalow, which meant the tunnel team might be spotted moving in and out of the entrance by guards. Happily, however, the sump chamber was close to the window of one of the ablution rooms of the bungalow. The distance to the end of the bungalow nearest to the wall was about 35–40ft, after which it would be necessary to dig out to and under the wall itself. Walker Brown passed on his idea to his tunnel syndicate and in due course it was approved by the Escape Committee.

The initial task was to demolish the side of the brick chamber that faced towards the wall. Working in such a small area, this would be no easy task. The lid of the chamber would of course have to be closed whilst the work went on, and indeed at all times. Walker Brown's team therefore recruited the smallest team member they could find to carry out this tricky operation – a 5ft tall Indian Army officer – and secreted him in the chamber. Giving such cover as was possible, they found it took between two and three minutes for a man to exit the ablutions room window and conceal himself in the chamber. The small officer worked away diligently in the hideously confined space, and within a few days had managed to remove all of the bricks of the chamber in the side that faced the main camp wall. Beyond the bricks was the earth that lay under the concrete pavement surrounding the bungalow. Tunnelling proper could now start. Walker Brown notes that the only tool that they had was a fire poker about 11in. long. It was with this that the Indian officer had managed to remove the bricks. The spoil from the chamber, and later the tunnel, was hidden between the double skins of the bungalow wall – a space originally intended to be part of a heating system for the bungalows.

Tunnel 4 began on 18 March, and the tunnel team was headed by Major W. H. L. 'Bill' Gordon, Royal Signals, and will be described in detail below. Again, this route started from a drain beside his bungalow (probably bungalow 2, since three of his tunnel team lived in room 5 of that bungalow, as did Captain Frank Stone).

There were others who preferred to try easier and quicker routes to freedom. Cross and Broad intended to get out of Campo 21 without having to dig underground. Since their plan to escape via the roof of the hospital had been approved the previous October, they had been working hard on the scheme, getting themselves as fit as possible. Because they intended to cross the Gran Sasso mountain range they also had had to wait until the weather improved and much of the snow was gone from the mountains. The appointed day for their attempt was 29 March. They had made their own compass and had collected the ingredients for their escape rations – biscuits, cocoa, bars of chocolate, Bemax, a marmite cube, sugar and condensed milk. These they took to the cookhouse, where the ingredients were turned into easily portable high-energy cakes. The

Escape Committee had provided them with a map and 200 lire each in cash. They made their attempt after dark. The first part of their plan was to climb up on to the roof of the camp hospital, so a ruse or 'rammy' was adopted to get the attention of the searchlight that normally covered the hospital wing of bungalow 1. Captain M. J. D'a Blackman, Sherwood Foresters, dropped a tin out of his room on to some steps, making sufficient noise to attract the attention of the searchlight. Broad went first, covering the ground to the bungalow and climbing up a drainpipe to reach the roof. Sadly, it was a very wet night and the drainpipe was slippery. In trying to grasp hold of the guttering that ran round the edge of the roof Broad slipped and fell 25ft down on to the ground. He was lucky to suffer only severe bruising and no fractures. He was also lucky that Cross and three other officers were quick off the mark and able to carry him back inside a bungalow before the searchlight could swing back and investigate. Cross wanted to go ahead and make the break on his own, but Lieutenant Colonel Cooper, head of the Escape Committee, refused to allow it. The attempt was a painful failure. At least this time they had not lost the map or cash that the escapers were carrying.

April 1943

SWIMMING IN SEWAGE

The Italian Military Authority, concerned about escapes and the fact that many soldiers and civilians could not easily identify the different uniforms issued to Axis and Allied troops, had issued an order that all Allied prisoners should wear bright red patches on their uniform top and trousers, in order that they could be easily identified as prisoners of war. There had been a running battle over this for some time. Lieutenant Colonel Gray, with the full support of his men, initially refused to accept the patches, maintaining that to mark them in that way was a breach of the Geneva Convention. In response, the Italians went so far as to raid all the dormitories in the middle of the night, uplift the prisoners' clothing, and return it all in due course with the patches sewn on. The prisoners cut the patches off again. So things had gone on, until finally Lieutenant Colonel Gray, realizing that in the long term this was not a battle that they could win, reached a compromise with the Commandant and Croce to the effect that they would wear the patches, in exchange for a resumption of walks outside the camp. Early April appears to have been the time when the patches were finally sewn on to the prisoners clothing and accepted by them. The walks had been resumed in late March and were much welcomed, most of the men simply enjoying the opportunity to see something of the world outside their prison, though many took the opportunity to study the countryside outside the camp with a view to eventual escape.

That April 3rd was the Websters' first wedding anniversary and Sam wrote home to his wife and parents: 'Well today is my wedding anniversary, and I'm not singing: "I wish I were single again" – never will either. I sure would like to be there now and have a nice quiet party for three. Oh Well! We'll have it next year and make up for this one we're missing. I hope you have a nice big supper or something tonight as I'll be there in mind if not in body'. Webster knew, of course, that there was absolutely no chance of his wife reading the letter until long after the anniversary, but no doubt writing his thoughts to her on what for both of them must have been a very poignant occasion was good therapy for him. The reference to 'a nice big supper' was not untypical of the prisoners' obsession with food, as they struggled to avoid starvation. Although Webster's family by now knew that he was alive, he still did not know anything about the birth of his daughter two months before. Indeed, Webster finished his letter by saying, 'Tell Sam III Hello', guessing that the baby had safely arrived and was a boy.

The weather was hot and with improved supplies of equipment, organized games were on the increase. For those who enjoyed them and could find the stamina, outdoor sports now took up a lot of their time. There were tournaments arranged in various sports, between a variety of teams. The increasing number of American servicemen in the camp meant that their favoured games became more prominent. The British sometimes complained at how noisy the American games were. Baseball, or its more practical version within the confines of Campo PG 21, softball, was not surprisingly the Americans' first love. The British, who had been mainly playing basketball, with some soccer, tenni-quoits and rugby, quickly took to softball too. The Americans were happy to provide coaches to teach British teams the rules and techniques of the game and then took them on in a series of matches. Not surprisingly, to begin with, the British always lost.

Whatever the sport might be, there were endless variations on the teams who might take part. Settore 1 played against Settore 2, bungalows played against other bungalows, there were championships within individual bungalows, and there were regimental competitions, under the overseeing eye of Bill Bowes' sports committee. As softball caught on, leagues were set up for the various teams. Frank Osborne played for the British other ranks against teams such as the All Americans and the Rascals (the latter being a team from the RASC captained by Freddie Brown). The Americans produced national sides and played against the British or the Empire. The vast majority of the non-American prisoners in the camp were British (the South Africans had been moved away in October), but there was also a handful of Canadians, Australians and New Zealanders. For both individual and team competitions, 'silver' cups were manufactured out of empty Red Cross tins by the theatrical workshops, suitably inscribed.

A number of basketball and baseball games were regularly in progress, as what was to become a summer of entertaining competitive sport began. Bill Bowes had sent a prisoner-of-war postcard to his Yorkshire and England teammate Herbert Sutcliffe, sending his best wishes and those of Freddie Brown to all his cricketing friends. He told Sutcliffe that he was in good health and making the best of his enforced idleness. The *Hull Daily Mail* published the news that all was well with Bill Bowes on 2 April 1943.

Sometimes, games or sport would provide a chance for guard-baiting. Apparently, a group of prisoners with a sense of humour in one of the bungalows decided to create a special game of snakes and ladders, with a giant board painted on the floor. The biggest snake was provided with the large and obvious head of Benito Mussolini, the Italian 'Duce', spouting a forked tongue. When the guards saw this they very quickly painted it out, and for a while a sentry was posted to prevent its reappearance.

The Americans also made a significant contribution to the camp theatre. In early April, they put on what Webster described as a Minstrel Show. Popular in the United States at that time, such shows involved white actors blacking their faces and performing musical, burlesque and comedy acts. They were later echoed with success in post-war Britain, most famously in the televised Black and White Minstrel Show of the 1950s, 1960s and even the 1970s (though controversy about racial stereotyping had already arisen and in that decade they came to an end). Sam Webster performed in one of the sketches and commented in a letter home: 'I hope that burnt cork will come off easily else I'll have a slight tan for several days.' Webster, despite his painful separation from his family, remained upbeat. The war was going well and he, like many others, firmly believed that he would be free sooner rather than later.

Nonetheless, the tunnelling carried on. It took a long time and required a large supply of workers. For would-be escapers, although they hoped for their tunnel's success in due course and kept working with their team, the temptation was always there to look for a quicker route. Peter Glen and Tony 'the Ronc' Roncoroni decided to make another attempt at going through the wire into the guards' compound. They would be the third team to try it. Although Peter Glen had successfully got under the wire when he went with Toby Graham, this time both he and the Ronc got hopelessly caught up in it, as Claude Weaver had done on his attempt. Lieutenant R. A. 'Tony' Davies, Royal Horse Artillery, recalled that the sentry who first noticed them fired his whole magazine at them as they lay trapped. Luckily, he was so excited that every shot missed and both men were eventually marched off to the cooler uninjured.

The first ten days of April were a period of success for the Italian tunnel detectors. Three tunnels were found, one in the washhouse of D Block, one in the theatre latrines, and one in room 6 of D Block. The team of fifteen men who had been digging from the theatre latrine included Charles Napier Cross, Captain D. B. Haslehurst, Worcestershire Regiment, Captain Richardson, Royal Artillery, and Flying Officer K. Pollard, RAF. Unhappily, Richardson and Pollard were actually caught underground – happily, the Italians did not throw a grenade down there. Both men were sentenced to 30 days in the cooler and fined a total of 4,000 lire for 'damage to camp property'. The Escape Committee paid the fine.

The Italians did not find the tunnel that ran from the other ranks' cookhouse, tunnel 1. Digging through the Chieti clay in early April, Spowatt struck a sewer, which he reported that he believed ran in the direction of the perimeter wall. He thought it must be a tributary to the main sewer that served the whole of the camp. As it happened, on a walk outside the camp two days after this discovery, one of the team, Gordon McFall, spotted what he thought was a manhole to the main sewer about 20 yards down from the main gate on the other side of the road. The obvious conclusion was that if the team could break into the sewer, and if it was big enough for a man to crawl through, then they could reach the manhole and exit that way to freedom. Spowatt duly made the break, and the sewer proved to be about 2ft 6in. (75cm) square – just big enough for a man to crawl through. It seemed therefore that a crawl of 100 yards could bring a man to freedom. However, it does not take great imagination to realize how dreadful conditions would be for anybody crawling through the sewer. Though it began as a tributary, even that served the needs of several hundred men each day, many of them far from well. Because of the lack of water, the lavatories had to be flushed with buckets, and there was a considerable build up of human waste. The smell was simply appalling, and because of the blockages and sediment it would be extremely difficult for a man to force his way through. Also, the lavatories continued in use each day. But – at the end of the sewer, there might be freedom.

The story of the sewer tunnel is a telling illustration of the strength of mind and determination of some of those prisoners who were intent on escape. If the descriptions of the camp theatre, orchestras and sporting contests included here give the impression that Campo 21 was a happy place, they are misleading.

Beneath the surface most prisoners of war were miserable and longing to get home. Some were truly desperate to escape. Getting out of the camp was, of course, only stage one on the route to eventual freedom, and the possibility of using the sewer brought with it problems that many a sane man would not have contemplated. The first priority was to try to clear enough of the accumulated sewage from the tributary tunnel for a human being to be able to crawl through it. This was a purely practical problem and the prisoners' ingenuity soon solved it. The sewage was dammed up at the nearest end of the sewer to the lavatories, and those lavatories nearest to the dam were put out of bounds. Above the dam, the water level in the sewer was built up as much as possible by running the taps in the washroom when the water was on, and by adding water from buckets when it was not. Thus a big head of water was built up behind the dam, which was then deliberately burst, so that the water would force its way down through the tributary, taking much of the blocked sewage with it into the main sewer. This achieved, it was now possible, although still unbelievably unpleasant, for a man to crawl through the tight confines of the tributary sewer.

On 8 April 1943, two 'volunteers' were instructed to crawl down the tributary and explore the main sewer, in order to discover if indeed it led under the wall and across the road to the hatch. Claude Weaver was one of those who went down, together probably with Corporal Campbell, returning after fifteen minutes covered from head to foot in filth and reporting that the main sewer was virtually impassable. It seems that it was not very much bigger than the tributary, measuring about 3ft 6in. (107cm) square, but of that about 2ft was taken up by almost solid sewage, leaving only 18in. clear. The movement of a human body had the effect of pushing the compacted sewage forward, blocking the tunnel almost completely. The sewer was in fact performing as a cess pit, with very little flow through. Again, this was no doubt due to the lack of sufficient water over the months and the overuse of the lavatories by the too numerous occupants of the camp. Further, the dreadful smell of the two men when they returned was so strong that it seemed unlikely an escapee would get far on the outside without being noticed, even if he had a bag of clean clothes to change into. Washing oneself properly clean after full immersion in sewage is no easy task and much harder in their circumstances. Thus even if stage one of the escape could be achieved, stage two, the journey out of Italy, would be even more difficult than anticipated.

The tunnel team were naturally rather disheartened and took some time to decide how to solve the problem. Their dilemma became more pressing the next day, 9 April, when the Italians announced that 40 of what they regarded as the more troublesome officers were to be transferred from the camp on the following Monday, 12 April. They included Toby Graham and many others of the sewer tunnel team.

One of the tunnel team, Peter Glen, the US ambulance man, no longer needed to worry, since he had received the happy news that he was after all going to be repatriated. Glen went off on a Saturday morning, either 3 or 10 April, after a 'last breakfast' party. He duly reached London, where he was able to report on conditions in Campo 21, and write to or speak with a number of the relatives of the prisoners that he had met. Amongst others, Glen made contact with Toby Graham's family, and with Gordon Lett's uncle Hugh and other relations, to whom he spoke highly of the role that Lett was playing in Campo 21. On 6 May, Glen wrote to Bill Wendt's mother to reassure her, and to confirm that he was actually in Campo 21. His letter was upbeat, and he described the positives of the camp, including the orchestras, library and education courses, saying: 'All this helps to make one forget being a prisoner, although with a nine foot wall surrounding the place, it seems very much like a penitentiary. If you have a chance of sending anything over from the States, send chocolate, condensed food, raisins and saccharine tablets. Mail, however, is the important thing, and although it has been slow and inconsistent in arriving, it is beginning to be a little better, so do write yourself, and have all your friends and relations do likewise.'

The Italians had been foolish to agree to Glen's repatriation, because after holidaying for a while in the United Kingdom, Glen applied to the US Army for a commission. However, as he put it in a letter to Lett's uncle and aunt, he got fed up with writing to the US authorities (who apparently showed no interest in him), so made the journey to India, where he was accepted into the British Indian Army for training. November 1943 found him in an officers' training school in Bangalore. From there, he wrote to the Letts in London, asking for any news of what had happened to Gordon Lett after the Italian Armistice in September 1943.

After Glen had departed, on the morning of 10 April, the sewer tunnel team (tunnel 1) including his friend and fellow American Bill Wendt, gathered for a crisis meeting. If many of the officer members of the team were to be moved on Monday, 12 April, for them it was now or never for the sewer tunnel. Toby Graham had come up with the idea that it might be possible to skim over the top of the blocked sewage in the main sewer on an inflatable lilo bed, which had arrived in the camp either courtesy of the Red Cross or a next-of-kin parcel. Graham's plan was to keep his body on the lilo and to propel himself along with only his legs deep in the sewage. That, he hoped, would avoid the problem of the sewage piling up in front of him, and would save most of his body from becoming coated with sewage. As it was his idea, Graham was asked whether he would like to go down the tunnel and try it out. Andy Spowatt, the miner, would go with him. Many years later, telling the story at a Monte San Martino Trust luncheon (happily after the meal had been served and consumed), Toby Graham confessed that he wondered how he had been prepared to undertake such a dreadfully difficult and unpleasant task. The only answer he could give was that he had been very young, ready to try anything, and had been asked by a more senior officer if he was prepared to give it a go. In those circumstances, he had automatically agreed.

On the afternoon of Sunday, 11 April, Graham and Spowatt prepared themselves for the expedition. They put on old overalls, tying the sleeves tight at the wrist and trousers at the ankles with string from Red Cross parcels, in an attempt to keep the sewage from seeping into their clothing. Each of them carried a home-made lamp, since there was of course no light in the sewer. The lamps contained oil (any inflammable oil would do, including cooking oil or Italian hair oil) with a wick, usually made from a bootlace or pyjama cord. Graham's was the more sophisticated version, having the naked flame enclosed in a KLIM tin with a reflector, while Spowatt's had an open flame. Neither gave much light, but they were better than nothing. Graham found getting into the tunnel very difficult. The oven which he had to enter first was very small for a full-grown man, and then he had to manoeuvre himself through the narrow tunnel into the tributary sewer. He went first and Spowatt followed with the lilo. Both men were stretched out, propelling themselves along with their hands and feet in an extended crawl as they made their way through the tributary sewer, which now contained a relatively small depth of sewage. Progress was not too difficult. Then, to Graham's horror, he encountered an unexpected problem as he reached the main sewer – the floor level dropped by about a foot. Stretched out as he was along the tributary, he could only slither head first into the main sewer. With nothing to support his hands and keep his upper body above the level of the sewage, he found himself diving headfirst into it. The smell was indescribable when he surfaced and his stomach heaved uncontrollably a number of times. Then his nasal passages seemed to go numb and thankfully he was no longer able to smell the stench. Spowatt arrived behind him and Graham took the lilo from him. He told Spowatt to stay at the junction, whilst he went on exploring. He rested his trunk on the lilo, and slowly pushed himself along using his legs. It was a very slow business, because it was difficult to push his legs through the glutinous mess of sewage. In the first five minutes, he travelled about five yards. He was surrounded by buzzing insects and other unknown but horrible creatures in the sewage itself. Still Graham pressed on. He felt that once he had forced a way through, the passage would be a lot easier for whoever followed behind. If the full length of the sewer did indeed prove to be 100 yards, then progress of 2 yards a minute would bring him to the end of the sewer within an hour. Graham's idea of using the lilo to avoid a build-up of sewage in front of him was working well.

Then came disaster. Having covered about 20 yards, Graham heard a terrible roar behind him and felt two explosions. Looking round he saw a wall of blue flame rolling towards him. Graham brought the lilo round to use as a shield, but found himself surrounded by fire and hardly able to breathe in the heat and lack of oxygen, as he sought to fight off the flames. The struggle seemed to him to go on for an eternity, but then suddenly it was over and the fire died down. What had happened was that the naked flame of Spowatt's lamp had ignited pockets of methane gas created by the sewage. Graham called out to Spowatt and was thankful to receive a reply; he then battled his way back to the tributary sewer. Spowatt confessed that he was 'a bit burned, nothing much', and led the way back to the entrance to the tunnel, crawling in front while Graham followed, holding his legs. Thankfully, they finally wriggled their way up to and out of the stove. One of the medical officers in the camp was quietly asked to attend. Both men had suffered burns – Spowatt had in fact suffered quite severe facial burns, bad enough for him to be confined to bed by the prisoner doctor for several days. Graham ended up with his head swathed in bandages. His cover story was that he had been burned when doing some cooking in the other ranks' cookhouse. Spowatt was said to have been the victim of a fat fire in the same cookhouse. Miraculously, both not only recovered well, but got away with their cover stories; the tunnel was not found.

On Monday, 12 April, Graham and many of his friends were put on a train and taken north to a new camp at Fontanellato. The group included Captain Michael Gilbert. 'Ownership' of the tunnel now passed to those members of the team remaining in Campo 21, who included Gordon McFall, Claude Weaver and Bill Wendt, and new members were brought in also. The tunnel would be continued and did eventually serve a very valuable purpose, even though it was discovered that the exit from the main sewer was blocked by a substantial iron grill, so that possible escape route was abandoned.

On the same day, 12 April, there was another visit from the Protecting Power. The inspector on this occasion was again Rudolf I. Iselin. He was well aware, of course, of the problems that had existed in January, and hoped to see considerable improvements. Lieutenant Colonel Gray made sure he was fully prepared for Iselin's visit, since he by now realized that whatever he himself wrote by way of complaint to the Protecting Power would never be sent on. In recent weeks he had written on 11 March and sent a telegram on 20 March, neither of which had been received by the Protecting Power. Therefore, Gray had prepared a detailed written list of complaints, which he intended to read out in front of all the prisoners once the representative had arrived. Only in that way could all the men be confident that their complaints were being made known to the Swiss. Rudolf Iselin no doubt already had strong views on the way the camp was being run. When confronted by Gray's request that the list of complaints be read out before a full parade of the prisoners, he readily agreed. In those circumstances, Massi could hardly refuse. His stance, anyway, was that he could not deny the shortcomings of the camp, but that his pleas to Rome for improvements went unanswered.

Iselin noted that there were now 1,328 prisoners in the Chieti camp, 84 of them from the United States. Lieutenant Colonel Gray duly read out his lengthy list of complaints to Iselin in front of the parade. However Massi, no doubt prompted by Croce, would not allow Iselin to take the list of complaints away with him for onward transition to the British Government. The heads of complaint were sevenfold and Iselin summarized them in his report: serious overcrowding, living accommodation desperately bad, water supply entirely insufficient, eating arrangements disgraceful, lighting in many of the barracks very bad, lack of hygienic washrooms and lavatories very dangerous, and recreational facilities totally inadequate. Iselin endorsed all the complaints, saying: 'Walking through the camp we could see that the conditions mentioned are really most unsatisfactory.'

Arriving at the canteen, Iselin was shown a list of charges that the prisoners complained were unjustified. The rule was that the prisoners should be able to use any profits that they, as opposed to the Italians, made by selling goods through the canteen for the general benefit of all inmates. However, in Chieti, the cost of all sorts of items was being deducted by the Italian administration (i.e. Croce) from the canteen's profits. The prisoners were charged for such items as the cost of bricks for paving a road in the camp; for an adding machine for the camp administration office; for overalls worn by Italian personnel working in the canteen; for 'presents' to the interpreter (Croce); and 54 lire for vermouth offered by the Camp Commandant to the representatives of the Protecting Power. The last item Iselin found particularly outrageous. If the Commandant offered him a drink, why should the unfortunate prisoners have to pay for it? In total, Iselin recorded that unjustified deductions and 'expenses' of this sort amounted to about 50,000 lire. The rate of exchange was 72 lire to £1 sterling.

As to recreation, Iselin's report recorded: 'The only space for open air games is the space between the bungalows, which, unfortunately, has been decorated with some miserable little trees so that games like football cannot be played here. Nothing at all is done for recreation.' Mail remained a problem. A statistician amongst the prisoners calculated that only 1 in 70 letters written from inside the camp reached its destination. A list of those who had little or no post from home formed a part of Iselin's report, and included Gordon Lett. Also, it was noted that a batch of telegrams given to the Camp Commander before the new year were only despatched in March – again, no doubt the hand of Croce. Iselin recorded his general impression of the camp as 'decidedly bad'. He echoed what he had said in January: 'We shall make immediately strong representations with the higher military authorities in Rome about conditions in this camp and shall propose to close it unless the necessary improvements can be brought about in a short time.' The real problem for the Protecting Power was that if the Italians refused to do anything about its complaints, it had no real power to do anything. It could pass a copy of its report to the Allied governments, but could take no effective action itself. It could only rely upon the fact that Italy had ratified the Geneva Convention, and that the Italians knew that the Allies held many of their own people as prisoners.

On 21 April, Jenkins was again able to go out of the camp for a walk. He thoroughly enjoyed it, commenting in his diary: 'It was pleasant on the hill with the smell of earth and fresh growth and the sound of birds. We rarely hear birds around the camp, although a nightingale performed for two nights last week.' A delivery of sports kit from the Red Cross also brightened the lives of many. It included soccer and rugby balls, and cricket bats. Sadly, there was no room to construct anything approaching a proper pitch for any of those sports.

On 24 April 1943, Easter Saturday, Captain A. L. Cullen, Essex Regiment, wrote home to his mother in Essex. The Fascist press were complaining that Italian prisoners of war were not properly fed, and Cullen wanted to get the message home as to what was happening in Campo 21. He said:

Food here consists almost entirely of rice or macaroni or onions – other vegetables very rarely because of supply difficulties – and five and a half ounces bread daily; of the rice and macaroni stews we got three small plates in two days. Living conditions are disgusting – 30 men living on rough wooden bunks crowded into a small room – described by the Protecting Power representative on his last visit as equivalent to 'a 3rd class country prison'. Water is short even now, and we get a hot shower once a fortnight – sometimes. Hope this passes the censor. However, all very cheerful, and hoping to say goodbye to it soon.

Surprisingly, the letter got past Croce and the Italian censor. After his mother received it, she passed it on to the War Office, where it joined a growing file of material on the unsatisfactory conditions in the Chieti camp. Happily, a decision was taken in the camp towards the end of April or the beginning of May to centralize the supplies arriving in Red Cross parcels and to use Red Cross ingredients as part of the daily food issue. This gave the SBO, Captain MacKenzie (Red Cross Mac) and the cooks a chance to improve everybody's diet. All cookable food from the parcels was sent to the cookhouse and used to supplement the general ration, creating more edible and sustaining meals. Only chocolate and sweets would be handed out to the prisoners individually. Later in the year, when fruit and vegetables again became available to buy, this too was done centrally by an appointed quartermaster. Hunger remained a significant problem, particularly when consignments of Red Cross parcels failed to be released into the camp, but the general quality of food issued through the prisoners' cookhouse improved.

At the end of April came a development that caused very great concern. In the middle of the night a parade was called and it was announced that 52 officers were to leave the camp. They would travel in two parties – 34 junior officers would be transferred to the Fontanellato Camp near Modena, and 18 more senior officers were to go to Veano, near Piacenza. The latter included Lieutenant Colonel Cooper and virtually the whole of the Escape Committee, and Lieutenant Colonel Gray's HQ staff at the camp. Major Gordon Lett, head of the CNA, also found his name on the list. The accuracy with which the leading players in the escape organization had been identified led many prisoners to believe that there was indeed a spy amongst their ranks. Since all his staff was being 'deported' the SBO, Lieutenant Colonel Gray, insisted that he go too. Perhaps not surprisingly after nine months in Chieti, he had had enough of his command, and shorn of his staff had no wish to start all over again. Lieutenant Colonel William Marshall, another Indian Army officer, agreed to take over. Marshall immediately appointed Major Sam Derry, Royal Artillery, as the new chairman of the Escape Committee and Derry began to gather as much information as possible from the departing members of the committee in the short time available. It did not take the nominated officers long to gather together their sparse belongings.

Sam Derry had been a Territorial officer in the Royal Artillery when war broke out, had gone with the British Expeditionary Force to France, and had been successfully evacuated through Dunkirk. He was sent to North Africa, was captured and escaped in early 1942 and captured again in July near the El Alamein line. This time the Germans held onto him and passed him over to the Italians. Thus, he had eventually ended up in Chieti. Derry had been impressed by the size and breadth of activity of the Escape Committee and in due course became a member of it. His responsibility in the early days was to secure the rations for escapers and tunnel builders. This meant the manufacture of 'escape cakes' which Derry describes as hard as teak and tasting like sweetened sawdust. However so full of nutrients were they that a pocketful could sustain an escaper for a fortnight.

For those remaining in the camp, the search for the spy began immediately. Suspicion first fell upon one of the orderlies working in the prison hospital, Joe Pollak. Pollak was a multilingual private who spoke flawless Italian. He was often seen chatting with the Italian guards and was a bit of a loner amongst the prisoners. It was believed, certainly by Sam Derry, that Pollak was probably the traitor, and he was put under careful surveillance, but did not put a foot wrong over the months that followed. Indeed, the whole of the hospital was put into 'quarantine', and attempts were made to prevent any sensitive information from reaching it. In fact, they were barking up the wrong tree entirely. Joe Pollak was a Czechoslovakian Jew, one of ten children whose parents had been deported to Germany and then Auschwitz, where they died. Pollak himself had left Czechoslovakia in 1939 and had been studying to be a doctor when war broke out. He had joined up, and had served in Libya and Greece before his final capture. Pollak was no friend of either the Germans or Italians. Later, at the armistice, Pollak would escape and, ironically, would become a vital part of Sam Derry's Rome escape network, working with Derry and an Irish cardinal, Monseigneur O'Flaherty, to help hundreds of other escaped prisoners of war. Whoever the spy in Chieti was, it was not Pollak. However, for the time being

Pollak remained under suspicion. There were, of course, other ways for the Italians to gather information, covert listening devices being one of them, as we shall see later. One of the reasons why the tunnels in Stalag Luft III were named Tom, Dick and Harry was so that if mention of them was overheard by the German guards, they would not automatically be associated with escape. 'How far has Tom got? Any problems with Harry?' were not the sort of questions likely to raise suspicion.

Derry, having been unexpectedly elevated to head of the Escape Committee, set about his task with enthusiasm. He decided that the future for tunnels lay in mass production, and ensured that from then on there were always at least six of them under construction. Derry's idea was to drive as many tunnels under the wall as possible, then hold back any escape until all could go at once. He envisaged a mass exodus using all the various tunnels that had gone beyond the wall. The advantage would be both surprise and numbers – if all went well the Italians would find themselves chasing the numerous escapees all over Italy.

THE MURDER OF OUTERBRIDGE: QUESTIONS IN THE HOUSE

The hopelessness of their situation hit many of the prisoners in early May. Despite good news on the progress of the war, they remained confined to Campo 21. On 1 May, John Jenkins wrote in his diary: 'The months fly by. Soon be a year now. A year of wasted life! But perhaps we have learned some lessons here ... Tunisian show still drags on. How long now? Hope! Hope! Hope!'

The party of more senior officers heading for Veano were due to leave the camp early on 1 May 1943. It was clear to them that Croce, who doubtless was the guiding hand behind all the transfers, had decided to remove at a stroke all those whom he believed, from whatever source, to be involved in escape or resistance. Amongst other things, Croce desired that the Chieti News Agency, which was doing damagingly good propaganda work, should be broken up. Thus Gordon Lett was on the transfer list. Lett, however, was determined to stay. He felt that the CNA was doing worthwhile work. He was also something of an optimist, believing that an Allied invasion of Italy was bound to commence soon and that the Allies were most likely to invade from the south. Thus, he did not want to be transferred to a camp further north. His group of transferees were given twenty-four hours' notice of their departure. This gave Lett time to arrange one of the very few 'reverse escapes' in prisoner-of-war camps. Lett found another officer who sufficiently resembled him, Captain Nick Rennie, Royal Artillery, and the two agreed to change places. Rennie, like many others, no doubt fancied his chances of escape from a train or lorry. Lett shaved off his moustache (moustaches were very much the military fashion amongst officers) and the two swapped badges of rank, so that Lett became a captain and Rennie became a major. Then, at 0730hrs on the morning of 1 May, Nick Rennie paraded as Major Gordon Lett when the departure squad formed up near the main gate, and the real Major Lett, minus his moustache, made himself scarce. Unfortunately, although perhaps predictably, Croce had decided to come and see the group off. He and Lett had crossed swords too often for him not to realize that the 'Major Lett' now leaving the Camp was an imposter. Nick Rennie was immediately arrested and a hue and cry started throughout the camp for Lett. However, the remaining members of the transfer party had a train to catch, so they were marched off towards the station. There was no time to wait for the capture of Lett, who later commented on the search: 'The resulting upheaval was gratifying to one's ego. At the end of a couple of hours, I found myself in the cooler, on a month's solitary confinement.' He had in fact achieved his aim, because he had succeeded in missing the train. For Lett, as for many suffering the overcrowded conditions in Campo 21, solitary confinement was in some ways a pleasant relief – privacy was virtually impossible to find anywhere in the camp. After two weeks, Nick Rennie, who was also in the cooler, was allowed to join Lett in his cell. He came with a warning that the cell had been bugged with a listening device during one of Lett's exercise periods – so the two men had an enjoyable time discussing the more unpleasant characteristics of Croce and other prison guards.

In fact, solitary confinement never quite meant what it said. There was a system whereby the waiters who brought food from the cookhouse to a prisoner in the cooler would also bring and take back messages to and from the prisoners there. A Lieutenant Roberts (not David Alwyn Roberts), later a banqueting manager in the West End of London, presided over the officers' cookhouse, and Frank Osborne was one of those who acted as a waiter/courier. He described how he would carry written messages concealed in various bowls of soup (in which case they were tightly wrapped in cellophane), macaroni, cheese or fruit to Major Lett. Osborne or one of his fellow waiters would always be accompanied by an Italian guard and no talking was allowed. However, whilst Lett was sitting eating his food, Osborne would go through the motion of sweeping out his cell, and invariably Lett found a way to thrust a note into Osborne's hand as he busied himself close to where Lett was eating. Lett was gathering information from his guards and from listening to the camp radio, even as he sat in his cell. He would analyse it as usual and pass the result to Osborne. The messages Osborne took to Lett would carry new snippets of information gathered in camp and information gleaned from the Italian newspapers. Lett's messages would be passed on to a senior officer designated by him, and would then be fed into the news releases from the CNA. On one occasion, Lett passed a note of thanks to Osborne and his colleagues, which Osborne kept. It read:

Dear Osborne,

Many thanks to you, and Ryle, for all you have done. We are both most grateful to you both, as some of the notes were very important. You may be aware of the results soon, I hope one will be the acute discomfort, if not the departure of our friend Mr Cross [Croce].

Remember me to Mr Yates [probably Captain D.A. Yates, 7 Gurkha Rifles] and the lads. As a parting message, they might like to know that, now that we hold Tunis and Biserta, all medium bombers which we send from there can now reach as far as Genoa and back on raids. They can also carry bombs up to 3,000 lbs in weight, but not more, while doing it. So we can expect an air blitz at any time now. Pantelleria will probably be evacuated by the Wops [Italians] in a day or two, and so the next move might be the invasion of Sicily, Sardinia, or Italy south of Bari, when the moon is a bit later in setting.

Cheerio, and the best of luck to you all. If ever you should feel like dropping me a line, now or after we get out – the address is c/o Lloyds Bank, 132 Regent Street, London. I should like to hear how you get on, and we might have the chance of celebrating in beer, one day, who knows?

Gordon Lett, Major
P.G.21   14/5/43

P.S. Best wishes, too, to Chesters, Williamson and Spencer.

Lett clearly believed that he would soon be transferred from the camp, but in fact he was to stay on until early August, albeit much of his time was spent in the cooler as Croce tried to make his life as difficult as possible.

Although Lett had avoided the train north on 1 May, the others had gone. The group of more junior officers heading for the recently opened Campo 49 at Fontanellato included Claude Weaver, Eric Newby, the American War Correspondent Larry Allen, and Flying Officer James Outerbridge. In the opposite scenario to Lett, Claude Weaver was not meant to go, but wanted to. He believed, like others, that the train journey would present an opportunity to escape and there were a number of other young pilots who were his friends, also being transferred. Weaver changed his appearance, as had Lett, in order to assume another prisoner's identity. He had gone so far as to colour his blond hair black with boot polish in order to better resemble the officer that he was impersonating. Though Croce had spotted Rennie/Lett, he missed Weaver, knowing him less well.

Jim Outerbridge was one of Weaver's friends. Flying Officer James Edwin Outerbridge was eleven months older than Weaver, born on 5 September 1922 in Bermuda, where his family had lived for many generations. He was sent to Rossall School, in Lancashire, for an English public school education, between 1936 and 1940. There he excelled in athletics and boxing. He was still a schoolboy, just 17, when war broke out in September 1939. As well as being a good sportsman, Outerbridge was also academically very bright, winning the 1941 Rhodes Scholarship for Bermuda and obtaining a place at Trinity College, Cambridge. However, he did not take up his place at Trinity, instead he joined the RAF and qualified as a pilot. Spring of 1943 found him, now aged 20, on operational duty flying a torpedo bomber from Luqa airfield on Malta. At about 2120hrs on 24 March 1943, he and a crew of five others had taken off from Luqa in a Wellington Mark VIII, destined for an armed search of the Maritimo–Naples area. His potential targets were German U-boat submarines and enemy shipping. His Wellington was equipped with a Leigh Light – an airborne searchlight designed for picking out a submarine on the surface at night. The aircraft never returned to Malta and was presumed shot down in the Naples area. Happily, all six of the crew survived to be taken prisoner. A report that Flying Officer Outerbridge was now a prisoner of war reached London on 11 April 1943. He was sent to Campo 21. Jim Outerbridge was one of those who very suddenly found himself deprived of the dangerous, but glamorous and exciting life of an RAF pilot, and condemned to endure hardship, boredom and frustration within the walls of a prison camp. For him, there was also the prospect of spending his 21st birthday in prison and of an unknown number of his youthful years to be wasted in captivity. For an energetic and ebullient young man like Jim Outerbridge, captivity was desperately hard.

After only a relatively short time as a prisoner, Outerbridge was notified that he was one of a number of junior officers who were to be transferred from the overcrowded Campo 21 to the newly opened Campo 49 at Fontanellato, not far from Parma. The thirty-four prisoners were to be moved from Chieti to Fontanellato by train, accompanied by guards from their own camp until they were handed into the custody of new guards at Campo 49. The commander of the escort guard was Captain Ester Giovanni Nardone. He was not having a happy time at Campo 21, having been disciplined by Camp Commandant Colonel Massi for negligence when in charge of the hospital clinic, in March 1943. Two officers made an escape attempt and were missing from roll call. Captain Nardone was fooled by two 'stand-ins' into thinking that they were still present. He was sentenced on 16 March 1943 to five days' close arrest. It was later suggested that he felt some sympathy for the plight of his prisoners; in truth he may just have been a rather inefficient officer.

Escorting prisoners to another camp was doubtless not a very popular task with the guards, and Nardone was probably selected for it because he was out of favour with Colonel Massi. His squad comprised 14 soldiers and 3 *carabinieri*. Their rifles were loaded with both ordinary bullets and what was later described in a poorly translated Italian report as a 'spreading bullet' – apparently buckshot. The guards had orders to shoot at prisoners who escaped and did not stop at the customary warning of 'stop'. Most of the journey of well over 200 miles was to be on an ordinary civilian train which ran from Pescara to Ancona and on to Bologna. Colonel Massi issued strict orders as to how the prisoners should be guarded. The windows of the compartments containing the prisoners were to be kept shut, with the blinds lowered. This was particularly important when the train stopped at a station. Whilst stationary, an armed surveillance cordon should be put in place around the carriage containing the prisoners. The prisoners were not to be allowed to talk to, or have any contact with civilians.

Jim Outerbridge, one of the younger men in Campo 21, combined the ebullience of youth with a burning desire to escape. But he had little experience of captivity or the way that his guards were likely to behave. He saw the journey by train simply as an opportunity. Within the camp, all escape plans had to be vetted by the committee, but on the train it would be for the individual prisoner to decide when and if to attempt it. The party of prisoners travelling to Fontanellato was closely guarded. The officers were allowed to sit in the compartments of one of the train carriages, six or seven to a compartment. There was a corridor that ran the length of the carriage, past each compartment. Some of the time, an Italian guard would sit by the window of the compartment in case anyone was tempted to try to leave the train by that means. Other armed guards were posted in the corridors of the carriage and elsewhere on the train.

For young Jim Outerbridge, used to the freedom of the skies, the temptation to try to escape into the world outside was overpowering. Looking out from the confines of the camp at Chieti had been difficult enough, but now the open prospect of the villages, fields and mountains of Italy as they sped past the carriage window, seemed tangible. A more senior and much more experienced officer, Major Sam Derry, would later describe what he had felt before his own escape from a train carrying him from Sulmona towards Germany in the early autumn of 1943. The desire for freedom became so great that he found he was repeating to himself the words, 'I must get away ... I must get away' in time to the noise from the wheels of the train, and he became incapable of coherent thought. When he eventually jumped from the train it was an act of pure instinct, at what was a momentary opportunity.

The other officers who shared Outerbridge's compartment were much more experienced prisoners than he. Lieutenant Eric Lawton of the Worcestershire Regiment had been captured at Tobruk in June 1942, and had been an inmate of Campo 21 since August of that year. Lawton spoke fluent Italian and recalled later that the Italian guard in the compartment was one Guiseppe Papantonio, a 33-year-old from Foggia. The other officers in the compartment were also old hands: Lieutenant Charles Chamberlin, Royal Artillery, Lieutenant Hugh Thomson, Royal Artillery, Second Lieutenant Barry Nicholls, Royal Artillery and Second Lieutenant Ormsby Pritchford, Royal Northumberland Fusiliers. All had their own thoughts of escape, but were waiting for nightfall. The young SBS officer Eric Newby was in a compartment at the end of the carriage, as were Lieutenant Edwin Lee, Dorset Regiment, and Larry Allen, the American War Correspondent.

The journey to Fontanellato was a long one, well over 200 miles. Jim Outerbridge sat and watched the Italian countryside flashing past until he could stand it no longer. The train was carrying many normal passengers apart from the Allied prisoners of war, and stopped regularly at small stations along the route. Obviously, the chances of jumping successfully from the train were better when it was slowing to enter a station, or gradually picking up speed as it left one. To jump out when the train was stationary at a platform would be extremely foolhardy, since the guards would have ample time and opportunity to fire at any escaping prisoner and to make chase on foot. Outerbridge spoke to his fellow officers in the carriage, saying that he was proposing to make an escape attempt as soon as an opportunity presented itself. At one point, he went out into the corridor to get some air. The window in the corridor was open and the temptation to jump almost overcame him then and there. He readied himself, adrenalin pumping. But before jumping he looked quickly to left and right at the guards in the corridor, and realized that they were watching him carefully, their rifles to hand. He knew then that he had no chance of surprise, vital to any escape attempt, and abandoned the attempt. He returned a little shakily to his seat in the compartment, coming down from the adrenalin rush. Hugh Thomson noticed that he had gone very white and asked him what was the matter. Outerbridge told him.

To his companions Outerbridge appeared to remain agitated and they tried to calm him down, and to persuade him that any attempt should wait until after dark. After a while, they believed that they had succeeded and that all would be well. However, as the day grew hotter, Outerbridge asked that the window of the compartment be opened, and eventually Captain Nardone agreed (despite his orders), on the condition that one of his men sat beside the window, between Outerbridge and the outside world.

When the train stopped at a small station some distance south of Rimini, Outerbridge could not contain himself any longer. With a brief word to the others, he leapt up, got his feet onto the small table by the compartment window and prepared to launch himself through the window to the platform, past the startled Italian guard, Guiseppe Papantonio. Realizing it would be little more than suicide, the other five officers in the compartment grabbed him and hauled him back into his seat. They quietened him down as best they could, trying to persuade him of the realities of the situation and the suicidal nature of what he had just attempted. Eventually, the young man seemed to accept that he had been foolhardy in the extreme, and to agree that if he was going to make an attempt to escape, it should be at night, under cover of darkness. In reality, however, Outerbridge's emotions remained in turmoil – like Sam Derry some months later, he was unable to think rationally.

Guiseppe Papantonio's reaction to Outerbridge's attempt was surprising. For reasons known only to himself, he did not report the incident to Captain Nardone, but simply swapped places with his fellow guard, Francesco Barbarito, who was in the corridor. Papantonio later suggested that he had done this to avoid the possibility that he himself would be assaulted if another attempt to escape was made. Obviously, if anybody did succeed in getting out of the window, the guard in that compartment would have to be neutralized in some way.

As the train pulled away from the little station, Eric Lawton thought that Outerbridge had calmed down. He and the others relaxed. Sadly, they had misjudged the situation and when, before very long, the train again pulled to a halt in a small station called Gradara-Cattolica (nowadays simply Cattolica),

Outerbridge decided to try again. It was 1520hrs and broad daylight. Barbarito, the guard now in the compartment, seemed inattentive and was sitting with his legs stretched out under the table by the window. As the train began slowly to pull out of the station, reaching a speed of perhaps 4 miles per hour, James Outerbridge lunged for the window once more, this time catching everybody off guard. After a short scuffle he succeeded in pushing the Barbarito aside and clambered through the window, jumping down to the platform. On landing, he stumbled, but stayed on his feet. The platform was surrounded by wire fencing, so there was no easy way off it and Outerbridge had no choice but to run along the train. He began to run along the platform away from the engine towards the back of the train. In so doing, he had to pass by the other Italian guards posted in compartments further along the carriage. Barbarito now raised his rifle and began firing out of the window after Outerbridge, but Ormsby Pritchford knocked the gun up as he fired so that the shot went harmlessly wide. Pritchford, Nicholls and Lawton then managed to prevent Barbarito from firing again.

The train stopped immediately. Poor Outerbridge did not get far. Papantonio had remained alert in the corridor, and although he took no action to try to prevent Outerbridge from jumping out of the window, Papantonio now ran along the corridor to the carriage door, raising the alarm. The other guards on the train reacted quickly. In broad daylight, from the near stationary train, Outerbridge proved an easy target. Edwin Lee was some four or five compartments further down the carriage and said that as Outerbridge ran past his compartment, the guard in Lee's compartment fired out of the window and shot him from a distance of only three feet. Outerbridge was hit in the back and immediately fell to the ground. Eric Newby, who was in the same compartment as Lee, recorded that Outerbridge appeared to be hit low down towards the buttocks.

Outerbridge knew that his attempt at escape was over. Crying out in pain, he raised an arm from the ground in a gesture of surrender. To all watching it was obvious that he was no longer capable of attempting to escape and posed no possible threat to his guards. The train had come to a complete halt and Papantonio was now on the platform. Raising his rifle, he fired four or five shots into Outerbridge's prone body as he lay defenceless on the ground. Outerbridge collapsed, his arm dropped and he rolled over. One of those watching, Claude Weaver, now also on his way to Fontanellato, described how after shooting Outerbridge, Papantonio was still apparently not content and began to 'beat his brains out with his rifle'. Outerbridge's body was gathered up and put back on the train by the Italian guards and he was pronounced dead shortly thereafter. His body was taken off the train when it arrived at Rimini. The cause of death was recorded by the Medical Authority in Rimini as being: 'various wounds in the region of the heart by the bullets from a gun'. Sadly, Papantonio was a good enough shot and had been aiming to kill.

Captain Nardone was furious at what had happened. He had been in the train corridor at the other end of the carriage, and had seen virtually nothing of the escape, but had heard the shots. Once Outerbridge's body was back on board, Nardone went to inspect the compartment, to try to discover exactly what had happened. For reasons best known to himself, he summoned Papantonio into the compartment and proceeded to interview him there, in the presence of the remaining prisoners. Lawton was able to understand all that was said. Not surprisingly, Nardone was angry with Papantonio for not reporting Outerbridge's first attempt at escape, and pressed him as to why he had simply swapped places with Barbarito rather than follow proper procedures. Papantonio had no answer, other than that he had not wanted to find himself under physical assault from the prisoners.

When the incident was reported to Colonel Massi at Campo 21 (where all the guards returned after a few days), and up the chain of command to the headquarters of Italian IX Army Corps, the reaction was very different. The official view was that the guards should be praised and rewarded for taking prompt action to prevent an escape. An Italian report of the shooting dated 20 May 1943 claimed that in total four guards fired after Outerbridge. Barbarito, whom the report claimed hit Outerbridge when firing 'buckshot' from the train, was said to have fired simultaneously with Privates Papantonio, Ciccarelli and Santoliquido. All four were rewarded for their actions. Barbarito received ten days' leave and 200 lire, the other three received a reward of 100 lire each. It is suggested that Massi arranged for a group photograph of them to be taken. Two British officers, Ormsby Pritchford and Barry Nicholls, who had impeded Barbarito's attempts to shoot Outerbridge, were each sentenced to seven days in the cooler and followed by ten days' open arrest for their actions.

Once the remaining 33 prisoners had been delivered to Fontanellato, they immediately reported the murder of Jim Outerbridge to the Senior British Officer there, Lieutenant Colonel Dudley Norman DSO, East Yorkshire Regiment, and he conducted a formal enquiry into what had happened, hearing evidence from a number of witnesses, including Eric Lawton, Edwin Lee and

Larry Allen. A sanitized report of the findings of the enquiry (Papantonio was not named in it as the murderer) was handed by Norman to the Swiss Protecting Powers representative who visited Fontanellato in May 1943, and news of what had happened duly reached London. Outerbridge's family were notified of their son's death directly from Campo 21. Lieutenant Colonel Gray wrote to them, via the camp chaplain, based on the information that he received when the Italian guards eventually returned to Chieti. Outerbridge's mother found it difficult to understand why he had attempted to escape in the circumstances, commenting: 'It has all been so sudden and it was such an unexpected thing for him to try and do. He has always been so sensible over things. I suppose homesickness and monotony got him down and made him feel he just had to take a chance.' No doubt she found it difficult to understand the frustration, for a 20-year-old used to the freedom of the skies, of a sentence of indefinite imprisonment in the conditions of a camp such as Chieti.

 The first eye-witness report of Outerbridge's killing to reach the Allied Authorities came from his friend Claude Weaver, after he had escaped through Allied lines following the Italian Armistice in September 1943. He was debriefed by MI9, the wartime intelligence department set up to deal with prisoners of war and escapees. Weaver did not know the full name of Outerbridge's killer, referring to him as: 'Antonia Pietro Guissepi, a prison guard at Camp 21 who lives in Foggia'. Undoubtedly this was Guiseppe Papantonio, born in Foggia in 1910. Claude Weaver had not remained in the Fontanellato camp. He was much saddened by his friend's death and when the Italian authorities realized he should not be there, soon owned up as to who he really was. He had not been able to escape on the journey to Fontanellato, but perhaps the journey back to Chieti would offer an opportunity. However, Weaver was in due course successfully returned by the Italians to Campo 21. There Weaver recommenced his escape activities and, as we shall see later, eventually succeeded. Sadly however, he was killed in action on 25 January 1944. Eric Lawton also escaped following the Armistice and his account was more precise. Lawton spoke fluent Italian, and had listened carefully to the questioning of Papantonio by Captain Nardone after the shooting. In a statement dated 25 November 1943, Lawton named the guard who had murdered Outerbridge as Guiseppe Papantonio, son of Raffaele Papantonio, born in Foggia in 1910.

Returning to the story of Campo 21, back in London on 2 May 1943, a summary arrived from Berne of the Protecting Powers' 12 April report on the camp. It included Lieutenant Colonel Gray's list of complaints and finally seems to have alerted the British Government and War Office to what was really going on. It confirmed the matters that had been complained of in the occasional prisoners' letters that had got through, including the insufficiency of food. The summary of the report came to the Prisoners of War Department at the Foreign Office, who passed it on to the War Department with a request that the Protecting Power (through whom all communication with Mussolini's government had to be undertaken) be asked to inform the Italians that unless they remedied the breaches of the Geneva Convention immediately, the British Government would demand that the camp be closed. Also at around this time, the British authorities began to receive first-hand witness evidence from former inmates of Campo 21. Glen was repatriated, as was Captain J. W. Creamer, Royal Army Medical Corps, and both supplied full accounts of what had been going on there.

It has long been the British way that citizens have the right, if they are concerned about something, to raise it with their MP. The conditions in Campo 21 were raised in the chamber of the House of Commons on 11 May, by Tom Driberg MP. Driberg was a colourful character who worked as a journalist for the *Daily Express*, setting up the now famous 'William Hickey' gossip column. He was at this time an independent (he had formerly been a communist and later joined the Labour Party), who had won a previously Conservative seat on 25 June 1942, during the disquiet following the surrender of Tobruk. Some knew him as the 'Tobruk MP', and perhaps it was appropriate that he was the first to raise the question of the mistreatment of prisoners in Campo 21 in the House of Commons. Driberg began by asking the Secretary of State for War whether he had any information on conditions at Campo PG 21, Italy, about which complaints had recently been received, particularly with reference to the supply of water. Unfortunately, Sir Percy James Grigg, replying, had been badly briefed, and was not aware of the true situation. He claimed that the camp had been inspected three times by the Protecting Power and was generally satisfactory, except that water was usually short. Driberg then put to him that in January of that year conditions had been found by the Protecting Power to be very unsatisfactory. Relying, it seems, on the original Trippi report from October 1942, Grigg replied that the bathing and washing arrangements were modern and almost luxurious, and the only complaint was that there was not enough water to put in them. It was an unhappy mistake, but no doubt not Grigg's fault. Two days later, on 13 May, a memo from the Prisoner of War Department advised the Secretary of State that 'conditions in Campo No 21 are certainly worse than his answer may have implied.' This was followed on 18 May by the High Commissioner for Canada drawing the Government's attention to the 'extremely serious conditions' in Campo 21, where three Canadian officers were being held. As it happened, on that same morning, a formal protest had been sent by the British Government, via the Swiss to the Italians, demanding the closure of the camp unless radical improvements were made. However, all of this remained unknown in Campo 21 and had no effect upon their unhappy state. After the shooting of Jim Outerbridge, life went on.

The Dramatic Society continued to come up with ideas to entertain the prisoners. On 15 May, they held a 'Happy Hampstead Night', with shows, stalls and fancy dress. On 17 May, news reached the camp that North Africa had finally fallen to the Allies. There was much celebration. On 20 May, one of Gordon Lett's aunts, Olive Cranko, wrote to him, not knowing of course that he was in a punishment cell. She sent him love and best wishes, referred to news of him received from Peter Glen ('P.G. a young Yank you will remember'), and gave him news of the success of his father Lewis's most recent book. Hidden in the text she sent him an important message – the capital letters are the author's – 'at first you know … Nobody Obviously Realizes That Her Apparent Frigidity Really Indicates Courage And Openheartedness Under Rather Severe and plain features, poor dear…' Decoded using the first letter of each word, the message is plain: NORTH AFRICA OURS. In fact, that news had already reached the camp. The letter successfully passed the censor and eventually reached Lett in Chieti. Lett had by now sent a number of letters containing a rather more sophisticated code than that he had used to his uncle Hugh in November 1942. These letters were passed on to another uncle, Major Lawrence Bird, who was working in the War Office. Just what Lawrence Bird's real job was there is obscure, and there is no record of whether the coded passages were successfully deciphered and proved to be of use. Also on 20 May, Kenwyn Walters recorded that he was barred from his bungalow all day. The Italians were finally disinfesting the accommodation of its unwanted extra inhabitants – bed bugs, lice and other unpleasant insects. On 24 May, there were celebrations of Empire Day.

An American, a medic called Alan R. Stuyvesant, had been repatriated from Campo 21 in mid-May, since medical staff belonged to a category described as Protected Personnel (as was ambulance man Peter Glen).

Frelinghuysen describes Alan Stuyvesant as being about 40 years of age, with laughing eyes, bright red cheeks and a beard but no moustache. The two had been friends when Frelinghuysen was at college, and Stuyvesant had been living in Tranquility, western New Jersey. Stuyvesant was a fluent French speaker, and was driving an ambulance for the American Field Ambulance with the Free French Forces when captured in North Africa. Frelinghuysen says that Stuyvesant's repatriation, like Glen's, was in fact a mistake by the Italians, since Stuyvesant had privately declared that his wish was to parachute into France to fight with the French Resistance. Once repatriated and in London, Stuyvesant was able to add his account to the stream of information now reaching London about conditions in Chieti. Stuyvesant was a friend of Bill Wendt's and he, like Glen, wrote to Wendt's mother in reassuring terms. He commented that the climate was excellent, the view of the Gran Sasso was beautiful, and thanks to Red Cross parcels, the food was adequate. Stuyvesant emphasized that morale amongst the prisoners was high and that Mrs Wendt should not worry about Bill, but added: 'However, if it is possible and you can send him things, please do so. Books, American cigarettes, tobacco or cigars, a pipe, soft baseballs, socks, shaving kits, toothbrushes, powder, towels, muffler, underwear, sweaters, chocolate, any canned foods, spam, cheese, meat roll, etc, maple syrup, peanut butter, and jam would give them great pleasure … Letters mean even more to POWs than to anyone else. Few arrive. They [POWs] write you two letters a week but I doubt if you receive any of them. Please write Bill often and get all his friends to do so too.'

On 26 May, Bill Wendt wrote to a friend, Randolph E. Brown in Glenwood, Minnesota, saying: 'I have had no mail from the States yet, but I have had a few from England from a friend there.' He had been a prisoner for six months without hearing from his family.

On 30 May, the Honourable Artillery Company (HAC) held a dinner for its members and their guests. Arthur Green was the secretary of the Dinner Committee, and kept careful notes and calculations as to cost, and as to the arrangements that were made. Planning took a number of weeks and began in April with permission being sought and granted by the SBO, at the time still Lieutenant Colonel Gray. There were to be decorations, including flowers, and decorative menus. Richard Edmonston Low was responsible for these. There would be a band, and each HAC member who was coming could invite one guest. Official guests who sat at the top table included the Church of England padre, Major Chutter, Lieutenant Colonel Kilkelly, and the Senior American Officer, Colonel Max Gooler. Certain items had to be bought from the Italians. Edmonston Low spent 150 lire on flowers. In total 798 lire was spent by the committee on extras, including wine, anchovies, sardines, clams and fish paste.

Since it was summertime fruit and vegetables were available to buy, and happily the camp was not very far from the sea, so that fish was also occasionally available. Thus the food was somewhat better than that served at dinners earlier in the year. Each of the hosts had to pay up to 25 lire towards the cost of the extras. The required contribution of food from each man illustrates the true poverty of their rations: one Oxo cube or similar per host, half a meat roll, one spoonful of jam, two biscuits, one orange or apple, one tablespoon of condensed milk, and so on. Menus were drawn, with the arms of the Honourable Artillery Company and its motto, *Arma Pacis Fulcra* on the front cover. As always the basic food was exotically described: '*Delices de fromage; Hors d'oeuvres parisiens, Crème St Germain, Croquettes de Poisson; Sauté de galantine, petit pois frais, riz anglais; trifle; Welsh rarebit; Café moka; Vin du pays.*' A seating plan was drawn up and 88 guests attended the dinner, which was a great success.

June 1943

SPORTS AND ENTERTAINMENT

Finally, at the beginning of June, Sam Webster received a letter from home. He had spent six months as a prisoner worrying about the well-being of his wife and wondering whether their child had safely arrived. Now, news began to come through. Several other letters followed during the month and soon he received photographs of little Mary Ray, and news of her progress.

Tunnelling continued in the better weather. Sam Derry and his Escape Committee were kept busy and sometimes had problems with with over-enthusiastic young would-be escapers who had not thought through their plans properly. One such was apparently Lieutenant Dennis Bossey Rendell, of the Middlesex Regiment and 2 Para, who had been captured in Tunisia as a part of Operation Torch. Rendell, who eventually achieved the rank of brigadier, commented many years later: 'I quickly got down to escape activities, and dug a number of tunnels, one of which a mule fell down when we got outside [the wall]. I had a row with the Escape Committee, I was young and stupid, had no real idea how to get out, I just wanted to get out. I wasn't very popular with Sam Derry...' Generally, however, things were going well. The prisoners had learned from their early setbacks and there were now a number of long-term tunnels under construction.

A letter from Lett to his Uncle Hugh, dated 16 June 1943, fell foul of the censors and much of the text was blacked out – including a description of conditions in the camp. However, one coded passage was left untouched. It read: 'Very glad to hear through Sheila that you have seen Peter [Glen] at last – please tell him that I have now qualified for full membership of the club which he and Dennis [Duke] and Tony [Roncoroni] founded – in fact I now find myself its "doyen".' This actually referred to the Cooler Club, where Lett had been spending much of his time since 1 May.

With the successful conclusion of the war in North Africa, the Allies had turned their attention to Italy. Mussolini's African Empire had been swept away, and in order to mount an invasion of mainland Italy, the Italian off-shore strongholds had to be dealt with. There were in essence two of these, both part way between Africa and the Italian coast – the heavily fortified islands of Pantelleria and Lampedusa. Pantelleria, known as Mussolini's island fortress, surrendered to the Allies on 11 June 1943. Lampedusa surrendered on the following day. The Allies now drew breath and prepared for the next stage of their invasion of the European mainland. Their plans were of course highly confidential, but in fact the target was Sicily. All this was of course of the greatest importance for the prisoners, when it reached their ears.

The entertainments staged by the theatrical and musical departments continued to improve in quality, variety and ingenuity. Efforts were made to replicate some of the entertainments of a typical British summer. There was a village fete, opened by the Dowager Duchess of Chieti (Lieutenant M. C. D. Sykes, Royal Tank Regiment). The fete boasted stalls with a variety of produce, and various games and sideshows, the most ingenious of which was a milking competition. Lacking a real cow, the udders were made from football bladders, and the milk was the KLIM powdered version.

On 6 June, a 'circus' came to Chieti, with clowns, acrobats and pantomime horses. There was a Chamber of Mysteries, waxworks, a wall of death, acrobats performing with 'animals', and 'sea lions' with a ringmaster, a fairground with freak shows, including a giraffe-necked woman, and penny-a-shy stalls, where one could topple a bucket of water over a 'ravishing blonde' if one hit the bullseye. There was a hammer and bell sideshow, but since the bell was at the top of a fairly high drainpipe and the diet was dreadful it defeated even Bill Bowes.

Always there would be music. At the summer's sports meetings, the Chieti Colliery Band played, resplendent in uniforms cobbled together with much ingenuity by the theatrical costume department. The stars of the theatrical costume department were Captain A. A. Galpin, Royal Army Service Corps, and Second Lieutenant A. Mateer, Royal Artillery, who created the most convincing collection of stage costumes, as well as costumes for events such as these. As additional recreation there were also Race Meetings in the camp. These were variations on the Race Nights still much favoured today as charity fund raisers. In Chieti, the jockeys lined up on stools and their progress was decided by the SBO, who threw dice for each horse. These races were always popular with the sporting fraternity, who would bet on most things. Eventually, there was a sweepstake on the date of the Allied invasion of Italy, which became worth £600.

Events were held to raise money for camp funds that could then be used to buy instruments, sports equipment, educational books and so on. A two-day casino was set up, where the prisoners could play mouse roulette – this was a circular board with holes around its circumference. Each hole would have a playing card in front of it on which a gambler could place a bet. A mouse was then released from a box in the centre of the table, and would chose a hole to disappear down. The card that he crossed to do so would then be the winning card. The house took a percentage of the stakes for camp funds. The fun and games were only superficial, of course – a form of escapism to avoid the reality of their unhappy lives. Freer Roger confirmed that despite the larks, 'we had our times of depression when the walls felt as though they were closing in and suffocating one'. June, for many, marked the first anniversary of their capture in North Africa. A year is a very long time in a young life – time goes quicker only as one gets older and many of the inmates in Chieti were still in their early twenties or even late teens.

At least the news of the Allied victories brought them hope. Also the garden in Chieti was beginning to produce, so that the prisoners' diet started to improve. Walters noted on 17 June that he 'had radishes from garden'. A working cinema now arrived in the camp, and the Italians installed a projector and screen outside. The films were supplied by them and were of their choosing, the first two being shown on the nights of 19 and 20 June. One turned out to be an American musical, dubbed into Italian but with the songs still in English. The audience of prisoners found it comical, but enjoyed the music and the rare opportunity to see a pretty girl or two. The other evening was not so entertaining, with a third rate Italian film that in any case started over an hour later than the advertised time. Kenwyn Walters was one of those who didn't think much of it.

For the prisoners, hope soared and sometimes fell equally dramatically as news of the Allied campaign arrived, yet time went on and their captivity continued. On Saturday, 19 June, Jenkins wrote:

A year ago the attack which finally landed me here had begun. A year! It seems almost yesterday and now the whole of North Africa is in our hands, and Pantelleria and Lampedusa, and Europe is standing by for an invasion. What next!! Hopes are high. I hope they are not shattered. Camp life changes little. We have an athletic meeting today, with the influx of Americans baseball takes precedence over basketball. Deck tennis is in vogue again, and volley ball caught on quickly. Food has improved enormously since we started centralising parcels. Fruit is becoming plentiful.

But on 20 June he wrote:

A date I will remember all my life, just like 1066 or 1492. A day of unutterable despair and disillusionment. Today marks a year of captivity. I hesitate to think how chaps captured at Dunkirk must feel [they had been prisoners for three years]. Oh God! How long now? How long to peace and freedom?

As Jenkins noted, the American population of the camp was steadily increasing, most of the arrivals being billeted in a wing of bungalow 5 as they formed a community of their own. The American way was different to the British, but the two communities got on well together. Apart from sport, there were a number of crossover societies. Every week there would be a meeting called the Chieti Triangle, the triangle being Chieti, London and New York. A topic would be chosen, and talks would be given on the subject, for instance schools and education, from the American and British point of view. For each nationality, it was a method of increasing their understanding of the lives that their allies had left behind.

Back in London, the British Government tried to increase pressure on Italy to improve the conditions in Campo 21, and sent a further memorandum to the Italian government. With the war in North Africa won, and the islands of Lampedusa and Pantelleria captured, they no doubt hoped that the Mussolini government might finally listen. Invasion, and the day of reckoning were coming closer. The memorandum registered a formal complaint at the fact that the Commandant Colonel Massi (through Croce) had refused to allow Lieutenant Colonel Gray's written list of complaints to be taken out of the camp on 12 April. It further complained of the extremely bad conditions in the camp which had existed under Lieutenant Colonel Barela, and 'the most improper and inhumane treatment accorded to prisoners of war by this officer during the autumn of 1942'. It then listed seven specific complaints against the Barela regime: insufficient water for the prisoners' most elementary needs; failure to provide clothing; failure to provide bedsteads for the officers; confiscation of valuables without receipts; strip searches in the open air, in front of Italian sentries and *carabinieri*; collective punishments of prisoners; and the opening of all Red Cross tins, leading to the hopeless mixing up of foodstuffs in whatever container a prisoner had. The memorandum concluded: 'His Majesty's Government consider that the Commandant at the time of these incidents, Lieutenant Colonel Mario Barela must be considered responsible for the ill-treatment of prisoners of war, and accordingly demand his trial and punishment…' But the British complaint seems, in fact, to have had very little effect on conditions in Campo 21. Barela was long gone, but Massi and Croce remained and things carried on much as before.

On 22 June, Tom Driberg MP asked a further question in the House, and this time elicited the concessions that conditions in Campo 21 required radical improvements, and if these were not carried out immediately, the Government would insist on the closure of the camp. When Driberg not surprisingly complained that he had been told something quite different a month earlier, he was told, 'There is a war on, and communications are not quite as effective as they are in normal times.' When the issue was raised in the House for a third time later in the summer, Sir Percy James Grigg informed MPs that, unsurprisingly, no reply had been received from the Italians to the British Government's demand that the camp be closed unless drastic improvements were made.

On 23 June, Sam Webster wrote to his father, mother and wife, saying: 'Have received several letters from each of you, with pictures of you and Mary Ray. Words just can't express how glad I was to get them. I sit for hours now reading and looking. Mary Ray's the cutest little thing I've ever seen … wish I was there too. You're perfectly right, I wouldn't swap her for twelve little boys!! … I am still feeling fine except for missing you and waiting to see Mary Ray. I can imagine her kicking around and trying to laugh. When I do get back, I'll be the happiest man in the world. Maybe it won't be so long. Tell Mary Ray to be a good girl.'

On either 27 or 29 June, there was a Country Fair and a band played on the cookhouse veranda. Sam Webster wrote home again on 30 June, saying 'We had a World Fair of our own last night – everything from sideshows and rodeo to throw a ball and duck the 'lady'. Bill Harrison and I took it all in, tried all the games, and lost all of our money. We didn't have cokes and ice cream but had substitutes – after a fashion. It's really remarkable how good it was, considering what we have to work with. We even had a Gypsie Rose Lee.' Bill Harrison was a fellow American prisoner who like Sam had a young daughter. He and Webster spent many hours sharing photographs of their little girls. Webster finished his letter home: 'I miss you all so very much, and hope to see you soon.'

Meanwhile the matches between Great Britain and the USA at softball were becoming more serious. Bowes was a thinking sportsman and was doing his best to work out the weaknesses of the American teams and how to exploit them. Bowes was modest about his achievements at softball, saying that he let the side down with monotonous regularity, although he was regarded by the British players as their star pitcher. He confessed that he could only occasionally produce the beautiful fast one which would raise the hearts of his team, saying: 'The Yanks did eventually begin to treat my pitching with some respect, but the inglorious fact remained that whether they challenged us or we challenged them, the result was always the same – defeat.' A contrasting account was given by Lieutenant H. W. Bonnello, Royal Artillery, however. Bonnello recalled that Bowes was 'absolutely magic at softball, because he could pitch the ball just above the knee, and for softball, you have to have the ball coming in just around shoulder height. With Bowes pitching them above the knee, it was virtually impossible to hit them. The US would say: "Come on you big bastard, pitch them up." And the Empire continued: "Strike one, Strike two, Strike three, you are out." They didn't take it very kindly.'

Nonetheless, the competitor in Bill Bowes wanted to defeat the Americans at their own game. A part of Bowes' job as 'Head of Sport' was to discover what sports, if any, new arrivals in the camp could play. To his delight, one day a Canadian whom he recalls as being called Cowan arrived, and Bowes discovered that he was a first-class softball pitcher. Canadians, of course, played for the Empire or Rest of the World team, not for the United States. At the selection meeting for the next 'international' softball match, Bowes persuaded the selection committee to drop him, and to play the untried new arrival instead. There was always a lot of betting on these matches, and with the dropping of Bowes from the team, the odds against England rose from 2 to 1 to 3 to 1. What would make it more exciting was that the Red Cross had sent a real brand-new softball into the camp, which was being carefully preserved for this match.

The match took place on a lovely sunny day. Freddie Brown captained the Rest of the World team. Cowan turned out to be something of a showman, according to Bowes turning up, despite the warmth, in a fur-lined flying suit. He limbered up while the captains tossed, and then the teams moved into their positions. Cowan was to pitch. When all was ready, he stripped off his flying suit to reveal a battledress blouse. This also came off and Cowan then dramatically signalled that he was ready. The star American striker took his position. Then, Cowan uncoiled and delivered the first ball directly into the catcher's gloves at incredible speed. The striker never even saw it and had not moved. The watching British members of the crowd roared with delight. The same thing happened with the next ball, and the one after that, and the Americans' star striker was out. Cowan was able to make the ball swerve and dip in the air. The American strikers followed in a steady procession, few able to see or hit a Cowan-propelled ball. The Rest of the World duly scored a first and emphatic victory over the United States, 14–5. Bowes clearly revelled in the satisfaction of having beaten the USA at their own game, particularly having suffered so many thrashings at softball in the past. He wrote later that it was his second best day in Chieti, bettered only by the Village Cricket Match.

The British then offered the Americans a return match, but with a sense of fair play, the teams this time were to be the West Atlantic versus the East Atlantic, so that Cowan played with the Americans. Surprisingly, the East Atlantic (the British) won this match also, though by a much closer margin of 8–5. Freddie Brown said: 'I think one of the reasons we did [win] was because most of our players, being cricketers, hit the ball on what would be the off side of a cricket field, whereas the Americans' only stroke appeared to be the pull-drive. By the time that they had woken up to the fact that they needed some fielders in the covers, we had won the match. Another reason for our success was the pitching of Bill Bowes, who had devoted just as much time to studying the weaknesses of his opponents as if he had been playing in a Roses match.'

Bill Bowes, as is I hope clear from other passages in this book, was one of those who understood perfectly what needed to be done to survive in the harsh conditions of Campo PG 21. He knew that it was important to stay busy and to throw yourself fully into whatever your chosen activity was. He was undoubtedly an excellent team man and spared no effort to achieve the objective of the team. As he himself put it: 'Never in the lives of the 1,700 of us had ingenuity, skill and enterprise meant so much or, to corrupt the Churchillism, never did so many do so much from so little.' When not arranging sporting events or playing sport himself, he would take part wholeheartedly in other activities in the camp, developing, amongst other things, a career on the stage – acting, singing and dancing. However, he commented that much of their success, particularly that of keeping the necessary rooms free for entertainment, library and indoor recreation, was at the cost of personal discomfort and overcrowding in their sleeping quarters.

The baiting of the guards remained a popular unofficial sport. An American B-26 pilot, Curtis Church, noted a rather childish game that some of the British prisoners played. It was widely believed that Italian soldiers were overly superstitious, and the practice developed whereby a few British prisoners would stand by the wire near to the wall and fix the sentry in the sentry box with an unwavering stare. The sentry would, in due course, notice that he was being stared at, and would become uncomfortable, either believing that he was being given the Evil Eye and that a spell or curse was being placed upon him, or wondering what the prisoners might be plotting against him. The increasingly nervous sentry would eventually complain to his unit commander, and the prisoners would then receive an ultimatum to desist from staring at the sentry or risk being shot. They would at length disperse, satisfied with the result of their game.

Harold Sell remembered that one night the Americans took baiting to a new level. At 2230hrs, the lights in the bungalows had to be switched off, leaving nothing on but the dim security lights in the barrack rooms. The Americans in bungalow 5 baited a trap. They carefully removed all the bulbs from the security lights in their part of the bungalow, so that their rooms would be pitch black when the normal lighting went off. Then they quietly waited until not long before 2230hrs, before bursting into song with carefully orchestrated, very rude and very loud, anti-Fascist songs. The singing became louder and louder, until the guards had no option but to turn out in their full kit to quell the disturbance. The timing was perfect, and they burst into the American barrack rooms just before the normal lighting went off. The Americans immediately stopped singing and a few moments later the lights went out, leaving the room pitch dark. An American then shouted out, in Italian: 'Get your razors out!' In the dark, not knowing from where attack might come, the guards panicked, bursting from the bungalows through whatever window or door they could find. Not a finger was laid on any of them, but jeers and catcalls followed their speedy retreat from the bungalow. The guards reacted once they had reached a safe distance by picking up stones from the ground and hurling them through the windows of the bungalow. The Americans fielded some and threw them back at the guards, who then lost control and started firing through the windows of the bungalows at targets that thankfully they could not see. At the sound of firing, the Commandant and the whole of the guard turned out, but proper order was not restored for about three hours. Perhaps miraculously, none of the shots hit anyone and the Americans ended up with nothing more than a few bruises. Despite the hideously dangerous nature of the situation, the Americans were well pleased with the havoc they had created.

During the summer, American numbers had continued to increase. One new inmate in late June was Flight Officer James E. 'Jim' Beck, of the United States Air Force. He had been shot down in his P-40 fighter off Sicily on 15 June 1942, and had landed in the sea. He had lost his life raft during his descent by parachute, and had been fortunate to be picked up by an Italian boat. He was eventually brought to Campo 21, along with a P-38 pilot called Bruce Campbell, at the very end of June or early July. Beck described the living conditions in the camp as generally poor. Sanitary conditions were still bad and in order to 'have a bath', it was necessary to draw a bucket of water from the well behind your block, then get a fellow prisoner to pour the bucket over you while you washed yourself down. For the Americans, news was disseminated by Larry Allen who, according to Beck, spent a number of periods in the cooler when the Italians disliked his bulletins, in the same way that Lett did. Beck commented: 'We were allowed to write cards to be mailed through the Red Cross. I wrote many cards but none ever reached home before I did [in late 1943]. I never received a letter while I was in the POW camp. The most distressing thing about being a prisoner is that you did not know how long you would be there: it might be a few months or it might be years.'

July 1943

THE CRICKET MATCH

The Village Cricket Match

There is perhaps nothing more English than a village cricket match. In the world of Campo PG 21, escapism was essential and anything that could take the prisoners out of their depressing existence for a few hours was enormously popular. Thus the theatre was well attended, as were the fairs and circuses that were staged. Bill Bowes and his sports section now decided that they would put on a proper English village cricket match in the confines of the prison compound. Daunting though such a project would be, it would raise morale, show the Americans the beauty of the English national game as a riposte to the invasion of softball, and no doubt reduce the Italian garrison to a state of total bemusement, since there was little chance that their captors would understand what was going on. Two teams of the best cricketers in the camp would play each other – with Freddie Brown of Surrey and England captaining one side, and Bill Bowes of Yorkshire and England captaining the other. The creative arm of the theatrical department was enlisted to help create as realistic an environment as possible. Happily, since the invasion of Italy was expected imminently, and Lampedusa and Pantelleria had already fallen to the Allies, the Italian administration was rather less obstructive than it might have been the previous autumn.

The first hurdle was to create a wicket on which a proper game of cricket could be played. Bowes decided that this would have to be a stretch of the tarmac road that ran through the centre of the camp. It was hard and flat, but sloping, with one end appreciably higher than the other. It would no doubt prove to be pretty fast for bowlers such as Bill Bowes, with plenty of bounce. However, it was the wrong colour. The outfield was never going to truly resemble that of an English cricket field, but the appearance of the wicket was felt to be all important. Therefore, using prisoners' camp funds allotted for the purpose, Bowes arranged to buy a quantity of green distemper from the Italians, and having no doubt paid far more than the market price, used it without objection from the guards to paint a length of the road green. The prisoners had their pitch. Cricket bats had come from the Red Cross, and making the wickets was no great problem. Broom handles were cut down, and soon a set of stumps and bails were available. The next trick was to obtain a supply of good quality cricket balls. Here, the skills of Major Dennis Lamplough, Royal Army Service Corps, were employed. From the materials available in the camp, Lamplough created a cricket ball which, Bowes later claimed, could easily have been sold in any cricket shop. Apparently, the leather came from boots stolen from Italian guards. Having produced one ball that performed as it should, Lamplough then proceeded to manufacture a set of six balls for the match. Hopefully, that would be enough.

With a fast wicket, and decent cricket balls, the next consideration had to be protective clothing for the players. To provide the wicketkeeper and the batsmen with pads, cardboard from the stout Red Cross parcel boxes was compressed and moulded into shape. Although the resulting products would not have met English County Cricket standards, they would have to do for the Chieti village cricket ground. A skilful thief managed to acquire a pair of Italian motoring gauntlets which, once improved with extra padding, became the keeper's gloves. The batsmen would be equipped with batting gloves, which provided far less protection. There were no cricketers' boxes to protect their most vulnerable parts. Tim Toppin, who never used such protection anyway, would find himself well suited to Chieti village cricket. Since this was to be as serious and realistic a game of cricket as possible, etiquette required that all the players be dressed in white. Sheets were spirited away from the stores and passed on to the experts of the theatrical costume department. Twenty-two sets of white shirts and 'flannels' resulted. For the umpires, two white coats had been 'acquired' from the hospital, apparently by bribing one of the Italian orderlies there. And so the game was made possible.

But the elaborate preparations did not end there. Challenged to create an authentic English scene, the theatrical department excelled itself. A bungalow facing the cricket 'square' was appointed as the pavilion. On the roof of this bungalow was built a huge pavilion clock, out of odd bits of wood, bunk boards and cloth. The clock had two large hands which would be moved manually throughout the match by a man hidden inside the clock, keeping up with the actual time, so that the drama would be maintained as the match approached close of play. In front of the pavilion, a members' enclosure was built, complete with deck chairs and rails. Beside the members enclosure rested a mock roller for the pitch. Beside the pavilion the theatrical department built a bandstand and then a large scoreboard, visible from all parts of the camp. Two sightscreens were erected at either end of the ground, made of sheets. It was arranged that the cookhouse staff would serve afternoon teas to the spectators during the course of the afternoon. The effort was extraordinary, but by the end of it an English cricket ground had appeared in the centre of the camp, overlooked by the Italian sentries with their machine guns perched in the sentry boxes on top of the 4-metre high surrounding wall. The outfield remained stranger than any seen on an English ground, with a rough stony surface and various small trees, drains and ditches making fielding a rather hazardous affair, but a serious game of cricket could now take place. The players took the time to study the outfield with care, so that the batsmen could decide where best to place their shots, and the bowlers where to place their fielders.

Despite their efforts this was not England, so 3 July was a fine summer's day. The match was to start at 1400hrs. At 1340hrs, amid glorious Italian sunshine, two appointed 'groundsmen', Mr Long and Mr Short, went out to 'roll' the pitch with the mock roller. Next, the groundsmen painted the white lines of the creases on the roadway, and then they erected the two wickets – each being fixed into wooden blocks placed on the roadway. At 13.50, the two captains tossed: Bill Bowes' XI would bat first. Immediately after the toss, the two umpires, resplendent in their white coats advanced slowly to the wickets and put the bails in place. At 13.55, Mr Freddie Brown led out the fielding team, to considerable applause from the large crowd of spectators (including quite a number of Americans curious to see how the game was really played). The batsmen followed and took their guard. As the hands of the pavilion clock moved to exactly 1400hrs, an umpire called play.

The details of the game perhaps hardly matter. It was hugely enjoyed by all who watched it. Soon the crack of handmade leather ball was heard meeting the bat and the calls of the batsmen, and the appeals, rang around the ground. Bill Bowes was later to write: 'There was one day when we succeeded in forgetting the walls and the barbed wire, the sentries and the tommy guns that surrounded us. It was the occasion of the cricket match, a real match that took us back to the village green, and was the greatest and most memorable match in which I ever took part.' Thus spoke a veteran of the 'bodyline' series, numerous English Test Matches and countless games for Yorkshire and the MCC.

The Italians did not really know what was going on. In the middle of the match, Captain Croce and two orderlies decided to assert themselves by walking slowly down the middle of the wicket, thereby disrupting play. It is rumoured that the bowler at the time was Bill Bowes, and that he was encouraged to 'let one go!' Bowes replied, with a twinkle in his eye, and in the broadest of Yorkshire accents: 'Ah would, but tha never knows, I might kill the bugger!'

Bands played, Pitso's orchestra performing in the appropriate intervals until tea, Tommy Sampson's band playing during the second session. Afternoon tea, Chieti style, was served by the cookhouse staff. Not surprisingly with such distinguished cricketers involved, the play was of a very high standard, despite the difficulties caused by the most unusual outfield, covered in dust and pebbles, with ditches and random trees making fielding more difficult. Bowes assessed the game:

There was some excellent bowling by Freddie Brown. An Indian officer named Gardener achieved the hat-trick, Beaumont [Yorkshire] played a fine back-to-the-wall innings, and Bull of Essex batted most academically. Boundary shots and more especially sixes were equally a matter of applause and concern. We had only six balls in stock, and five of them were hit far away into liberty. Fortunately the last one saw the game to a finish … And what a finish! To describe it as close would be an understatement. Men never raced against time with such dogged effort and exciting effect. All the while, time – and the players – were being deftly egged on by the careful manipulation of the great hands of the pavilion clock.

Freddie Brown describes Bowes himself thundering down the road to bowl, wearing ammunition boots, but delivering the ball with aplomb. Brown claimed later to have scored about 30 runs, although he admitted that he was caught second ball off Tim Toppin, but was not given out by the umpire. He did not walk! What is perhaps most interesting is that in the many references to the match that still exist, I have been unable to find anyone who recorded the actual result. The occasion was too glorious somehow. Arthur Dodds was one of those who played in the match, and much later, after he had escaped from Italy and returned to England, he went to see Mrs Bill Bowes in Yorkshire to bring her news of her husband, as he did with other wives and families. To Mrs Bowes he gave a full description of the cricket match, with the result that an account of it appeared afterwards in the *Yorkshire Evening Post*.

There were many Americans in the crowd, whose reactions to the game amused the British prisoners. It was perhaps inevitable that someone should raise the idea of the Americans playing the English at cricket. There had already been a number of encounters between British and Americans at softball. It was agreed that a match should take place in three weeks' time, on 25 July 1943. The British lent the Americans a coach, who was also allowed to play for them on the day. Coaching a baseball loving nation to play cricket in three weeks was an impossible task, but the Americans took up the challenge with gusto.

Other sport continued, and on 7 July Osborne was delighted to record that he had taken six catches in a softball game between the British other ranks (captained by Harold Beaumont) and the North Americans, albeit that they had lost 6–9.

MUSSOLINI FALLS

Rumours began to circulate around the camp that the prisoners were to be allowed out to swim in the Pescara River. Happily, this rumour was one of the few that proved to be true. On 17 July, John Jenkins was one of a lucky group to be taken down to the river to bathe. In the hot summer weather, the shortage of water became critical, and although they might enjoy the sunshine, the men were unable to freshen up with a shower after sunbathing or playing sport. K. J. Bowden recalls that after a particularly hot spell, when there was a violent thunderstorm with heavy rain, hundreds of prisoners stripped off and ran about naked, revelling in allowing the rain to wash them all over. The swimming trips were, in themselves, quite extraordinary. The bathers would be surrounded by guards with machine guns who obviously did not trust the prisoners at all, even with their word of parole. They were forbidden to put their heads under water, presumably lest they should seek to swim away from their guards beneath the surface. The depth of the water varied; John Speares remembered a bathing trip when the water was 5ft deep, but most recall it being fairly shallow. No doubt it would depend whether there had been a recent thunderstorm to put the river in spate. Sam Webster wrote home on July 21: 'Yesterday, we went to the creek for a swim – wade is the correct word … It wasn't deep, but at least we cooled off for a few minutes.'

Bombing raids on Italy increased in number and ferocity and, on 10 July, the Allied invasion of Sicily finally began. News reached the camp at 1300hrs. Everyone in Campo 21 began to follow the news very carefully. From the prisoners' point of view, the Allies were finally getting quite close. However, the battle for Sicily was bitterly fought, and the capitulation by the Italians that all the prisoners were hoping for still did not come. The camp guards stepped up security, and searches became more frequent and more thorough. On 18 July, a speech was broadcast on Italian radio explaining that Italy had a mere handful of men and a small strip of land, and was fighting against two of the largest nations in the world (the United States and Great Britain). On 19 July, Rome was bombed for the first time, and Italian radio emphasized the outraged protests from Roman Catholic communities everywhere. On 21 July news came that Enna, a key stronghold in Sicily, had fallen to the Allies, and Jenkins wrote in his diary: 'Everything in the garden's lovely.' The Italian newspapers ceased to arrive in the camp, as did the prisoners' mail – a sign that Allied bombing had disrupted their communications again.

On 22 July another Italian film was shown, which Walters described simply as 'rot'. One of the films that the Italians chose to show their prisoners that did go down well was a Laurel and Hardy comedy, rather clumsily dubbed into Italian. Bowden remembers gales of laughter as Stan and Ollie referred to each other as Stanlio and Olio. Bill Bowes, who had met both Laurel and Hardy during an England cricket tour in the 1930s, must have laughed harder than most.

Lett and the CNA had long been searching the Fascist press for signs that Mussolini's grip was weakening, and had noted any apparent gesture of conciliation to the titular monarch of Italy, King Victor Emmanuel III. For some time, the Italian guards had been at pains to make clear to their prisoners that they really had no dislike for them, and that traditionally Italy and Great Britain had been friends. Historically, that was true. During the First World War, Italy had fought with the British and Americans. She joined a little late, in 1915, declaring war first on her neighbour, Austria, and then on Germany in 1916. She had suffered alongside her British and American allies. Italian casualties during the First World War were 578,000 dead and 530,000 captured, for whom there was a 20 per cent mortality rate in the Austrian prisoner-of-war camps. Thus, until the arrival of Fascism there had been no hostility between ordinary Italians and the 'Anglo-Saxons', as Fascist Italy liked to refer to British and American forces. Most Italians had regarded the British and the Americans with greater affection than they had the Germans. Over the years, many Italian and British families had intermarried and figures for emigration from Italy to Great Britain and the United States had always been high. Nonetheless, Italy had been dominated by Fascist propaganda for more than twenty years, and since 1940 British forces had been killing Italians, including many civilians who were dying as a result of the bombing raids. There was no reason to believe, in July 1943, that the Italians would regard the British and Americans with anything other than hostility.

On the morning of 25 July 1943, a rumour had circulated around the camp that there was to be an important announcement made on the loudspeakers at 1100hrs. The inmates expected the usual bombastic speech, but were delighted instead to hear an announcement that Mussolini had been arrested and that the Fascist regime had collapsed. The announcement finished with the vague statement that 'the war continues'. Lett was only recently out of the cooler, where he had spent much of his time since 1 May. Happily, he was 'at liberty' within the camp when the announcement was broadcast. An Italian major of the camp garrison happened to be standing beside him, and after the announcement, overcome by emotion, he seized Lett's hand and shook it warmly. 'Signore, at last we are free,' he said, and then hurried away towards the Commandant's office. News spread around the camp like wildfire. Irrespective of whether they had their own secret radio, as Lieutenant Colonel Marshall says, now operating successfully, the CNA had little difficulty in eliciting information from the camp guards, most of whom seemed very happy that Mussolini had gone. They believed that finally the war would now finish. The 20–year reign of Mussolini's Fascists had come to an end and the trams heading up the hill to Chieti town carried flags in celebration. However, as a result of the work that the CNA had been doing, no one felt real surprise at the news – for a number of months now, the CNA had been suggesting that Mussolini's support was ebbing away.

In the happy atmosphere that followed the news of Mussolini's fall, the international cricket match between the United States of America and the Rest of the World took place. A large American crowd turned up to cheer their team onto the pitch. Much amusement was caused by the fact that all the United States team turned up in white vests, with USA emblazoned on the front, and numbers on the back (not so different to the modern one-day game). They clearly had far from understood the complex rules of cricket. Bonnello commented that they were always on the wrong foot, and if they hit the ball, they felt that they had to run, even if they were run out. Ronald Hill remembered that their catching was good, but that if one umpire refused an appeal to give someone out, they simply appealed to the other umpire instead. They made no attempt to stump anyone, clearly not having understood that manoeuvre. Freddie Brown, who had spent some afternoons helping to coach them, said that their bowlers never mastered the technique of a straight-arm bowling action, or the concept of batting with a straight bat, but he did praise their catching and throwing. The American crowd were enthusiastic and patriotic, cheering on their team at every opportunity, and barracking the English bowlers for going too hard at their batsmen, but to no avail. England (or the Empire or the Rest of the World, whichever they were on the day) scored 221 in their innings, and bowled the USA out for 101, of which their English coach scored 67. It was a match played in the very best of spirits on both sides and hugely enjoyed, but many English observers felt afterwards that the Americans did not at all get the point of the game. Sam Webster, who by the tone of his letter may have been one of those who played in the match, wrote home some days later to say: 'We had that cricket match – English vs Americans – and we lost. Took a bad beating too. It takes more than that to dampen our spirits now though.' By the time he wrote his letter, the fall of Mussolini meant that the world for the prisoners in Campo 21 had changed substantially.

From now on, bulletins were posted daily on the bungalow noticeboards as to what was believed to be happening outside the camp walls and on Sunday, 1 August, Lett would finally have the opportunity for which he and his team had been waiting for a very long time – giving a CNA news summary which confirmed the fall of Mussolini. They had been predicting that this would happen under the pressure of Allied success on the battlefield for many months, and now finally the moment had come. A huge wave of optimism swept through the camp. Surely, it could not be long now?

On 28 July, Prime Minister Churchill sent a note to the king of Italy via Swiss intermediaries. It said simply: 'Expect no mercy if you deliver our and allied prisoners of war now in your hands to the Germans.'

August 1943

WAITING FOR FREEDOM

In his CNA talk on Sunday, 1 August, Lett endeavoured to construct from the numerous accounts received what had actually happened, and to predict how long the war in Italy was now likely to continue. In a lecture entitled 'E Finito Benito', he gave a short history of Mussolini's reign and then moved on to summarize the events that had led up to Il Duce's fall on 25 July. He drew a picture for his audience of the scene at the final meeting of the Grand Council of Fascism (which had long been the organ through which Mussolini had ruled) in the Palazzo Venezia in Rome. He described Mussolini as being furious at having to be there at all, and his ministers as being terrified at the prospect of the fields and cities of their country being turned into blood-sodden battlegrounds. He told how the meeting had soon descended into confusion and anger. Finally, a motion had been proposed that all power was to be returned to the king of Italy, and that he was to be trusted to 'liquidate the crisis arising within the country, and to decide on all matters of defence and internal relations.' At 0300hrs in the morning of 25 July, a vote was taken. There was a clear majority against Mussolini. Thus Benito was 'finito' and Marshal Badoglio, a veteran Italian general, took over.

Looking to the future, Lett told the meeting:

The fate of Mussolini is at present obscure. One rumour has it that the mob found him in the Palazzo Venezia, and murdered him on the spot. Another says that the Duce committed suicide after handing in his resignation. A third says that he is under arrest awaiting trial by the state. [This third rumour represented the true position.] The situation at present, then, can be summed up as follows: the Italian government wants to extricate Italy from the war as quickly as possible. The Allies want to get on with the destruction of the German armies without unnecessary delay. The Germans have to make up their minds – and doubtless have already done so – as to what they are going to do about it. Meanwhile, for us, what seems to be this unnecessary waiting for freedom is tiresome enough, and it is bound to become more so before the end. But, you will realize, I hope, that it cannot be avoided. I cannot believe that the Allies are prepared to give the Germans more than a week in which to clear out of Italy. It is natural to expect some opposition from them, they might even decide, as a last resort, to hold the Plains of Lombardy for another month whilst they evacuate all they can in the way of war material, troops, and perhaps even prisoners from Italian camps in that area. So, to conclude, we must endure the irritations and delay of the coming week as patiently as we can. There is a chance – just a faint chance – that the termination of the war between Italy and the Allies might be announced on the radio tonight. If on the other hand, no such declaration is made tonight – and I would emphasize again that it is only a very slender chance – then it seems to me that we may expect Allied intervention on a very large scale before next Sunday.

Lett was undoubtedly right that the Italians would decide to withdraw from the war if they possibly could, but that was by no means straightforward. Only unconditional surrender was going to stop the Allies continuing their campaign to conquer Sicily, and thereafter to battle for the Italian mainland. There were German troops also fighting in Sicily alongside the Italians, and many German troops in mainland Italy. Adolf Hitler, in July 1943, was showing no inclination to surrender. If the Italians wished to sue for peace, to cut themselves free of their ill-chosen alliance with Nazi Germany, and to avoid an outright and complete surrender, negotiations were likely to take some considerable time. As we shall see, Lett's predictions were subsequently proved to be over optimistic, but it is clear every prisoner appreciated that although the Italians were now bound to try to withdraw from the war, the Germans might not be too keen to leave Italy. The vast majority of prisoners in Italy had been captured by the Germans not the Italians, and there were estimated to be in excess of 80,000 Allied prisoners now in Italy. Many believed that the Germans would be unwilling to abandon such a vast number of prisoners to be repatriated and to rejoin the enemy forces against them. The prisoners were also understandably apprehensive as to how the Italian public presently viewed the Allies. They had been able to listen regularly to Allied bombing raids on the town and port of Pescara and had seen squadrons of Allied aircraft overflying the camp on their way to attack other Italian towns, ports and airfields. They knew that these would inevitably have resulted in an increasing number of Italian casualties, both military and civilian. They fully expected the Italian population to be hostile towards them if and when they got out of the prison camps.

In Campo 21, the last days of July had passed in confusion, most prisoners experiencing a mixture of strong emotions. Italy's Fascist press had fallen with Mussolini, and many journalists from the pre-Fascist era were emerging from enforced retirement. For a while the papers were full of anti-Fascist sentiment, before the new Head of Government, Marshal Badoglio, imposed fresh censorship. In August, the days and then the weeks passed in a whirl of rumours of all kinds. The wiser heads knew that they must simply get on with life and await developments. The tunnellers kept on digging. The music, theatre, and education continued. Croce disappeared from the camp for a week after Mussolini's fall, and was presumed to have gone to Rome to get instructions from his masters, whoever they might now be. Not long after the CNA's 'E finito Benito' talk, Croce reappeared. Many of the prisoners were enjoying the sunshine and watching a softball match arranged by the Americans when Croce came striding up the central pathway of the prisoners' compound, as immaculately dressed as ever. He paused for a moment, to impress on the prisoners the fact that he was there, then spoke to one of the junior officers, saying: 'You are looking very pleased with yourself today, I suppose you think that you will soon be free.' 'I certainly do,' replied the lieutenant. Croce placed his monocle in his eye and stared at him for a moment. 'I assure you that you are mistaken. You will not be released for a long time yet.' With that, Croce turned on his heel and swaggered off. His words, and the fact that he had returned to the camp, had the effect that he no doubt desired. As the days passed and nothing really seemed to change, morale plummeted.

Croce now finally managed to get rid of Lett. One afternoon in early August, Lett was informed that he and a handful of others would be transferred to another camp on the following morning. At this time there were already rumours circulating that because of the uncertainties of the situation, all prisoners might be transferred to Germany. Certainly that was what Lett feared the next morning when he was put on a train travelling north. However, he was in fact being transferred to the Veano camp near Piacenza, many miles to the north, but still well within the borders of Italy. Lett thought he was nonetheless unlucky to be so much further north, but events proved to the contrary. Officers being transferred rarely knew where they were being sent to. Sometimes, they proved to have been lucky with their transfer, sometimes not. Captain Peter O'Bree, 4th Gurkha Rifles, was an energetic young 23-year-old who had been captured in the 'Knightsbridge Box', and was amongst those very keen to escape. He was in Sulmona but involuntarily drew the short straw when he was transferred to Campo 47 at Modena. Sulmona proved to be a good camp to escape from, Modena the opposite.

Croce showed his true colours by expelling another group of prisoners from the camp. They had been banded together against the danger of the Germans taking over at Chieti, but it is unclear whether this was organized by the SBO, Lieutenant Colonel Marshall, or by Major Sam Derry, the head of the Escape Committee. The group of officers were known as 'the Fighting Squadron' or simply 'the Squadron' – either name clearly demonstrates what they were intended to do if an Armistice was declared and the Germans tried to take over Campo 21. They would seize vital points in the camp to defend it, send out scouting patrols to ascertain the whereabouts of the enemy, and seek to make contact with advancing Allied forces. However, there had been a breach of security, and a list containing the names of the Fighting Squadron somehow passed into the hands of Croce and the Italian guards. Lieutenant Norman Charles Johnson, Lincolnshire Fusiliers, one of the selected squad, believed that they could have been betrayed by loose talk in the cooler, where the Italians had a listening device fitted (as Lett and Rennie had known during their incarceration). The result was that Johnson and all the others on the list were transferred to Campo 19 at Bologna. However, at Chieti, they were simply replaced by a new 'Squadron'.

The question of what action Germany would take now became the main topic of conversation amongst the men. If the Italians surrendered, would the Germans withdraw from Italy completely, would they fall back on a defensive line to the north of Italy, or would they take over the whole of the country and treat Italy in the same way they had treated so many countries whose territory they had occupied? Although the prisoners did not know it, the new Italian government under Marshal Badoglio was holding Mussolini in custody, eventually in a mountain prison on the Gran Sasso, the mountain that could be seen from Campo 21. The Italians commenced negotiations for an Armistice with the Allies.

It seems inevitable that Adolf Hitler and his High Command had seen the fall of Mussolini coming for some time. If Lett and the CNA could predict it, so could the Germans with their infinitely greater resources. Once Mussolini was dethroned, the Germans clearly expected the new Italian government to manoeuvre to get out of the war. With Fascism gone, so were the dreams of an Italian Fascist Empire – the new Roman Empire that Mussolini had sought to build. North Africa had already been lost and the Italians had nothing to gain by fighting on. The speed of the German reaction confirms that they had been planning against the possibility of Italy surrendering long before the Armistice was eventually announced on 8 September 1943.

Field Marshal Rommel, the Desert Fox who had done so well in North Africa with his Afrika Corps in 1941 and the first half of 1942, was now closely consulted by Hitler as to the Italian situation. Hitler did not want to give up possession of Italy, and to allow the Allies a firm foothold on mainland Europe. He wanted to keep the door to mainland Europe closed. What troubled Rommel the most was the possibility that the Italians, in their efforts to get out of the war, would try to close the Brenner Pass and the other northern passes into Italy, and to hold Italy intact for the Allies to occupy. One effect of this might be to cut off the not inconsiderable German forces already in Italy. It was agreed that action should immediately be taken to keep the passes open, and to reinforce the German troops already within Italy's borders. On 29 July, four days after Mussolini had been deposed, Rommel ordered General Feurstein, a stocky black-moustached Austrian who was a first-class mountain warfare specialist, to move his 51st Mountain Corps through the Brenner Pass. By 31 July, much of Feurstein's Corps had passed into Italy without resistance. All the passes were seized and secured by the Germans and troop movements into Italy continued. The Italians, in confusion and still nominally Germany's allies, did nothing to stop them.[3]

On 15 August 1943, Rommel was appointed Supreme German Commander, Northern Italy. He was, at that time, generally regarded as Hitler's top general, and he was committed to preventing the surrender of Italian territory to the Allies. As he put it in a letter to his wife: 'It is better to fight the war in Italy than here at home.' If there was to be a new European front, it should not be on German soil. Extraordinarily, the Allied High Command seem not to have appreciated that the Germans were almost bound to stay in Italy, or how perfect the Italian terrain was for defensive action if they did stay. All indications

---

[3] See *SAS in Tuscany 1943–45* by Brian Lett.

are that they believed that once they had landed on the mainland, the Italian Campaign, if one remained necessary, would be won well before Christmas 1943. Lieutenant General Bernard Montgomery, who was taking credit for the British victories in the desert, seems to have totally failed to realize how difficult to defeat a determined resistance by the Germans in Italy would be. The campaign on Sicily lasted for 38 days before victory came, and was far from easy. Regrettably, the majority of the German forces on the island were able to withdraw to mainland Italy. The island was eventually secured by 16 August 1943 and the next move was to be the invasion of the mainland. In the background, the Armistice Commission continued its work, seeking some form of peace agreement between the Allies and Italy. The prisoners in Campo 21 followed the news as best they could. Many now believed that freedom was, at most, only a few weeks away. Their guards also obviously expected that the war would not last much longer.

In the camp, the water situation remained very bad. On 19 August, a first round of TAB anti-typhoid injections was given to the prisoners, courtesy of the Red Cross. The second round of innoculations was due on 25 August. Again, it is perhaps no coincidence that on the day after the first injections, 20 August, a further inspection took place by the Protecting Power. On this occasion, the Swiss Inspector was Georges Bouvant. He noted that, despite the transfers to other camps, there were still 1,334 prisoners, of whom 178 were now United States servicemen. There had been no improvement in the overcrowding. The US prisoners had their own senior officer, Colonel Gooler, but his authority was not recognized by the Italians. Massi said that the regulations allowed only one official camp leader or prisoners' representative. However, Bouvant commented that relations between prisoners and the camp authorities seemed better since Lieutenant Colonel William Marshall had taken over from Lieutenant Colonel Gray. Gray, it must be remembered, had carried the burden of his command through the worst of times, from August 1942 until the beginning of May 1943. He had finally been reduced to reading out a list of complaints to the Swiss Representative on 12 April, in front of a parade of the prisoners. Gray had found that all his written protests about conditions in the camp had been intercepted and had never reached the Protecting Power. He had experienced the worst of Croce and three Camp Commandants. Marshall's experience was rather different. By the time he took over as SBO, the problem of clothing had been resolved and some of the other failings of the camp had also been addressed. It was summertime, the weather was good and sports equipment and musical instruments had arrived. The food was still poor, and the water shortage was increasingly a problem in the summer heat, but Marshall had a relatively easy ride compared to Gray. Also, by late August, many of the Italians (Croce being a notable exception) were adopting a line something like 'we want to be your friends, we did not want to fight, oh the terrible Tedeschi [Germans]'. Harold Sell described the new SBO: 'Marshall carries out his duties with vigour and does not spare himself. In his early fifties, he is a recluse by nature, seeking no company or counsel but his own. His decisions are carefully weighed, but in his mind alone. He lives a lonely life…' Marshall certainly seems to have developed a closer relationship with Commandant Massi than Gray had done, and many of the prisoners in Campo 21 came to believe that Massi exercised an undue influence over Marshall's subsequent actions.

Bouvant commented in his report that the overcrowding and shortage of water remained problematic. Some of the officers, he said, had to form a chain each morning from the nearest well to their latrines for cleaning purposes. However, trips to the river to bathe had now been arranged. Five detachments of 70 officers now went regularly to the river. Sell was one of those who went swimming and very much enjoyed it. He describes how they were ordered to wear suitable bathing dress, so as not to offend any ladies who might pass by. They were taken to a section of the river which had been roped off, where the river was about a foot deep. Although the guards would stand over them with their rifles at the ready, Sell commented: 'How marvellous it is to be wet all over with cool water.' Other walks, however, had been suspended, as they had all over Italy. Generally, Bouvant found the camp improved since the last inspection in April.

In late August, Allied air activity increased, and during the night of 24 August there was a long air raid nearby. On 27 August, when Walters went for a swim again at 0845hrs, he noted that there was an air raid in progress. It was over by the time he returned to camp at 1100hrs, but at 1115hrs he and his friends saw two large flights of aircraft going over at a great height, and another air raid subsequently began. The prisoners could not tell where or exactly what the targets of the air raids were, but the port of Pescara was one of the more obvious ones. There were no longer any films to watch in the evenings since communications had apparently been interrupted by Allied bombing, and anyway the Italians did not want to risk any lights showing after dark, in case they became the target of a raid. Also, in late August, the guards seemed to be short of weapons. It was noticed that the sentries would hand over their rifles to their successors when relieved, which had never been necessary in the past.

The Allied invasion was clearly having an effect upon supplies and munitions. Everything was needed in defence of the motherland. On 31 August, John Jenkins noted in his diary: 'At the moment we are getting practically no food from the Ities, and parcels have been reduced to a half per week. However, the end must be near now.'

September 1943

TUNNELS CONTINUED

On 1 September Pescara was bombed. The prisoners actually identified and watched the Allied bombers going over the camp. Life in Campo 21 went on as normally as possible. The theatre was showing Oscar Wilde's *The Importance of Being Ernest*. Tony Baines was presenting a series of Promenade concerts, based upon the Henry Wood Promenade Concerts at the Albert Hall in London. Sam Derry's plan for a mass escape was nearing fruition. Five tunnels had survived all the searches by the Italian tapping teams, four of which now stretched under the main wall. Toby Graham's tunnel 1, the 'sewer tunnel' from the other ranks' cookhouse, which had been left in the hands of Spowatt, McFall, Weaver, Wendt and others, had also progressed over the months. The team had given up the idea of using the sewer as an escape route, and dug round it in order to continue. They too were now under the wall and ready to complete their work.

Gordon-Brown, Pennycook and Gregson's tunnel 2 had progressed over the months. They kept the lid of their entrance well concealed, preserving a quantity of grey dust to brush over it when closed. As spring had turned to summer, their security system included spreading a rug over the entrance, upon which two men would sit – sometimes sunbathing, reading a book or painting, or pursuing some similar occupation. In due course, the tunnel passed under the foundations of the main wall, which went down a couple of metres into the earth. They worked three regular shifts – morning after first roll call until 1200hrs; 1400hrs until before evening roll call, which was usually about 1700hrs; and an evening shift which was often just to dispose of the spoil excavated during the earlier shifts. Like others, Gordon-Brown's team hit a sewer, but in their case not until after they had crossed under the main wall. This they broke into, but found it a very narrow passage. They did send a very small tunneller in to explore, but when he suffered the same fate as Spowatt and Graham and set off an explosion of methane gas, it was decided that the sewer was only fit for storing spoil, in the same way as others used theirs. As they progressed, they found the air quality became extremely bad and the lamps would hardly burn for the lack of oxygen. Therefore, they constructed an air pipe by fitting together empty tins from Red Cross parcels. A hand-powered pair of bellows was made out of wood and part of an old canvas kit bag (supplied by Gregson), and the contraption worked well enough to give the diggers just enough air to work. The fact that the sewer that Gordon-Brown's team had run into was beyond the wall helped greatly as they approached their exit point, because it meant they had a far shorter distance to transport the spoil in order to conceal it. They planned to complete the tunnel by 20 September 1943.

Having made the break through the wall of the small initial chamber, Walker Brown's team, in tunnel 3, had begun digging toward the main wall. For the first 35–40ft the task was straightforward. They dug forward at as shallow a depth as possible under the concrete pavement. Because they were at no real depth they had little problem with moisture, and the concrete roof above meant that they did not need to consider any sort of shoring. Like moles, they made their way towards the main wall. The earth was loaded into old Red Cross boxes and then quickly handed up from the tunnel entrance and through the window into the bungalow, to be distributed in the space between the two skins of the wall. Once they reached the end of the pavement, it was necessary to drop the tunnel down about 6ft, to ensure that the roof did not collapse on them. Six feet down brought them to just above the water table, in the damp clay of the Chieti ground. The tunnel was very narrow, just wide enough for a man's hips to pass through and just high enough for a man to crawl. It was impossible to turn round, and had there been a collapse or had the Italians discovered the tunnel and dropped a grenade down it, as they threatened to do with tunnels that they found, any man still inside would have stood little chance of survival. The air was foul and oxygen sparse. The diggers took small homemade lamps with them, but these would burn for only twenty minutes. Initially, only two men at a time went down the tunnel to dig, but as the tunnel progressed, so the digging party increased to three and then four. Only one man could dig at the tunnel face, but the spoil then had to be passed back down the length of the tunnel for disposal. When they got about a third of the way towards the main wall, the diggers struck the concrete of a sewer. Sewers ran all the way round the camp and many tunnellers ran into this obstruction. Walker Brown's team duly broke into the sewer – the smell was appalling and they were not tempted to try using it as a means of escape. However, for them as for others, it served an extremely useful secondary purpose as a dumping ground for the spoil from the tunnel. This gave the great advantage that it would not be necessary to carry the spoil above ground – always a hazardous task. They could simply transport it back from the face of the tunnel and dispose of it in the sewer. However, they realized that if they simply dumped it onto the floor of the sewer, they would eventually block the sewer and flood their own tunnel. Therefore, they used bed boards from the bunks to create a form of decking across the sewer, so that the sewage could flow freely underneath the decking, while the spoil could be spread out on top of it. Distributing the spoil was a very unpleasant task for those who had to go onto the sewer decking to do it, but it was very effective. The tunnellers dug on, beneath the sewer and towards the main wall. This tunnel used no shoring, they were relying on the solid clay soil above and upon the fact that they were burrowing as narrow a tunnel as possible.

The digging had taken many months. It was regularly disrupted by surprise roll calls, searches and other alarms. At one stage, Walker Brown's team worked at night, because numerous daytime roll calls were making work impossible. They would go down the tunnel after evening roll call, and would arrange for dummies to be put into their beds in case of a nighttime roll call. They would then be listed as sick, and the guards would be invited to glance at the dummies to confirm that the men were still in camp. This apparently worked, so the dummies must have been quite convincing – no doubt made with the help of the theatrical department. Working at night was an extremely unpleasant experience – the earth was damp and cold, yet mosquitos seemed to thrive underground. Once the maximum amount of work possible had been done, the diggers had to sleep where they lay in the tunnel in their sweat-soaked underclothes until the morning light made it possible for them to leave the tunnel and slip back to the bungalow. There was a night curfew for all prisoners and anyone seen outside a bungalow during forbidden hours would be shot at. Each sentry box was equipped with a searchlight as well as a machine gun and it was simply not practical for a tunnel team to check that the coast was clear, leave the bungalow, open the tunnel, get the diggers out, then close up and conceal the tunnel entrance again. Such activity would be certain to attract the guards' attention, would lead inevitably to the discovery of the tunnel and might well prove fatal.

Even when Mussolini fell from power in late July, the digging continued. Nobody really knew what would happen next. The team working on tunnel 3 aimed for a fig tree, the top of which they could see over the main wall – the thinking was that if they came up through the roots of the tree, there would be less danger of a collapse. Their navigation was good and when in early September they decided to tunnel upwards, they found themselves amongst the roots of the tree. Only now did they resort to bunk boards to shore up the exit shaft. They were understandably concerned that as they came closer to the surface, the likelihood of a collapse would increase. Finally, after many months of difficult and unpleasant work, Walker Brown's team were ready to go. In total, they were about 30 strong – apart from the diggers, a tunnel needed many others helping to ensure the success of the team. Their sense of achievement that September was enormous.

Bill Gordon's tunnel team kept working on tunnel 4. His team included John Jenkins. They had been digging since 18 March and they too were under the wall. Having got through the original concrete with a hammer stolen from the Italians, they had had to cross two sewers before they reached the main wall. Both were fortunately upstream tributaries of the main sewer, and carried only rainwater and waste from the camp barber shop. The team had built an air pump and air duct, a pipe made of biscuit tins sewn up in cloth, so for the last section of their tunnel air could be sent along through the duct. They had also constructed a trolley, nicknamed 'Susie', to haul the spoil back from the face of the tunnel to the disposal point. Susie had metal runners and was pulled back by a rope. Like other teams, they disposed of their spoil down the sewers, which they boarded so as to provide a platform above the flow. They too had started at a drainage sump by a concrete path around their bungalow, and they had cleverly tapped into the guttering drains that led down from the bungalow roof to provide air from the outside world for the first stretch of the tunnel. They shored up much of their tunnel between the end of the concrete path and the main wall with bed boards, but once past the wall they relied on the durability of the clay soil. They had covered up the digging by asking friends to give lectures in the small courtyard where their tunnel started, and if warning came that a guard was approaching one of the team would throw a mattress over the entrance and lie on it. Horace Crabtree was one of the tunnel 4 team, and worked at disposing of the soil down the sewer, into which he only just fitted. One day, Crabtree got jammed in the sewer and it took two of his team to pull him out. Bill Gordon's team finished their tunnel on 7 September.

On 3 September 1943, the Allies invaded mainland Italy. It was the fourth anniversary of Great Britain's declaration of war. Unknown to all but the very few, on the same day the new Italian government signed an armistice with the Allies. It amounted to surrender: all Italians would cease fighting immediately. The agreement also stipulated that all German forces were to leave Italian soil forthwith. It was the best that the Badoglio government could do to resolve the disaster that the war had become for Italy. For various reasons, the Armistice was not announced on that day, but was only made public during the evening of 8 September, at which point the Italians officially ceased fighting. During the five intervening days they continued to suffer further losses on the toe of Italy and Allied bombers continued to attack Italian towns and cities.

Larry Allen was one of the few who remained a pessimist. He began taking bets with other prisoners that they would not get out of Campo 21 for months, even if the Italians did drop out of the war, and certainly would not be home by Christmas. Among those who took his bet were Flight Lieutenant Danny Newman and Bill Wendt.

ARMISTICE

When the announcement of the Italian Armistice finally arrived in Campo 21 on the evening of 8 September it was followed by considerable rejoicing, as much among the guards as the prisoners. The 2030hrs Italian news was broadcast as usual over loudspeakers from the camp radio, and before the first few words were out of the announcer's mouth the cheering by the Italian guards began. The news spread like wildfire around the camp. At last, after so long in captivity, the men could finally taste freedom in the air. One rowdy group of prisoners lit a bonfire made from a broken up bunk bed, as Lieutenant Colonel Marshall struggled to maintain discipline. However, this seems to have been the only real incident of disorder, as the command structure amongst the prisoners had maintained a fair degree of military discipline. Harold Sell, perhaps one of the more aggressive characters, says that the popular idea amongst the prisoners was to exact immediate retribution on their captors by hanging the Commandant and lynching the security officer, Captain Croce. Although it demonstrates the degree of resentment that many felt against the Italians who had treated them so badly, not surprisingly absolutely nothing came of that idea. Within a short space of time, each individual became fully absorbed in his own thoughts and plans for the future. Fifteen months after the surrender of Tobruk, they finally believed they were to be freed. Thoughts of home and family were foremost in everybody's mind. Men like Bill Bowes and Tony Maxtone Graham, parted from their wives and children for three years, would at last be reunited with them. Arthur Green would see his bride of two weeks again and Sam Webster his bride of four weeks – and his daughter for the very first time. For the youngsters, the wasted months were done with, and they would soon be able to get back to their lives. The war against Germany and Japan would no doubt continue, but the defeat of Italy was a major victory which must speed the final cessation of all hostilities. A huge wave of huge optimism swept over the camp.

All the same, John Jenkins commented: 'We have waited so long for this day, and somehow I expected such a wild feeling, and instead I am left quite empty and incapable of expression. Thank God it is all over and please God the world is at peace soon. The Italians seem more pleased than we are ... we are not free yet.'

Ronald Hill had been inside his hut when the news came. He wrote: 'At 8.30 pm, just as soon as cocoa had been served, there was a sudden surge through the hut, and a cry: "It's peace." There was a mad rush by everybody to get outside ... I had exactly the same feeling as when I was captured, I could hardly believe it and wandered about in a dream. The Italians seemed pleased ... outside the camp people were singing ... Everybody is too excited to go to sleep ... What were the feelings at home? I thought very much of everybody, and the things to come.'

Lieutenant Colonel Marshall went to see the Commandant Colonel Massi to discuss the situation. As the Swiss inspector, Georges Bouvant had observed, Marshall's relations with Massi throughout the summer had been far more cordial than those of his predecessor. Lieutenant Colonel Marshall now found Massi apparently conciliatory and helpful and the two men discussed how to progress matters until the expected arrival of Allied forces at the camp. Even Croce appeared to have completely changed from an attitude of unswerving hostility to one of friendship and helpfulness. How quickly a leopard can appear to change his spots! Marshall also had discussions with Colonel Max Gooler, the senior American officer in the camp, with whom he regularly liaised. Using the loudspeaker system in the prisoners' compound, Marshall then addressed the Allied prisoners. Lieutenant J. R. Goody, Sherwood Foresters, was one of those who was not impressed. He described Marshall as a gnarled middle-aged soldier, commissioned from the ranks, who started his address rather like a schoolteacher or chairman of school governors when confronted by a microphone, saying: 'Do I speak down here?' The author has not been able to discover whether Marshall did indeed serve initially in the ranks. He was commissioned into the 103 Mahratta Light Infantry as a lieutenant on 4 April 1917. He served in the First World War, reaching the rank of acting captain and adjutant in April 1918. He continued in the peacetime Indian Army between the wars, being promoted to major in March 1934, and served in the Western Desert, promoted to acting lieutenant colonel in March 1941. Thus the vast majority of his service had been in India, where a number of the younger prisoners in Chieti (Stuart Hood amongst them) felt that the army, although undoubtedly courageous, was very old-fashioned in its approach to soldiering.

In his speech, Marshall summed up what was generally believed to be the present situation in Italy, namely that the Italians had signed an armistice and had ceased hostilities. The Allies, who had invaded the toe of Italy five days earlier, were now expected to sweep up country and arrive in the region of Chieti within a few days. There were still Germans in Italy and an Italian division had been diverted to the Chieti area in accordance with the terms of the Armistice, to ensure that no German troops would interfere with the Allied prisoners in Campo 21. In the unfortunate style of Chamberlain before the war, Marshall flourished a piece of paper which he said was a written assurance from Commandant Massi that he would do his duty and hand them over to their own forces. Marshall went on to say (no doubt relying on what Massi and Croce had told him) that German strength in the area was not believed to be great, and certainly that they did not have sufficient transport in the area to move the prisoners. Therefore, if the ex-prisoners, as they now were, remained quietly in the camp and did not make a nuisance of themselves, all would be well. Roll calls would be immediately discontinued, as would the *carabinieri* patrols within the camp. The prisoners could sleep outside their bungalows at night if they wished and there would be no curfew. In addition, and most importantly, Lieutenant Colonel Marshall announced that in any event he had some time before received an order from London on the prisoners' secret radio that in the event of the Italians surrendering, all Allied prisoners must remain where they were in their camps, to be collected by Allied troops in due course. Marshall emphasized that he was now enforcing the order in Campo 21 and that all inmates must remain at the camp. A similar order had been received by the American troops from their High Command. Citing the King's Regulations (the military bible) Marshall said that since they had all been captured by the enemy, there should now be held a court of enquiry or court martial in accordance with those regulations. Their capture, said Marshall, had to be considered by the court to determine if it was an act of cowardice and whether it could have been in some way avoided. Therefore, they had to wait for their own forces to collect them and were not free to leave on their own.

So extraordinary may this situation seem to the modern reader that it requires some detailed examination and explanation. Marshall had indeed received such an order, but he was wrong when he asserted that there had to be a court of enquiry or court martial for each and every prisoner of war. The War Office had been aware for some months of the possibility of a collapse by the Italian Armed Forces or an Armistice. As early as March 1943, plans had been drawn up in relation to what prisoners of war should do. It was indeed decided that all prisoners should remain where they were, in their camps, under the command of their senior officer. Once the Armistice had been signed, they would all revert from being prisoners of the enemy to being serving soldiers again and would, in the normal way, be subject to orders. To disobey an order from an SBO would be a disciplinary offence. Food was to be rationed, and a 14-day supply would be sent to each camp, if necessary by means of an air drop. Should the prisoners not be released by the Italians despite the Armistice, then there remained a duty to escape (since in that case they would still technically be prisoners). If they were no longer prisoners, then there was a duty to avoid recapture. However, it had been decided that there would be no courts of enquiry except in: a) cases of conduct at capture already known to the War Office; b) similar cases only known to fellow prisoners of war; c) cases in which offences had been committed in the detaining country during captivity or pending repatriations.

What became known as the 'Stay Put' order had come from the offices of Brigadier Crockatt's MI9 in the summer of 1943. It was issued to all prisoner-of-war camps in Italy and Germany in June 1943, either via the secret radios that many had, or by means of the secret codes that MI9 used. The order appears to have been successfully received in all the Italian camps well before the Armistice. It was made clear that to leave the camps would amount to a court martial offence – not only for disobeying a direct order, but also for desertion. No document proving the origin of the order has ever surfaced, but historians speculate that it emanated originally from Lieutenant General Bernard Montgomery. It is suggested that Montgomery gave the instructions to Brigadier Crockatt, the head of MI9, to send out the order covertly to all prisoner-of-war camps. Montgomery is said to have been concerned that thousands of escaped prisoners, lacking proper military discipline after a year or more in prison, would roam about Italy and get in the way of his organized advance. If some were armed or had explosives, they might attack and blow up bridges that Montgomery's troops wanted to use – in fact, generally make a nuisance of themselves.

In the light of what came next, the order was clearly a grave error. The thinking had been that the Allies knew where most of the camps were and could supply them by air with food, and with small quantities of arms to resist any rioters or looting. Hospital emergency cases could also be evacuated by air, while the chaos and confusion that might result from mass escapes could be avoided. But whatever the thinking may have been in the midsummer of 1943, by September the situation in Italy had changed. The dethroning of Mussolini on 25 July had given the Germans ample notice of what was likely to come, and as has been previously mentioned they had been throwing reinforcements into Italy since the end of July. It had been originally intended to follow up the first Stay Put order by pamphleting the camps with a repeat order in September, days before the Armistice was announced. Field Marshal Alexander, the Supreme Allied Commander in Italy, vetoed this, appreciating that there might be reasons why in particular areas the order was no longer appropriate. Sadly, however, no action was taken to contact the SBOs direct to withdraw the order.

Of course, it has long been established in military law that a commander in the field may disregard an order if the situation has changed in such a way that the order is no longer appropriate or 'out of date'. Indeed, the British Army's official Field Service Regulations laid down that *an order ought to be disobeyed* if 'some fact which could not be known to the officer who issued the order made disobedience necessary to comply with the known intentions of the superior who had given it.' However, such a commander would have to have full confidence in his decision and a considerable degree of personal courage, since he would be likely to have to account for his actions later. In some other camps, the SBOs did disregard the order. In Veano, to which Lett had been sent, and where also at the time of Armistice the ex–SBO of Campo 21, Lieutenant Colonel Gray was incarcerated, the serving SBO, Lieutenant Colonel Younghusband disregarded the order because of prevailing conditions. The camp gates were opened and all the prisoners dispersed into the hills. Another exception was at the camp at Fontanellato, to which Toby Graham, Tony Roncoroni and many other ex–Campo 21 inmates had been sent, where Lieutenant Colonel Hugo de Burgh was SBO. There too, all the inmates evacuated the camp. Many both from Veano and Fontanellato eventually found freedom. From the nearby camp at Sulmona, a similar mass escape took place. At Bologna, the SBO Brigadier Mountain personally opened the camp gate and attempted to lead his men to freedom. Unfortunately, that camp was already surrounded by German troops. At Modena, however, the camp to which Peter O'Bree had been sent, the SBO initially enforced the Stay Put order, only to find himself betrayed by the Italian camp commandant, who encouraged the Germans to take over the camp, which they did on 9 September.

One contemporaneous commentator was Captain Christopher Soames, who was appointed to lead No. 2 Field Escape Section of A Force in Italy on 30 August 1943, in preparation for the Allied invasion of the mainland. The purpose of A Force was to assist escapers and evaders to come through the lines. The very existence of A Force may seem to contradict the Stay Put order, but of course there were a number of evaders who had never been prisoners of war – shot-down air crew being the obvious example. Soames was highly critical of the order. In November, after an estimated 50,000 prisoners had been shipped to Germany, he said in a memo to his own HQ: 'The broadcast to Prisoner of War camps which was interpreted to say: "Do not escape – prepare nominal roll", or words to that effect, is surely a mistake of severe magnitude which brought dire consequences to many would be escapers, and ought on no account to be overlooked.' The attitude of Soames' bosses at A Force, however, remained surprisingly lukewarm towards escapes at this stage. A memo of 5 September 1943 states that although there would be no pamphlet campaign in support of the Stay Put order, no attempt should be made to provoke mass breakouts. Individual escapes could be encouraged, but only in areas near the front line.

The reply to Soames's memo, dated 25 November 1943, puts the case for Stay Put:

This must be taken in its proper perspective. The instructions to camps were passed in June 1943, and were in the nature of 'standing instructions' to deal with conditions likely to arise at the end of the war. These instructions were not specific to the Italy invasion, and of course there was no time in which to get messages through to deal with the peculiar circumstances which arose when Italy capitulated but the Germans fought on. [Any historian is bound to comment that Germany's action in remaining in Italy was entirely foreseeable. Even the occupants of the PoW camps foresaw it.] Incidentally, my own personal opinion is that, taking a broad view, what did happen may have been the best that could have happened. I can visualise some 75,000 unarmed and (on the whole) poorly clad prisoners of war in poor physical condition spreading over the countryside in large bodies interfering with the German war machine with the result that mass murder by the Germans would have taken place had the ex-prisoners of war not given themselves up in accordance with the proclamations issued by the Germans. Certainly, more might have reached Allied lines, but many more would have been killed without necessarily helping the war effort.

This view, which is unsigned, presumes that prisoners of war had lost their discipline and good sense, which was simply not the case. It also ignores what the true purpose of escapers was. Those who did escape from the camps after the Armistice were simply intent on getting home as soon as possible. They generally took to the mountains and did their very best to keep out of the way of the Germans.

Nonetheless, the order had been issued and Lieutenant Colonel Marshall cannot be criticized for enforcing it on the night of 8 September. In all camps, that night was one first of shock and then of celebration. On the following day would come an appraisal of what the local situation was and what action, if any, was necessary. Even at this early stage, many of the prisoners felt a sense of strong dissatisfaction at the Stay Put order, but Marshall made clear that he had the support of Colonel Gooler and that anyone leaving the camp, or attempting to, would be committing the serious court martial offence of disobeying a direct order. Such an order from a Commanding Officer is difficult to disobey. Horace Crabtree believed that Marshall had actually asked Massi to keep the Italian guards on the wall in order to ensure that the Allied prisoners did not leave – in other words, to enforce Marshall's order that they stay. Marshall seems to have gone to more extreme lengths in enforcing the order than any other SBO in Italy. The events of the next 12 days seem to a modern commentator quite extraordinary, yet they took place upon Marshall's orders, with the agreement of Gooler, the Senior American Officer, and other senior officers under Marshall's command.

When 9 September dawned, after a night during which few of the prisoners had been able to sleep, the significance of the Armistice finally began to sink in. Hill's diary reads: 'Woke early still very excited. Free Free Free. Removed some red patches.' On this day, everything in the camp seemed relatively peaceful and arrangements were quickly made for more formal celebrations to take place that evening. The Camp Commandant and guards were being friendly and confirmed that there was an Italian division in the area to protect them from any trouble with stray German troops. Many prisoners believed that unopposed Allied troops would soon reach them. Croce went out of his way to be helpful, even going up to Chieti town on one occasion to obtain a part for the prisoners' radio set. Also on 9 September, the Allies landed at Salerno, on the Amalfi coast south of Naples. In the evening, the celebrations started in earnest and the officers enjoyed a Victory Dinner. The reserves of Red Cross parcels were dug into and most of the officers over-indulged.

On the following day, 10 September, the camp was suddenly flooded with books as the Italians released thousands of volumes that had been held under lock and key pending the approval of the censor (or Croce). This only went to prove what many had believed – namely that a lot of the comforts had arrived but been held back. Rumours of all sorts were rife and the prisoners had still not received any definite news of how and when they were to be released. The position was equally difficult for their families and loved ones at home. The news of the Italian capitulation had by now reached all corners of the globe, but nobody knew quite what was going to happen. In the months of chaos that followed, the prisoners disappeared from any official Red Cross records and in most cases their families simply did not know where they were, or even whether they were alive or dead.

The inmates of Campo 21 now discovered the misfortune of being on a main road. Running directly outside the main gate to the camp was the main road from the east coast at Pescara towards Rome. After tea, German trucks were seen travelling in both directions along it, carrying amongst other things fighting equipment and some women. Rumour had it that the German diplomatic staff had passed by the previous night and that this was the rest of the German staff trying to get out of Italy. The reason for traffic in both directions, it was suggested, meant that they were finding it impossible to get through – supporting the notion that Allied troops were not far away. That night, 10 September, the British other ranks held their own Liberation Dinner and were entertained by a camp jazz band, the Hot Club de Chieti. However, many were worried at seeing the German road traffic during the course of the day, if only because it demonstrated how vulnerable the ex-prisoners were should the Germans decide to take an interest in them. Nonetheless, the SBO, when asked to relax the Stay Put order, refused, and he also declined to order the Fighting Squadron to secure the camp and send out patrols.

Dawn of 11 September brought the prisoners in Campo 21 their third full day as 'free men'. The understandable disquiet about their vulnerability was growing. The prisoners tried to pass time as normal in the camp while they awaited developments. However, as they were playing a game of softball in the centre of the camp (the diamond was on one side of the central path, the outfield on the other), orders came from the SBO that prisoners should stay clear of the centre in case passing Germans became inquisitive. Column after column of German transport passed by the gates during the course of that day and the view from the main gate was directly down the middle of the camp. The optimists speculated that these were the German rear guard retreating. John Jenkins described it simply as: 'the most amazing situation that I've ever been in'. Official news seemed very scarce, and the Italians at the camp did not seem to have any idea themselves of what was going on. The Italian guards still remained, but were now nominally there to defend the occupants from outside interference. Lieutenant Hill noted that the guards on the wall now had boxes of hand grenades with which to 'protect' the prisoners. Alpini troops, said to be a part of the Italian division that was in the area to protect them, climbed up on to the walls to talk to the ex-prisoners and seemed extremely friendly.

Then, at 2030hrs, the Italian government announced that effectively they were now declaring war on the Germans and were joining the Allies. The Germans had refused to leave Italy. Marshal Badoglio made a public broadcast saying: 'We cannot tolerate the Germans acting towards our country as if it were conquered by them. Therefore there is only one duty for everybody, only a single command: "Out with the Germans!" We will collaborate with the Anglo-Americans who have accepted our fighting potential to chase the Germans out of the peninsula.' Badoglio's speech went on to remind his fellow countrymen of Italy's alliance with the British and Americans in the First World War and concluded by saying: 'It is our strict duty to fight at the side of the Anglo-Americans against the Germans and those few Italians, no longer worthy of the name, who have placed themselves under their orders; to fight them with whatever means in every place and in whatever moment they present themselves.' Thus, the world had totally changed for the prisoners over the course of a few days. Their erstwhile captors were now their allies, fighting against the Germans, who had declared their intention to take control of Italy.

Still, Lieutenant Colonel Marshall continued to enforce the Stay Put. He consulted regularly with Commandant Massi and seems to have accepted all that Massi told him. Massi, of course, spoke no English, and what Marshall was in fact hearing was Croce's translation of what he said. Marshall addressed the camp again, telling them that they were (or had been) prisoners of Italy, and therefore under the Geneva Convention the Germans could not touch them. That day, Joe Frelinghuysen went to see Colonel Gooler, his own Senior Officer, to argue for permission to leave the camp, but to his anger, he was refused leave, and told to obey the Stay Put order.

On 12 September, the situation in Campo 21 moved from being confused and uncertain to chaotic. In the outside world, events were moving fast and were moving against the ex-prisoners. Although they had not known it, since 28 August the deposed dictator, Mussolini, had been held under guard by Italian *carabinieri* at a small hotel on the Gran Sasso, the mountain that they could see from within the camp. German intelligence discovered his whereabouts and Adolf Hitler ordered that he be rescued. Captain Otto Skorzeny of the Waffen SS took a squadron of parachute troops and landed by glider in front of the hotel on the Gran Sasso where Mussolini was being held. Despite their superior numbers, the *carabinieri* made no attempt to resist and Skorzeny and his men rescued Mussolini from the hotel without difficulty. He was then taken to safety by Storch light aircraft. Hitler had been planning for some time to rescue Mussolini, and to put him back on the 'throne' of Italy as a German puppet, to provide a focal point for Italian Fascists. On 18 September, Mussolini would declare the arrival of a new Italian Republic and the return of Fascism. Having freed Mussolini, the Germans formally announced that they were taking over Italy, which in fact they had more or less already done. Rome and a number of other major Italian cities were in German hands.

Inside the Chieti camp, news of the German stand arrived along with numerous unsubstantiated rumours. It must have been clear to anyone with access to either British or Italian radio (Marshall and his team had access to both) that there was very unlikely to be any quick victory for the Allies, or a speedy withdrawal by the Germans. Marshall and Massi now resorted to the utterly bizarre. They decided upon a pretence that Campo 21 was actually a lunatic asylum. The Italian guards on duty at the main gate, and any others who were visible from the road, donned white doctors' coats from the camp hospital to support the masquerade. Jenkins commented: 'This is a further precaution against Gerry interference. If things go on like this for much longer, we really shall all be crazy.' From now on, no Italian guards appeared on the walls during the day, only at night.

In the evening, a thanksgiving service was scheduled for 1915hrs, to mark the prisoners' liberation and the end of the war in Italy. To many, such a service must now have seemed markedly premature. The majority of the ex-prisoners were extremely worried about their future, and all over the camp preparations were being made for a breakout, whatever the SBO might say. Interestingly, Hill seems to have been one of the few on the SBO's side: '[There was] a broadcast that the Germans were taking over the country, seizing railways and government buildings. Sends great majority of officers in the camp into a flap, and start to make preparations for making a break should the Germans try to move us to Germany. This I cannot possibly see them doing. Getting their equipment out is far more important than a few prisoners … In the evening the SBO broadcasts that the Commandant is responsible for us, Italian division in the neighbourhood. Tells us to be cool, calm and collected. A very sensible speech.' But for others, such as George Hervey Murray, Marshall's speech was infuriating. His manner was that of a parade-ground martinet as he shouted his orders at the ex-prisoners over the loudspeaker system. The protests by the men in favour of being allowed to go were becoming very strong, but Marshall now informed them that should prisoners escape, the remainder of the camp would not be able to shelter behind the Geneva Convention, and would be totally at the mercy of the Germans. It is extremely difficult to see any force whatsoever in the latter argument. When the Armistice was announced, Larry Allen had immediately placed a news flash on his noticeboard that simply said: 'You are Free!' Frelinghuysen recalls that when Marshall and Gooler refused to let the prisoners leave, saying that they should remain 'cool, calm and collected', an outraged Allen posted another news flash on his notice board saying that the order was wrong, and ending with the words: 'Stay cool, calm and be collected by the Germans'. Lieutenant Colonel Marshall was furious, and ordered Allen's immediate arrest. Only Colonel Gooler's intercession saved Allen from the cooler and a threatened court martial.

Later that night, Tony Baines and the orchestra presented the third in a series of Promenade Concerts. It was a high quality performance, starting with the national anthems of Great Britain and the United States, both of which had previously been banned. No doubt it served Lieutenant Colonel Marshall's purposes well, and preserved a degree of calm in the camp. Freer-Roger was one of those who remembered what an excellent concert it was, since it featured as a guest producer Herb Parry, an American inmate who had been Walt Disney's musical director before the war. Parry reproduced with the orchestra all the music of *Fantasia*. To the modern observer, it is possible that the holding of the concert may seem reminiscent of the ship's orchestra on the *Titanic*, playing on as she gently slipped beneath the waves.

Although they had no way of knowing it, events had turned even more starkly against the interests of the 'free' prisoners of Campo 21 than they believed. Not only was Mussolini now free to rekindle Italian resistance to the Allies, but also the regiment of hardened German paratroopers from whom Mussolini's rescuers had been drawn were now in the general area of Chieti. The comparison must be drawn between the actions of Marshall and the actions of other SBOs not so very far away. To all who had listened anxiously to radio broadcasts as to the position of Allied forces in Italy and the reaction of the Germans, it was clear that the expected progress was not being made. The situation was now quite different to that envisaged when the Stay Put order had been issued. Long before the evening of 12 September, SBOs such as Younghusband in Veano and de Burgh in Fontanellato had read the war situation correctly, and with the assistance in each case of the Italian Camp Commandant, ignored the order and evacuated their camps. By so doing, they had given the men under their command a chance of escape. Marshall, in Campo 21, did the opposite.

Again, to be fair to Marshall it seems very likely that Massi and Croce were playing a dirty game. What emerged later, as a result of questions asked by an angry Prime Minister Winston Churchill about the Stay Put order, some weeks after the Armistice, was that once it was clear that the Germans were remaining in Italy in force, messages had been sent by Allied High Command to the prisoners 'through the Italian authorities'. These countermanded the Stay Put order and ordered them to leave the camps and work their way towards Allied forces. It had been a term of the Armistice that all Allied prisoners should be handed over to the Allied Commander-in-Chief. After the Armistice, when it became clear that the Germans were not going to leave, the United States' General Eisenhower had agreed with the Italian authorities that all the Allied prisoners should be released and provided with 10 days' food, and that they would do everything in their power to prevent them falling into the hands of the Germans. These instructions were delivered to the guards in charge of all the Italian camps, to be passed on to the ex-prisoners and put into effect. Thus, Commandant Massi would have been informed shortly after 8 September (certainly no later than 12 or 13 September) that he should supply the Allied prisoners with food and let them go. In the event, either Massi and Croce did not pass that order on or else, which seems inconceivable, Marshall ignored it. The logical conclusion is that Massi and Croce, both described as committed Fascists, were pro-German throughout and were deliberately deceiving Lieutenant Colonel Marshall as to the status quo.

Many of the ex-prisoners became restive and wanted now to leave the camp. Marshall's reaction, with the support of Gooler, was to establish a cordon of Allied officers to prevent anyone from going. The Italian guards, never very happy soldiers, had begun to disappear, taking whatever opportunity they could to abandon their duties and be off. Many of them had no wish either to do battle with the Germans or to come under German command, which clearly they feared might happen. The Italians were replaced by Allied ex-prisoners in the sentry boxes and patrolling around the walls. The new 'guards' were armed with rattles, not guns, but their objective was the same as their predecessors – to prevent escape from the camp. Sam Derry and his Escape Committee became increasingly concerned. They wanted to leave as soon as possible and to start heading south towards Allied lines. They divided the inmates of the camp up into units of ten, so that if it became necessary to go they would do so in some sort of order, not as a disorganized rabble. Initially, Marshall had forbidden the continuation of any tunnelling, but in the face of sustained protest he agreed that tunnels might be continued, but insisted that no break-out would be allowed through them. Thus, the tunnellers kept working to ensure that their tunnels were ready for an escape, should one become necessary at short notice, and escape packs were gathered together. Marshall was aware of the disquiet and called a meeting of all the escape teams. He repeated his orders that they must stay in camp.

As the situation worsened, and it became obvious that the Germans had no intention of leaving Italy, the disquiet grew. Rome was in German and not Allied hands, and Rome was not very far from Chieti. Harold Sell and those with whom he shared his barrack room held a meeting, concluding that they should leave at once while German troops were relatively thin on the ground. Things could only get worse. Sell went and presented their reasoned case to Lieutenant Colonel Marshall, and requested permission to go. He argued that London was far away and there they could not know of the rapidly deteriorating situation – the Germans were moving their troops much faster than the British and were heading south. Marshall was completely unmoved by Sell's representations and still insisted that the order be obeyed. He stressed that whatever might be the private opinions of Sell and his room-mates, Sell's duty obliged him to remain with Marshall in the camp and to control the situation as best they could. An unhappy Major Sell returned to his quarters, where he relayed Marshall's reaction to his comrades. Although certain that if they went now they would be able to get through enemy lines and rejoin Allied forces, they reluctantly decided that in the face of Marshall's insistence, their duty obliged them to remain with him. These were experienced and disciplined officers, and they felt that Marshall had left them no choice. Nonetheless, the tunnellers kept on tunnelling. At least now they did not have a problem about spoil. They could simply dump it out in the camp. They were also able to leave the hatches to their tunnels open, thus improving the air supply. Having worked so long and hard on the tunnels in the first place, they now intended to finish them off as an insurance policy, in case the Germans did, as they feared, eventually take over the camp.

Although most senior officers like Major Sell felt that they had to obey a direct order from their Commanding Officer, some of the more junior officers and other ranks felt differently. Gradually, after Mussolini's release, the camp guards were fading away. They, of course, had their own orders from Massi and Croce to remain where they were, and therefore could not leave openly by the main gate, but increasingly could be seen climbing up ladders leant against the wall and disappearing over it. The time came when it was estimated that only about 50 Italians remained to guard them, 25 officers and 25 other ranks. At the same time, German road traffic in the area was increasing. Suspecting that the Italian division said to be protecting them had also faded away, another delegation made representations to Marshall that the time had come for them to leave. As before, Marshall would not be moved and permission was refused.

Monday, 13 September was an uneasy day. Rumours again abounded and individuals could choose which, if any, they believed. One report said that the Allies had landed on the east coast, at Foggia. It was in fact untrue. The British Eight Army eventually captured Foggia and its airfields on 27 September, but the German defensive line, the Gustav Line that ran through Monte Cassino, was established south of Chieti and north of Foggia. In another rumour, the Germans were said to be very short of petrol and abandoning vehicles. When a pall of black smoke was seen over Pescara, an Italian sentry announced that the Germans had been machine gunning 150 of their own aircraft that they had to abandon and destroy. In the evening, the ex-prisoners were confined to their bungalows as a precaution, as frontline German troops (presumably paratroopers) were seen passing the front gate.

Rifleman Jack Collarbone had transferred to Campo 21 as an orderly, with the likes of Frank Osborne. He had been detailed to work in the Security Office collecting information for escape purposes, any up-to-date news, spare parts for radio sets when they could be found, and checking careless talk amongst officers and other ranks. As a lowly Rifleman, he could often pick up information that others could not. Collarbone was quite convinced that the Germans were about to take over the camp, and on the night of 13/14 September, he decided to go over the wall. He arranged that a friendly Italian sentry would help him. Collarbone took two officers with him and they duly made their break that night, only to be recaptured shortly after getting out of the camp by a British patrol, set up by Lieutenant Colonel Marshall. Collarbone was ordered to parade at the company office next morning: on the face of it, he and his two officer companions had committed the court-martial offence of desertion.

The next morning, however, Collarbone noted that all of the Italian sentries on the walls now appeared to have gone, so he, this time with Bombardier John Reardon and Private Markey escaped again. The three men had obtained civilian clothes. They got clear of Marshall's guards without difficulty and, using maps that they had with them, made good progress to the south, walking, then catching a train to reach Castel di Sangro on the river Sangro. The three eventually split up, and Collarbone went up into the mountains thinking that would be safer. There he waited in the hope that the Allied front line would overrun his position. This did not happen and eventually, on 15 October, Collarbone had the misfortune to be betrayed by two Italian guides who brought an American officer to him who had been in Campo 21, Lieutenant Charles Eberu. Both Collarbone and Eberu were taken prisoner again and were then sent to Germany.

Still, Collarbone was undoubtedly right to make his break when he did. Throughout the day of 14 September, German vehicles continued to pass down the road outside Campo 21. Then, not surprisingly, two German officers visited the camp. They were from German headquarters in Pescara and were carrying out a survey of the country. They wanted to know particulars of who was being held in the camp. Massi no doubt told them exactly who was there and the Germans then apparently gave a written assurance that provided the ex-prisoners stayed put, they would not be molested. This was passed on to Lieutenant Colonel Marshall. Marshall addressed the men and told them that provided they stayed where they were, the Germans would not interfere with them. One must conclude that Marshall believed that they would be left alone until the arrival of Allied troops. However, a more obvious interpretation of the German assurance runs, 'If you stay where you are, we will come and collect you when we have time.' That night, Warrant Officer Claude Weaver and three others decided to make their break for freedom. They had their prepared escape kits with them, essential for survival on the other side of the wall. Their plan was to go out over the wall, now a relatively simple exercise. However, they momentarily put down their escape kits in the cookhouse and left them unattended. When they returned for them a short while later, they found that Lieutenant Colonel Marshall had taken the escape kits. Weaver demanded their return, but after an argument Marshall would only agree to give the kits back once Weaver's team had given their word not to escape. Thus Weaver's escape attempt was frustrated for the time being.

While Marshall was upholding the Stay Put order for Allied prisoners, the Italian garrison had their own ideas. By the end of 15 September, practically the whole garrison had quit, leaving only officers and a few *carabinieri*. Kenwyn Walters estimated that 250 Italians had deserted and gone home. He recalls getting up on the morning of the 15th to see a young girl playing in one of the sentry boxes – and no Italian guards. German convoys continued to sweep past the gates. A small group of Italians appeared on the hill in view of the camp and signalled to the inmates that they should leave the camp as soon as possible. This was dismissed by the Marshall group as 'a few civilians who considered that they would be far safer if we escaped.' In the light of the enormous help given later to escapers by the local people, it was clearly the opposite – good advice and well meant. Also on 15 September, tunnel 4, belonging to the team under the command of Bill Gordon and including John Jenkins, was finally completed. For the first time, Jenkins made an oblique reference to it in his diary, saying simply: 'Today saw the completion of six months work, of which more anon.'

Some news of an incident at Campo 19, Bologna, had now reached the Chieti inmates and Marshall and those who shared his views used it to justify staying put, arguing that it was far safer than trying to evacuate the camp. Marshall emphasized that ex-prisoners would have no status wandering about outside the camp in hostile territory at the mercy of German patrols, and that an attempt to escape might well be met by a massacre, as he said had happened at Campo 19, where the Germans had machine gunned escaping prisoners of war. In fact, this was far from the truth, but it was a persuasive argument for some of the prisoners. Thus it is necessary to look briefly at what had actually happened at Campo 19. Some camps suffered the misfortune at the Armistice of being already close to or surrounded by a significant German garrison. Gavi, the Italian Colditz, was one. Perched on a hill, there was a substantial German presence in the town of Gavi that surrounded it. Campo 19 at Bologna suffered a dual misfortune – there was a German garrison in the district, and the fact that the prisoners were likely to leave the camp was betrayed to them early on. The SBO in Campo 19, Brigadier Mountain, had decided to disregard the Stay Put order before the Armistice was announced and had organized the camp for a mass break out as soon as the expected Italian surrender came. Apparently the plan became known to the Italians, some of whom were pro-German. When the Armistice was announced on the evening of 8 September, the SBO immediately called the men together and, since it was after dark, it was decided they should get some sleep and then make the break out at dawn on the 9th. Unfortunately, the Germans were ready for them and had already moved to surround the camp with troops, armoured cars and guns. The German presence, although not its extent, was noticed by the men inside at about 0130hrs on the morning of 9 September and the order immediately given to break out of the camp as soon as possible. At 0400hrs, Brigadier Mountain himself forced open the north gate of the camp, and prisoners began to flow out. At least three points of exit were used, and some of the inmates had got out and across the nearby road before the German firing began. The Germans were at this stage unaware of whether or not the prisoners were armed – it was entirely feasible that they might have disarmed their erstwhile Italian captors. When they realized that prisoners were escaping, they opened fire. Captain Johnson was shot dead and one other prisoner wounded before the Germans realized that the British were unarmed and began to fire over their heads. All but three or four who had got out of the camp were recaptured. The following day the Germans apologized for shooting the unarmed prisoners, and explained that they had been tipped off about a possible break out the previous day, and had been in position since midday. It was fortunate that the SBO, Brigadier Mountain, had destroyed the camp roll of personnel as soon as the Armistice had been announced, so that no meaningful roll call could be held. Most prisoners agreed that the Germans could not be blamed for taking the action that they did – there had been a rush of prisoners across the road and the Germans had fired, not knowing if the escapers were armed. A number of prisoners were still able to escape before they were all removed to Germany. Campo 19, therefore, was an unusual and unlucky case, but there had in fact only been one fatality. Some news of what had happened, seemingly grossly exaggerated, had obviously reached Campo 21 by 15 September. Marshall used it to justify his stance and Hill noted in his diary: 'Considering PG19 efforts, consider far safer to remain inside these walls for the time being.' Lieutenant Bonnello commented later: 'We stayed put and the Germans took over, but it might have been a blessing because there was one camp where they did rush out, and Germans were waiting with machine guns and mowed them down.' Some prisoners believed, probably rightly, that Commandant Massi was deliberately exaggerating the rumours to keep them from leaving the camp, and that he was in fact playing a double game, still sympathetic to the Germans and the restored Mussolini government.

On 16 September, many inmates of the camp were cheered by Tommy Sampson, who for the first time played the 'Reveille' to start the day. Jenkins noted that, 'Some experts have been able to alter the radio and thus obtain BBC radio broadcasts. Another visit from the Gerries today. Last night, Brett and I did *carabiniere* duty for an hour 0045–0145.' As an active member of a tunnel team, Jenkins was no doubt unimpressed by having to do duty as a gaoler for his fellow prisoners. However, given a direct order to stand guard, he had no option but to obey it.

The BBC still seemed confident that prisoners in Italy would not be sent to Germany. Marshall called a meeting of would-be escapers and resisters at 1500hrs. About 120 attended. According to Claude Weaver, Marshall now knew that the Germans had announced to Massi their intention to occupy the camp. He said that the fact that Germans were going to take over did not mean that they were intending to take the prisoners away. It was necessary from their point of view that they protect their lines of communication. Marshall ordered that all escapers whose plans were ready, and who intended to escape (to the prejudice, he said, of the rest of the camp), should reassemble at 1530hrs. Such was the lack of faith in Marshall that at the appointed time, only 14 officers turned up. Marshall then indicated to them that he would not permit any attempt at escape until the Germans had taken over the camp. After that, they were welcome to try. Marshall ordered that the Allied patrols should continue in the meantime and any would-be escapers should be stopped. Weaver recalled that this order was put into effect again that night, when an American officer climbed a ladder to cross the wire, and found the ladder being shaken by British 'guards'. The American lost his escape kit, but got out of the camp successfully. Captain Vernon

Sudbury, Sherwood Foresters, Lieutenant Peter Grigg Uglow, Sherwood Foresters and Captain Alan George Cameron, Cameron Highlanders, in a joint report, recorded that a Captain MacKay, Royal Artillery, also attempted to escape, but he was caught and put under close arrest. He succeeded in escaping later through a tunnel.

The extraordinary situation in Campo 21 on the evening of 16 September can be summarized as follows: 1,350 men had been incarcerated in difficult conditions in the camp for up to 14 months. They had celebrated their liberation eight days before. Their Italian guards had almost all gone and the Italian Commandant was said to be working for and with them. Any Italians who sought to resist the will of the ex-prisoners could be overwhelmed without difficulty. The ex-prisoners were free men (except from their own self-appointed guards) in contested territory. Allied troops were for the first time on Italian mainland soil, less than 200 miles to the south. It was known that there were German troops in the area, and that these had declared the intention of taking over the camp in the near future. If they remained where they were, they would become prisoners of the Germans. All this was within the knowledge of the British and the American commanding officers, yet they continued to imprison their own men within the walls of Campo 21 to await the arrival of the Germans.

On the following day, 17 September, the situation became still more bizarre. Kenwyn Walters records that the other ranks were allowed to go into the town of Chieti to collect rations and acquire other food. In town, they encountered ex-prisoners of war who had escaped from the camp at Sulmona and were now on the run. This they reported back when they returned to the camp, but Marshall remained unmoved. Kenwyn Walters and his friend Lieutenant John Collinge, Royal Armoured Corps, were amongst those ordered by Marshall to do an hour's guard duty that day, which despite their resentment they duly performed. Ironically, both men would later escape from a train taking them to Germany and make their way successfully to freedom through enemy lines.

The American prisoners were amongst the most rebellious, despite the fact that their senior officer, Colonel Gooler, was supporting Marshall. Still on the same day, 17 September, two US and one British officer succeeded in avoiding the Allied guards and escaping from the camp. One of them was young Claude Weaver, who escaped with a fellow American called Harold Rideout. According to Freylinghuysen, Rideout was a fighter pilot, like Weaver, known as 'Mouse'. Rideout's rank is unclear – one source suggests that he was a Lieutenant Colonel. The British officer was McKay. Weaver believed that the

Germans were showing far too much interest in the camp and was not prepared to stick around any longer. He took the view that his word not to escape, given to Marshall a few days previously, was no longer binding on him. Weaver and Rideout wore British battledress, and little blue skull caps – they were intending to pose as Spanish workmen. They carried forged identity passes, which had been created for them by Lieutenant C. A. Goldingham, Royal Artillery, a roommate in Campo 21 of Richard Edmonston Low and Guy Weymouth. Goldingham had become a painstaking and expert forger. Equipped with a steel pen and Indian ink, he could copy any printed pass so perfectly that it would pass the most careful inspection. The photographs that were required on many documents posed no great problem for him. A candidate would look in the Fascist newspapers allowed in the camp for an Italian or German face that looked sufficiently like his own, cut it out, and pass it over to Goldingham. The latter would then doctor the photograph with a special mixture of his own that would make the newspaper stiffen and take on a glossy appearance. He would then fix it to the pass and apply the appropriate 'stamp'.

Weaver and Rideout also had a map and home-made compasses. Wearing their 'disguises', they duly went over the wall and the wire. They were challenged by a sentry (presumably an Allied one), but called out 'Amigo' (Spanish for friend) and pretended to be drunk. The sentry let them go. They walked south for a total of 17 miles on the first day. They fell into company with two Italian youths who said that they wanted to go south to join the Allies, and on the morning of 18 September, caught a train with them to the south. They left the train at 1300hrs, and again began walking. They walked on for the next seven days. Just short of the German front line, Weaver sprained his ankle and could go no further. Rideout went looking for a way to help him, and managed to return with an Italian mule. Mounted on the mule, Weaver rode the last few miles through the German front and into Allied territory. He and Rideout reached safety on 25 September, after a journey of only nine days. By 27 September Weaver was in Malta, where he was interviewed by Air Vice Marshal Park and was allowed to do some practice flying. He was eventually flown back to the UK on 14 October. As mentioned earlier, McKay was unfortunately caught on the way out of the camp by Marshall's guards. Hill's diary reads: 'Another officer breaks in the night. Caught and put in the cooler. Bloody fool.' The situation had become quite absurd, with the British sentencing their own men to the cooler.

Following the extraordinary charade with white coats and the pretence that Campo 21 was a lunatic asylum, an observer may wonder what William

Marshall's mental state was at this stage. He obviously knew that there was much German activity in the area, and that Allied progress had been held up. He also must have known that the 'protection' he had been promised by Colonel Massi was so much hot air, since nearly all of the Italian guards and the Italian division supposedly looking after them, had now gone. He also knew that the Germans had declared an intention to take over the camp. Now on 18 September, the day that the freed Mussolini had announced the setting up of new Fascist Republic, another German officer visited the camp. He spoke to Commandant Massi and then left. According to the announcement that Marshall later made to the assembled ex-prisoners, the German officer had visited to see if all was well and to ask Massi if he required sentries, to which the answer was, 'No'. However, Marshall knew that Fascism was by no means dead in Italy and that whatever had been agreed in the Armistice, Mussolini was now at liberty, supported by the Germans and, as of 18 September, heading up a fresh Italian Fascist state. Thus, those who had abandoned Fascism on 8 September might well either publicly or secretly have returned to it on the 18th. That would include Massi and Croce, both of whom had been known to be committed Fascists. How could Marshall possibly trust the pair now? Yet he still enforced the Stay Put order. Marshall cannot surely have thought that London had contemplated the situation his men were now in. He may well have concluded that it was already too late, and that his men were now safer in than out, but by denying them the chance to escape he was removing any individual choice or chance of them returning to Allied territory, and to their homes and families. There is no doubt Lieutenant Colonel William Marshall was an extremely forceful and stubborn man. Kenwyn Walters characterized him as being the sort of man who loved his pink gin at lunch and started to drink whisky at sundown. Others complained that he was Indian Army, and not in touch with the realities of modern warfare. Despite all criticism and however strong the arguments made to him that the ex-prisoners should be allowed to leave, Marshall stuck to his decision to enforce the Stay Put to the bitter end, and did so with remarkable success.

For Ernest Lodge, all this was now too much. That it was now accepted that the Germans would take over the camp, while prisoners from other camps had already escaped, was the final straw. He had a friend, Flight Lieutenant Dennis 'Danny' Newman, a British-born US citizen serving in the Canadian Air Force, which he had joined in November 1940. Newman had been shot down in a Wellington bomber in July 1942, when on a bombing run over Tobruk (by then held by the Germans). The two men decided that they would ignore the Stay

Put and would make their break for freedom on the night of 20 September. In accordance with the order they had stayed in the camp for twelve days, but things only seemed to have got worse, not better. The correctness of their decision seemed to be confirmed when there came a further visit to Campo 21 by the Germans on the morning of 20 September, this time by two officers. In the afternoon, a German Storch aircraft overflew the camp three times, taking a good look at it. Still, Marshall was unmoved. That night, Lodge and Newman made their break. They had their escape kits ready, and waited until dark. The plan was to crawl through the wire into the Italian compound, thereby avoiding the Allied guards, and then to find a ladder such as many of the Italians had used to climb over the wall. They hoped that the wire barrier on the outside of the wall would no longer present much of a problem. The expedition started badly when Lodge and Newman lost touch with each other. Newman had crossed through the wire into the guards compound, before Lodge knew he had gone. Checking Newman's bunk in his bungalow, Lodge found that he was not there, and was told that Newman had already crossed. Not long after 2200hrs, Lodge made the same journey. Whilst an American chatted to the nearest Italian guard in his sentry box (a very few of the guards still remained), Lodge lifted and crawled under the wire. He succeeded in joining up with Newman and the two of them then walked, bold as brass, through the Italian barrack block, which they found completely deserted. Lodge noted that some of Marshall's Allied guards did apparently notice them, but did nothing about it. Most officers were deeply resentful of having to guard their own colleagues. At the back of the barrack block, Lodge and Newman crawled to a stable close to the wall, where they lay up for a short time. Unfortunately, an Italian guard now walked in on them. He appeared terrified of the Germans, whom he clearly expected to arrive shortly, but after something of an argument and the payment to him of a bribe, he allowed Lodge and Newman to climb up some mule cart shafts to reach the top of the wall. The wall itself was topped by a roll of wire. Lodge got over this without difficulty, but Newman got caught and had to fling himself down, relying on his body weight to get him to the ground. Happily he was unhurt. The wire on the outside of the wall did not prove to be a problem, and the two men dropped into a ditch and ran off as fast as they could. They got clear of Chieti Scalo and holed up in a cave for five days, living off their escape rations, and hoping for the promised Allied advance to reach them. That did not happen, so Lodge and Newman moved on. They received civilian clothes and a lot of help from local Italians, who told them of a boat that was said to be coming to pick up escapees off the coast. This was an A Force operation, carried out with the help of the SAS under the command of a Captain Lee, who had parachuted in. A Force was now doing its best to help. However, in the event this plan failed, and Lodge and Newman headed south on foot. They crossed into Allied territory on 28 October, after walking for about five weeks. Their successful escape, and that of Weaver and Rideout three days earlier, proved how wrong Marshall's decision had been.

John Speares, the signals officer who had worked on the radio, tells of an officer called Charlie Willmott, who had the strange habit of walking through his bungalow every so often predicting the number of weeks that they would all still have to serve. He had made himself very unpopular the previous summer by pronouncing, 'Only 153 more weeks to go.' Now, in September 1943, he was down below 100 weeks, but still predicting a lengthy period of imprisonment yet to come. He refused to be caught up in the justified optimism that followed the Armistice. For those who were transported to Germany, his pessimistic forecast was not far wrong.

THE ARRIVAL OF THE GERMANS

As it turned out, Lodge and Newman had made their escape only just in time. Between one and two hours later, shortly after midnight on 20/21 September, the Germans arrived in force to take over Campo 21. They were paratroopers, dressed in full battle order, and equipped with light automatic weapons. First they occupied the administration buildings, and once those were secure, they systematically took possession of the sentry boxes. Two roving patrols were introduced to the prisoners' part of the camp. The ex-prisoners were now prisoners again, back in the hands of the Germans, who had taken most of them prisoner in the first place. The men awoke next morning to find themselves in custody, now guarded by seasoned German paratroopers who would clearly stand no nonsense. Each sentry box atop the wall now contained two tough, steel-helmeted German paratroopers, instead of a single slovenly Italian sentry. For most it was a devastating realization. Richard Edmonston Low describes an orgy of recrimination and vituperation throughout the whole camp, directed at the SBO and his immediate entourage. Indeed, one wonders what Lieutenant Colonel Marshall's thoughts were when he awoke to discover what his dogged adherence to the Stay Put order had brought about. His men were furious with him, and a number complained formally about his conduct later. They suggested, correctly, that it had been obvious that London's Stay Put order had been overtaken by events and that Marshall had been entirely wrong to enforce it. They also suggested that Marshall had been unduly under the influence of the Italian Camp Commandant, Colonel Massi. They pointed out that escape had still been possible right up until just before midnight on 20 September, as illustrated by the successful escapes of those such as Weaver, Rideout, Lodge and Newman. Discovering later the actions of the SBOs at the Fontanellato and Veano camps, there was enormous bitterness at Marshall's stance, that in the event condemned so many to serve another 18 months in prison camp. Marshall of course suffered the same fate himself.

Marshall was eventually interviewed about his decision after the war had finished, on 11 July 1945. He appeared definitely sympathetic both to Colonel Massi ('quite a good commandant who had alleviated the lot of the prisoners') and to Croce ('quite a good interpreter but had a difficult manner which the prisoners disliked'). He denied that he had prevented escapes for anything other than the best motives. Marshall explained that by the time of the Armistice, the prisoners had made a wireless receiving set and were therefore able to hear the BBC news. He said that they heard of landings at Genoa and Ancona, to the north of them (such landings in fact never happened). He had received the Stay Put order and had also heard that arrangements would be made either by parachute landing or otherwise to assist them. He accepted that after the Armistice there would have been no difficulty in the whole camp walking out and dispersing into the hills. Marshall said that he had discussed the matter with his other senior officers, including Colonel Gooler, and it had been decided that it would be best to remain where they were. The British line to the south had still been some 200 miles away, and had the whole camp walked out, many of them might have been killed in the hills, as had in fact happened to a number of those who escaped from other camps. Marshall claimed that of those who had been transported to German camps from Chieti, only one had been killed as a result of a bombing raid on the Brunswick Prison Camp where they were held. He indicated that he was prepared to take full responsibility for the decision that he had made. A formal enquiry into Marshall's conduct later exonerated him from blame. He had, it said, simply been following orders.

In Marshall's favour, it must be said, of course, that not all the prisoners in Campo 21 were men of the calibre of Weaver, Rideout, Lodge, Newman and the tunnel teams. There were those who had allowed themselves to sink for many months into a state of despondency and inactivity. Harold Sell even suggests that there had been some attempted suicides. Such men would certainly have been at risk if left to their own devices out in the Italian countryside. Further, 15 months of inadequate food and harsh conditions had taken their toll on the health and fitness of many of the men. But to deny freedom to all, many of whom had the burning desire to escape and get home and who were fit and strong enough to do so, seems totally unjust. Marshall's argument that by keeping everybody where they were he managed to avoid casualties was not a true soldier's argument. Soldiers do not win battles by hiding in their bunkers.

The first thing that the Germans did at Campo 21 was to secure the camp itself. A roll call would wait until daylight. The attitude of the Germans was different to that of the Italians. These were front line troops, not gaolers, and their object was simply to move the prisoners out of the camp and off to Germany as soon as possible. The plan was to take them by road to the PoW camp at Sulmona (from which all its own prisoners had escaped at the Armistice, although a number had been recaptured or had returned) and from there they would be shipped north by train. Although very efficient soldiers and ruthless when necessary, the Germans did not have any detailed knowledge of the prisoners, and it is said by at least one source that they did not even bother to finish the first roll call.

As the prisoners awoke on 21 September, Sam Derry and the Escape Committee quickly realized that the German takeover that they had long feared had now taken place, and ordered as many of the tunnel teams as possible to go and hide in their tunnels immediately before the expected roll call. This many men did, but it was not possible for all of any tunnel team to hide in their tunnel. Also those who were slow to wake up, or who lived in a different area of the camp, found themselves without the time to get down into the tunnels before the roll call started. Now the entrances to the tunnels, which had been open since 8 September, also had to be closed and carefully disguised. This limited the amount of air that would be available to those hiding in them, and it was not possible for air to be let into the tunnels during roll call, since all the other prisoners still above ground would be on parade. About 50 men managed to secrete themselves in the tunnels for the first roll call.

The roll call was duly carried out by a German officer, with an Italian officer present to assist him. The Germans probably knew from the Italians that there should have been 1,334 prisoners in the camp (the head count from 20 August 1943, when the last Protecting Power representative had visited), and if they finished the roll call they would have known that the total now was appreciably short of that. However, they must also have known that the camp had been leaking prisoners since 8 September, and were no doubt quite satisfied (and perhaps somewhat amazed) that more than 1,250 still remained. They did not query the head count. The Italians themselves had little idea how many of the prisoners had already escaped. Once the roll call was over, those hiding in the tunnels returned to the surface. One disadvantage of the deception was that the rations per man issued thereafter by the Germans were about 50 short. For those tunnels that required further work to finish, the digging carried on with increased vigour. Gordon-Brown's team concentrated on enlarging the space inside their tunnel, so that more men would be able to hide when the time came.

Lieutenant Colonel Marshall remained in command of the prisoners. There is some confusion as to whether, even now, he gave permission for the tunnel teams to use their tunnels to escape, but the preponderance of opinion is that finally he did, but added that those escaping should be limited to the tunnel teams. There was not to be a general exodus, which Marshall decided was too dangerous and would lead to reprisals by the Germans against the rest of the prisoners. According to some inmates, Marshall still thought that the Germans would only guard them until Allied troops arrived and would then hand them over and withdraw from Italy. If that was indeed Marshall's view, then it tends to confirm that he was under Massi's influence, and being grossly misled by him. The situation was undoubtedly volatile and there was always the fear that the Germans would not bother to transport their prisoners to Germany, but would simply shoot them. Marshall indicated that in his opinion, the chances to escape would come if the Germans began to move prisoners. The prospect of jumping from trains or lorries was always attractive to prisoners of war. They felt, rightly, that they were more difficult to guard when on the move. Over the next couple of days, when the roll calls were repeated, the same number of men would hide down the tunnels (although not necessarily the same people), so that the numbers parading remained constant.

The Germans had no intention of allowing the prisoners to remain for long in the Chieti camp. They arranged for enough lorries to take them in batches to the prisoner-of-war camp at Sulmona, now also in their hands, and then north by train to Germany. Allied aircraft had been attacking many of the railways and communication routes, but trains apparently still ran from Sulmona. Assembling the transport and the necessary troops to guard the prisoners took time, but with Teutonic efficiency the Germans were able to move the first batch on 23 September 1943. For the tunnel teams, the plan now was to wait until the last batch of prisoners was to be transported, and then to hide down the tunnels until shortly before the camp was clear of enemy troops. Since the 50-odd tunnel men did not now officially exist, it was not difficult for them to delay their departure until the last convoy of lorries appeared on 25 September. The teams then descended into their tunnels and the entrances were concealed by their comrades still on the surface.

According to the accounts of the prisoners, a total of 47 men finally went down five tunnels to hide. Seven others concealed themselves in other parts of the camp and remained unfound. Out of an original total of 1,334 prisoners in the camp, 54 was a very small proportion, and only five or six had been able to escape between September 8 and September 21.

Of the five tunnels used, four have already been described and given numbers in this account. The Sewer Tunnel, starting in a firepit of the other ranks' cookhouse, was tunnel 1. This was now used by a group of six: Captain Gordon McFall, Captain D. A. Blair, Captain Collingwood, Captain Borradaile, Sergeant Pilot Wendt, and Corporal J. Campbell. Campbell had worked tirelessly in the foulest conditions in the main camp sewer over many weeks, and he was to be recommended by Captain Blair for a Military Medal for his efforts. Sergeant Spowatt, the miner who had done so much work on the tunnel, particularly in its early stages, did not get a place in the tunnel. Perhaps he had been in the wrong place when the first roll call had begun.

Tunnel 2 was the one that Pennycook and Gregson had been working on, under the leadership of Lieutenant Hugh Gordon-Brown. Into that tunnel now went a group including Pennycook, Lieutenant Guy Weymouth, Royal West Kents, Lieutenant James Cleminson, Army Air Corps, Lieutenant A. D. B. 'Sandy' Hope, 10 Hussars, and of course Hugh Gordon-Brown, in a party of 15. Hope later described the tunnel as 70 yards long, and as being 14 feet deep. About 30 men had worked on it.

Tunnel 3 was Bob Walker Brown's. Only 9 men finally decided to hide in the tunnel. Walker Brown himself went down, together with Lieutenant Ken Bangham, Royal Artillery, Captain C. L. Thomas, Hampshire Regiment, Second Lieutenant J. Tegid Jones, Royal Artillery, Lieutenant W. J. Waldie, Highland Light Infantry, and 4 others. The party for this tunnel had originally been 32 but when they had all tried to hide down the tunnel together, after 20 minutes they discovered there was not enough air. The party was reduced initially to a total of 15, with the others deciding to take their chances elsewhere, and then finally to 9.

Tunnel 4 contained Bill Gordon, the team leader, Second Lieutenant Peter Stern, Royal Engineers, Lieutenant E. C. 'Badgie' Lyte, Royal Artillery, Lieutenant Bob Evans, Captain Vernon Sudbury, Captain Alan George Cameron, Lieutenant Peter Grigg Uglow, Sherwood Foresters, Lieutenant John Jenkins, Lieutenant D. C. Brettell, Royal Engineers, Lieutenant Crabtree, and Lieutenant Clifford Boiteaux-Buchanan, 2 Battalion, Parachute Regiment, captured in Tunisia, making a total of 11 men. The tunnel team had drawn lots as to who might go down and these were the lucky men.

Tunnel 5 was far from complete. It ran from the boiler house and had been going for only four months. It had not got far enough to be used for an escape outside the camp. Amongst those working on this tunnel was Captain J. D. MacKay, Royal Artillery, a Canadian who had served in the regular army since 1933, and who had been caught by Marshall's guard and had suffered the indignity of a spell in the cooler. There were also Lieutenant D. T. Bourhill, Royal Artillery, Lieutenant H. M. Stephens, Royal Tank Regiment, Lieutenant Wright, Lieutenant William Murray, and Pilot Officer Otten, RCAF, another Canadian.

It was not only in tunnels that prisoners now hid. The camp offered a variety of possible hiding places, some more hazardous than others. Three officers, Captain Peter Vaughan, Coldstream Guards, Lieutenant James St Clair-Erskine, Coldstream Guards, and Lieutenant St John Cobley, found room in the loft over the boiler house. On 24 September, as the Germans were collecting the last batch of prisoners, they climbed into the loft, taking with them a plentiful supply of water. Once all the prisoners had gone from the camp, 12 German soldiers were left behind to guard the Red Cross parcel store. The Red Cross officer, Captain MacKenzie ('Red Cross Mac'), was assigned the job of supervising their onward transport to Sulmona. He returned to the camp two or three times, taking the opportunity when he could of whispering messages to those in the tunnels or other hiding places as to the number of Germans still in the camp. His last visit was on the evening of 25 September, when he indicated to Vaughan that he thought the rest of the Germans were about to depart with him and the final batch of Red Cross parcels. During the time that Vaughan and his companions waited in their loft, they were joined by a number of tunnel 5 refugees, who had found the air in their incomplete tunnel simply too foul to breathe.

On Sunday, 26 September, Vaughan and the others felt that the time to come down from their hiding place had arrived. Emerging from the loft, they found that all the Germans had gone. Some Italian guards remained, but they did not interfere with the prisoners. The loft group divided into two and each in turn went over the wall, half an hour apart. St Clair Erskine's group were actually guided across the wall by one of the remaining Italian guards, who then took the men directly to a local peasant farmer's house only a hundred yards or so from the camp, where they were given food and drink. From then on they were rarely without a guide, as they marched for many hours to the south, passed from Italian helper to Italian helper. Just short of the river Sangro, they came across two other escape parties from Campo 21 – Captain Blair, Captain Borradaile and Corporal Campbell from tunnel 1 in one party, and Captain Thomas, Lieutenant Waldie and another from tunnel 3 in the second party. On 1 October, the group crossed the Sangro (later to become the front line that ran also through Monte Cassino) and continued heading south through enemy territory.

About this time, St Clair Erskine found himself separated from the rest of the group, but kept going. He seems to have been the first to cross Allied lines, meeting up with British troops on 4 October. St Clair Erskine was then recruited into A Force and worked with them at Bari for about six weeks. He was, of course, exactly what A Force wanted, an escapee with very recent knowledge of conditions on the other side of the front lines. The others also kept going, and ran into outposts of the 4th Buffs on 16 October. They were then passed back to area HQ and eventually Termoli.

Four men had hidden in the camp water tower: Lieutenant R. C. Rickett, Northamptonshire Regiment, Captain E. R. H. MacDermott, Royal Engineers, Lieutenant Peter Gunn, Rifle Brigade, and Captain A. D. V. Hough, Rifle Brigade and 1SAS. The water tower had a locked door, but a 'burglar' had apparently copied the key. They moved into the tower on the night of 23/24 September, and stayed there until the evening of the 26th. It was a tight fit, and due to the necessary use of a lavatory bucket, unpleasant. Because of the close vicinity of German sentries, they had to remain absolutely silent at all times. They were, however, able to watch the Germans searching the camp as they evacuated the remaining prisoners. On 24 September, there was a scare in the morning when a British other rank made an attempt to enter the water tower. Then in the afternoon an Italian did enter the lower level of the tower and turned the water on. He didn't apparently spot them and left, locking the door behind him. This meant that the men were now locked in. It was very hot and they were plagued by mosquitos. Through 25 and 26 September they remained silent and still, and only on the evening of the 26th did they make their break. Hough recalls that they had been spotted in the water tower by children now playing in the camp. Once out of the tower (they had to break the door open) they left over the wall without difficulty and made contact with the local people, who turned out to be friendly.

Gunn and Hough decided to wait in the area for the arrival of the Allied 8th Army, but Rickett and MacDermott, rather more realistically, opted to move south straight away. Obtaining civilian clothes from local Italian helpers in Chieti, as well as much more help on their way south, Rickett and MacDermott crossed into Allied territory on about 10 October. Gunn and Hough waited in vain for Allied troops to arrive in the Chieti area, and eventually moved off with help from the locals. They had a more difficult time – they were still in hiding and dodging the Germans on Christmas Day 1943, when finally they became separated. Hough eventually managed to cross the front line to freedom on 28 December.

The men in tunnel 1 had entered their tunnel at 1200hrs on 24 September. The last party was due to be transported from the camp by the Germans at 1300hrs. Only six went into this tunnel, which was less roomy than some. They split up into pairs: McFall and Collingwood occupied the forward chamber under the outer wire, from which their exit would be made, Wendt and Campbell occupied the centre, and Borradaile and Blair the entrance chamber. All had their escape rations, home-made maps and compasses with them. They heard the last batch of prisoners leave, but activity continued above them for some time as the Germans apparently looted the camp. They remained in their tunnel overnight and continued to lie up all the following day. It was not until the night of 25 September that they made their break. They only had to remove six inches of earth from the exit to the tunnel to break out, and they found themselves outside the main wall, between it and the wire. The group now split into two parties. Borradaile, Blair and Wendt initially travelled together. Wendt then joined McFall and Collingwood, and Blair, Borradaile and Campbell continued together, reaching Allied lines on 13 October 1943. Wendt, McFall and Collingwood met up with the same SAS/A force operation that Weaver and Newman encountered, intended to lift them off the coast by sea, but that plan failed when a German coastal craft realized what was going on and opened fire. Wendt and Collingwood became separated from McFall, and later Wendt continued on his own, eventually crossing over into Allied territory on 6 November. He, like so many others, received substantial help from local Italians. Bill Wendt was one of those who fulfilled the escaper's dream of being home by Christmas. He commented to the British press that one of the most difficult things to adjust to when he arrived there, before heading back to the

USA, was the abundance of food – even in Britain, during rationing. He said that he did not know there was so much food in the world after going through his experience.

The men in tunnel 2 waited two days and nights, then broke out, split into small parties and made off. Gordon-Brown and Hope headed south. They also received a lot of help from the locals. After 12 days' hard walking, they lay up for a further 12 days in the hope that the Allied advance would overrun them. When it failed to do so, they became impatient and decided to creep through the German front lines. This they successfully accomplished, running into a patrol of the West Kents on the evening of 22 October 1943. Sandy Hope, a 25-year-old from London, and an old Etonian, was back in London well before Christmas. He was photographed there by the *Daily Express*, with cigar and drink in hand as he told the story of his escape. A large number of escaped prisoners had been and still were on the loose in Italy as a result of the Armistice, and the *Daily Express* referred to Hope as being 'one of Britain's Lost Legion'. At least three others from tunnel 2 also got through to safety – Pennycook, Cleminson and Weymouth.

The men in tunnel 3, Bob Walker Brown's outfit, numbered nine in all. This was a narrow tunnel in which it was impossible to turn round, with neither much space nor air. The nine men went in, like the other teams, before the last group of prisoners were transported from the camp, and other members of the team concealed the entrance for them from above. Walker Brown recalls that the air soon became very foul in there and that there was very little oxygen, since with the camp empty of prisoners, there was nobody to help by pumping air into the tunnels or aerating them in any other way. Eventually, Walker Brown and his team decided that the coast was clear and came back into the camp, then leaving it with little trouble. They split into smaller groups and walked south. Unlike various of the other teams of escapers, Walker Brown had little or no contact with the local Italians. He preferred to take no chances at all, and moved only by night. He and his two companions stole civilian clothing, leaving their better quality battledress in exchange. Despite being stopped at one point near to the front line by German troops, and recruited as 'Italian' labourers to dig defensive positions for them, happily, those Germans rapidly retreated in the face of the Allied advance, leaving their temporary labourers behind. About three weeks after leaving Campo 21, Walker Brown's group got through to Allied lines.

The men in tunnel 4 went inside at 0600hrs on 24 September, earlier than most, intending to remain there for 36 hours. They had with them one Red Cross parcel and an American emergency ration, plus a supply of water to keep them going in the horrible conditions. They also had their escape kits, including maps and escape cake. They had a 'pee tin' to pass from man to man during their stay in the tunnel, for obvious purposes. They planned to leave their tunnel at 2300hrs on 25 September, via the exit beyond the wall that they had completed on 15 September. At 0830hrs, the watchers helping them on the surface informed them that the main body of men was not now moving until 1300hrs, so they were able to come back out, enjoy the fresh air, eat and wash. They went back down at 1130hrs. Time passed painfully slowly, and the air worsened. They survived an awful night, with little sleep. Conditions were very cramped and there was little room to turn over. In most parts of the tunnel, the men had to lie stretched out head to toe, with only 18 inches of space above them. There was only one point at which it was possible to stretch a little, in the main shaft of the tunnel, where two people at a time could sit up. The air there was also slightly better. Every two hours, although it was a difficult manoeuvre, the two men in the main shaft would rotate with others, so all got at least a little relief.

In the morning, the air was very hot and thick. The hours dragged by. In the afternoon of 25 September they began to feel hopeful that, finally, they would soon be free. Then, at about 1600 or 1700hrs, disaster struck. The 11 dirty, tired and uncomfortable men heard a loud banging at the tunnel exit. They presumed that the Germans had found the tunnel and would soon come down after them – hopefully without throwing down a grenade first. An enormous sense of despair swept over the weary and filthy group. However, the banging stopped and all went quiet. After a suitable but very nervous wait, Alan Cameron crawled forward to investigate what had happened at the mouth of the tunnel. He found that it had obviously been discovered and had been filled in. It was no longer open to them to get out that way. According to Crabtree, they found out later that when the team in a parallel tunnel to theirs had broken out (either tunnel 1 or 2), they had asked the locals to fill in the exit for them, so that the Germans would not later spot it and come looking for escapers. But the locals had apparently filled in both exits, believing all the escapers to have gone. In tunnel 4, the team could not know this, and assumed it was the Germans. Cameron returned to report and a whispered conference was held. Morale was now very low and all the men were feeling pretty ill because of the lack of oxygen. Seven of the team decided that they would return to the surface via the entrance as soon as it was dark, and would take their chances at escaping through the camp. The other four, Gordon, Lyte, Stern and Evans, decided to stick to the original plan and stay where they were. If only four remained down, they hoped that the air might be a little more bearable. At 2000hrs, just after dark, Sudbury, Cameron, Uglow, Jenkins, Brettel, Crabtree and Boiteaux-Buchanan exited the tunnel, closed up the entrance, and crept into the bungalow. There, they cleaned themselves up and changed from their tunnel clothes into battledress. Looking out carefully from the bungalow, it appeared that the camp had more or less been abandoned. They could see that there were still a few Italian *carabinieri* around, and a single German sentry on the main gate. Sudbury and his team decided that they would make the break at once, after sending a message back down the tunnel that the coast was sufficiently clear for the others to come out. Watching from their bungalow, they could see that another tunnel team had come to the surface on the opposite side of the camp, presumably Bob Walker Brown's team from tunnel 3. Using a ladder, these men went over the wall near the water tower at a point far from the main gate. When Sudbury, Jenkins and the other five got to the same spot, they found the ladder had gone, so fetched a home-made bed-board ladder from their bungalow, specially constructed for just such a purpose as this. They successfully used the ladder to climb the wall and jump down to freedom. In the dark, with no sentries on the wall and, most importantly, no searchlights, they attracted no attention. Once out of the camp they split into pairs and headed for the nearby Pescara river, rendezvousing at a mill by the bathing place that they had been allowed to use. They then marched 5 miles in the dark, to put a safe distance between themselves and the camp, and lay up during the following day. Eventually, again with plenty of help from local Italians, they made their way south. Sudbury travelled with Cameron and Uglow, and the three men crossed into Allied territory on 12 October. All three had been captured at Tobruk, and had therefore been behind enemy lines for nearly 16 months.

Captain Clifford 'Bucky' Boiteaux-Buchanan, a racehorse trainer before the war and now a member of 2 Para, was also put in touch, by a friendly Italian, with Captain Lee of the SAS, who was collecting up as many escaped prisoners as possible. Boiteaux-Buchanan, with Brettel, Jenkins and Crabtree, waited with Lee and a number of fellow escapees at the beach for three nights. When the A Force attempt to evacuate them failed, the four men travelled south together on foot for some time, then they split up. Jenkins eventually got through the lines on 30 October. Boiteaux-Buchanan suffered an experience similar to Walker Brown's when he was rounded up by the Germans as an Italian, and put to forced labour. Happily, he spoke good Italian and was able to carry it off. He worked for two days without food, digging slit trenches on the north side of the river Sangro, where the Germans were creating a defensive line. When the work was done they let Boiteaux-Buchanan go and he crossed over south of the Sangro again. He was still in a German-occupied area, however, and noted a lot of bad behaviour by apparently drunken troops. The Germans were well aware that there were prisoners of war trying to move through the area and Boiteaux-Buchanan noted one particular tactic that they used. He observed SS troopers dressed as civilians, pretending to be escaped prisoners of war and approaching local Italians, asking to be put in touch with other escapers. At one point, because the Germans would only allow women out on the streets, Boiteaux-Buchanan dressed as a woman to go on a reconnaissance expedition looking for a way through the German positions. He found none. Fortunately, on 5 November the Allied advances forced the Germans to fall back and Boiteaux-Buchanan was able to make contact with his own side again. In the end, it seems that all seven of these escapers made it through Allied lines. He was awarded a Military Cross for his escape and for his efforts to help other ex-prisoners.

In the incomplete tunnel 5, six men were hiding: MacKay, Bourhill, Stephens, Wright, William Murray and Otten. They took down with them into the unpleasant conditions enough food and water to last for at least two days. They went into their hiding place at 1100hrs on 24 September and stayed in the tunnel until about 2330 on 26 September, two and a half days later. They were taking no chances. However, it can only be this group that sheltered for a time with St Clair Erskine, Vaughan and Cobley in the boiler house loft. When they finally emerged, they had no difficulty in going straight over the wall by ladder, and crossing the the wire on the outside. The two Canadians, MacKay and Otten, then travelled together and, with Bourhill, set out to walk south to Allied lines. They received civilian clothes, food and shelter and guides from local people along the way. On 8 October they had a shock when they were spotted and interrogated by two German soldiers on patrol. However, Bourhill spoke enough Italian to eventually convince them that they were just Italian peasants, and they were allowed to continue. They crossed over into Allied territory on 14 October 1943. The other group from their tunnel had in fact beaten them to it. William Murray, Cooper and Cobley had reached Allied territory five days earlier on 9 October.

In total, the author has been able to identify 54 prisoners who stayed behind in Campo 21 after the Germans had gone. Of these, a remarkably high proportion successfully made a 'home run'. In addition, Weaver, Rideout, Lodge and Newman, who had escaped against orders before the arrival of the Germans, also got through. Thus, it seems that the success rate for escapes was high. Applied to the camp as a whole, that would suggest that, even allowing for 'lame ducks', out of the total of 1,334 prisoners, more than half might have got through had they had the chance, and most of the others would have been recaptured and imprisoned in Germany. With the benefit of that hindsight, it is difficult to find any justification for Marshall's decision.

Toby Graham's basic rule for escapers was, 'If you are going to try to escape, do it as soon as possible.' That certainly applied after the Armistice in September 1943, with Italy in near total confusion. When it became clear that the Germans were going to make a stand in Italy, all sorts of people were heading south. Very many Italians wished to avoid further military service, and tried to reach 'free' Italy, while others took to the mountains to avoid being pressed into the new Fascist brigades once they were formed. Various other nationalities who found themselves in Italy when the Armistice was announced also sought to get south to Allied lines. All of this must have been obvious to those in Campo 21 who were analysing the general war situation. After 8 September, they could see with their own eyes the Italian sentries scarpering over the camp walls, heading for their homes. Lieutenant Colonel Marshall must have known all this. Other SBOs reacted appropriately, he did not.

In fairness, when looking at the success rate for escapes there was one factor that nobody anticipated and which enabled many to succeed who would otherwise have failed. This was the help given to many escapees by the Italian locals. Most of those who had been imprisoned in the camps expected hostility from local people when they escaped. After all, the Italians had just lost an expensive and bloody war against them, and Allied aircraft had bombed many of their cities and towns, inevitably killing many civilians as well as hitting military targets. Ex-prisoners of war might feel that they, as the victors, could demand a certain degree of assistance from the Italians, but had no expectation that help would be given voluntarily. This book is not the place to deal with the extraordinary self-sacrifice that many ordinary Italians made (particularly the peasant farmers in the mountains, the *contadini*) to help Allied escapers. Many were shot by the Germans and their homes burned to the ground because of the help that they gave.[4] Reading the accounts that the ex-prisoners from Campo 21 gave of their escapes, the vast majority had depended on the locals for food and shelter, and many were helped by local Italian guides. Bob Walker Brown's group were an exception, and of course Rifleman Collarbone was eventually betrayed by Italian guides. There were still Fascists about.

[4]   See *SAS in Tuscany 1943–45* by Brian Lett

Postscript

THE PRISONERS

Looking back later upon their periods of imprisonment, many of the ex-prisoners of war try to remember the positive aspects of the situation they were forced to be in. George Hervey-Murray comments: 'Whilst I would never wish it on anyone, I believe that the experience of having to endure the life of a prisoner of war is very character building. It taught one certain values and also how to exist with other men under conditions of extreme deprivation and hunger, and I am sure that some good came out of the experience. I learnt a great deal … which I would never have acquired under normal conditions.'

Despite the strongly critical views that many of the prisoners at Campo 21 had held of their Italian guards, those who escaped discovered a very different sort of Italian, often themselves dreadfully impoverished, who were prepared to shelter them and feed the ex-prisoners on the run, though under threat of death from the Germans and Fascists if they did so. The Monte San Martino Trust, mentioned earlier in this book, is a charity set up by Allied ex-prisoners of war to commemorate the sacrifices and generosity of the ordinary Italian people towards those escapees. Those who escaped, whether from Chieti or from other camps such as Veano or Fontanellato, from the Sulmona camp (where the ex-Chieti prisoners were held for a time pending transport to Germany), or from trains and lorries, have continued to support the Trust, together with their families, in an endeavour to perpetuate the gratitude of thousands of Allied prisoners. A significant number of those transported away from Campo 21 by the Germans escaped later. Osborne, Spowatt, Michael Murray and MacLucas and the US pilot Jim Beck were amongst those who escaped from

Sulmona. Sam Webster and his friend Bill Harrison also got out from Sulmona camp and were home in the USA by Christmas. The same was true of Joseph Frelinghuysen, who crossed into Allied hands on 15 November. The Welshman, David Roberts, attempted to escape from a truck that was carrying him from the camp at Sulmona to Sulmona railway station for transport onwards to Germany, but was shot in the foot. He was taken to the civilian hospital in Sulmona. Also held in the civilian hospital was Rodney Hill, who had been ill during the end of his time in Campo 21, and had been transferred to the hospital for a minor operation. Both men were supplied with civilian clothes by Italian visitors to the hospital, and on 8 October 1943, they climbed out of a window and escaped. After being sheltered by local helpers for three months, both men made the journey south with an Italian guide, and crossed the Allied front line on 15 January 1944. Roberts was awarded an MC for his escape, Hill a mention in despatches. Sam Derry, Kenwyn Walters, Richard Edmonston Low, Tony Baines and John Lepine were amongst those who escaped from trains. Some got home, some did not. Derry found his way to the Vatican City, where he was joined by Lieutenant John Furman, Royal Artillery, and Joe Pollak, and went on to set up the Rome escape network. Some of those who decided not to hide in the tunnels or other parts of the camp were therefore justified in their confidence that they would be able to break away from the Germans before they got to Germany.

The escapees enjoyed mixed fortunes. Some were recaptured after varying periods at liberty. Some died trying to get through enemy lines to Allied territory. A surprising number, however, succeeded in getting through and were able to rejoin the Allied forces and fight on. Many of those played a valuable part in the remainder of the war, and some gave their lives for their countries. Claude Weaver returned to action and won himself a Distinguished Flying Cross, but was shot down and killed on 28 January 1944. His friend Bill Wendt did not survive him very long, suffering a similar fate over France in June of the same year. Bucky Boiteaux-Buchanan was killed at Arnhem Bridge on 20 September 1944.

However, of those who, because of Lieutenant Colonel Marshall's insistence on adhering to the 'Stay Put' order, passed into German hands, the vast majority, including the likes of Bill Bowes, Freddie Brown, Gordon Horner, Paul Hardwick, Tony Maxtone Graham, Arthur Green, Ian Tennant and Pip Gardner VC and Gordon Norbrook were transported to Germany, where they served a further 18 months' imprisonment, much of it in Oflag 79, the Brunswick camp. As Marshall was to say in interviews later, they at least survived the war. Out of their incarceration grew the Brunswick Boys Club in Fulham, London, for which they collected money whilst in prison camp, and which did excellent work for youngsters for many years after the war and continues to do so today.

Three veterans of the Sewer Tunnel at Chieti, Toby Graham, Dennis Duke and Tony Roncoroni all escaped from Fontanellato at the Armistice, and eventually got through to freedom. Toby Graham at last crossed into Allied territory in company with Michael Gilbert. Graham, Roncoroni and Captain Peter Joscelyne, Royal Tank Regiment, had previously escaped from Fontanellato in May 1943, after burying themselves in the football field, but all three had been recaptured. Graham, Duke and Roncoroni all returned to battle, and each later won a Military Cross. Tony Roncoroni, sadly, later lost a different battle with cancer and died in 1952. Toby Graham enjoyed a long and very active life. He remained in the army after the war until the mid-1950s, and amongst other achievements was a member of the British Cross-Country Ski team at the Winter Olympics in Cortona in 1956. After leaving the army, he emigrated to Canada, where he became a professor of history and wrote several well-received books. He returned eventually to live in Yorkshire. In 2001 and again in 2002, I had the pleasure of walking with him on the Monte San Martino Freedom Trails in the Abbruzzo. In 2001 Toby, by then in his eighties, walked the entire route from Sulmona to Castel di Sangro over four days. In May of the following year he tried it again, but seized up on a snow-covered mountainside on day 3 of the trail, and had to be evacuated on a stretcher. On day 4, however, Toby was back on his feet, and duly completed the course. He died in March 2013.

After the war, Michael Gilbert developed his legal career and simultaneously began to write crime thrillers, and in due course stage plays. His first thriller was published in 1946 and his sixth book, *Death in Captivity*, published in 1952, was based on his experiences in Campo 21, and later Fontanellato. Many of the real-life incidents described in this book appear in *Death in Captivity* in a fictionalized form, and Gilbert dedicated the book to Toby Graham and Tony Davies, the two men with whom he escaped with from Fontanellato after the Armistice. In 1959, it was turned into a successful film, *Danger Within*, starring Richard Todd, Michael Wilding and Richard Attenborough. Gilbert was a prolific and highly successful author. He died in February 2006 at the age of 93.

One of the more dramatic Chieti reunions took place on 27 December 1944, when Captain Bob Walker Brown, now of 2SAS, parachuted with a troop of his men into German-occupied northern Italy to reinforce a band of partisans led by Major Gordon Lett, at this point an SOE liaison officer. Lett had not left Italy after his escape from Veano and had been fighting with the Italian partisans for over a year.[5] He was awarded a Mention in Despatches for his work with the Chieti News Agency and a DSO for his efforts with the partisans. Bob Walker Brown remained in the army after the war, and eventually became a lieutenant colonel of 22 SAS. Gordon Lett remained in the Army until 1948, but in fact was fully engaged on intelligence duties from the moment of Italian liberation in April/May 1945. He transferred to the Foreign Office, and remained in the intelligence community for many years.

As mentioned earlier, Paul Hardwick first appeared on the West End stage at the Piccadilly Theatre in 1946, playing Scarus in *Antony and Cleopatra*, alongside Edith Evans and Godfrey Tearle. He developed a very successful post-war career on the stage, also in film and television. He died 'in harness' on a Saturday night, 22 October 1983, a few weeks short of his 65th birthday. Tony Maxtone Graham went through a divorce, and Gordon Horner continued his artistic career, indulging his love of cars and becoming the staff artist for *Autocar* magazine, later working also for *The Motor Cycle* and *Classic Car*. Ian Tennant worked in Caledonian Associated Cinemas until they won the franchise for new Independent Television in the northeast and highlands of Scotland, and set up Grampian Television. Tennant became the chairman of Grampian Television in 1968, and was eventually knighted in 1986.

The sportsmen met with mixed fortunes. Bill Bowes, in his late thirties, returned to play again for Yorkshire, but not for England. He had lost more than 4 stone in weight during his time as a prisoner of war. With the cessation of hostilities, county cricket began to get back to normal in August 1945. Between 13 and 15 August, Bowes played in a Yorkshire vs Lancashire Roses match, for the benefit of the dependants of his long-time friend and colleague Hedley Verity, who had died of his wounds during the war. In a spell of 12 overs, Bowes took 3 Lancashire wickets for 11 runs, but then broke down with a badly pulled muscle. The following season, 1946, brought a reunion of Bowes and Harold Beaumont on the cricket field, with Beaumont playing 25 innings for Yorkshire. However, for Beaumont, his best years had gone. He played in only six first class matches for Yorkshire in the following season, 1947, again with Bowes, and failed to establish himself as a first choice Yorkshire batman. Bowes retired at the end of the 1947 season and neither he nor Beaumont played first-class cricket for Yorkshire again.

---

[5]   The full story of Operation Galia is told in *SAS in Tuscany 1943–45*, by Brian Lett.

Freddie Brown was the exception. He too had lost around 4 stone as a result of his time as a prisoner of war and returned only slowly to first-class cricket, concentrating first on his business career. In November 1948, however, he was asked if he would like to captain struggling Northamptonshire the following season, and he accepted that challenge. In 1949, Brown had a sparkling season, doing the double of 1,000 runs and 100 wickets for the second time. This led in the following season to a resurgence of his England career, and he captained England to Australia and New Zealand in the winter of 1950/1. He enjoyed two more golden years, falling one wicket short of doing the double again in 1952, before retiring at the end of the 1953 season. He remained involved in England cricket as a selector and tour manager for many years thereafter.

WAR CRIMES

Farrell

Farrell was sent to Campo 5 at Gavi, in breach of his agreement with Barela. Campo 5 was a medieval castle set on a hill, and on the hillsides and in Gavi town there was an enemy garrison. The escape rate from Gavi was even lower than that from Colditz, and although some got out of the castle itself, no one got away from the immediate area of the camp. When, on 8 September 1943, the Italian Armistice was declared and Italy nominally withdrew from the war, there was already a German garrison in place at Gavi and no opportunity for escape. When the time came for the prisoners of Campo 5 to be removed to Germany, some did manage to escape from the trains which carried them. Whitby, who had escaped from Chieti disguised as Croce, was one of them. He jumped from a train carrying him north to Germany, damaging his ankle in the fall but succeeding in getting clear. Masquerading again as an Italian officer, he travelled by train to Pisa, where his relatives were able to provide him with more money and clothing. Whitby then went into hiding with the Italian *contadini* in the mountains, until his damaged ankle healed. He eventually travelled on by train to Aquila and walked south from there, finally crossing the front line and making contact with Allied troops on 24 October 1943. Farrell was not so fortunate, and ended up in Oflag VIII F in Germany. It was there, on 20 April 1944, that Farrell first put into writing his complaint about Barela's treatment of him, in a statement witnessed by two of his fellow prisoners. However, it was not until after his release in April 1945 that Farrell was able to make a formal complaint, on oath, to the British Military authorities. An investigation then began, which in due course led to the arrest of Lieutenant Colonel Mario Barela. For a Camp Commandant to personally assault a prisoner in his charge in the way that Farrell described was clearly a serious breach of the Geneva Convention, and the threats and further ill-treatment that Farrell had received both from Barela and from the guards under his command compounded the crime. It was decided that Barela should be prosecuted under the War Crimes regime.

Under arrest on 11 April 1946, Barela made a written statement through an interpreter, to an investigator Captain N. E. Middleton of the department of the Judge Advocate General. In the statement, Barela demonstrated the arrogance that had been so resented by the Allied prisoners. He started by saying: 'I was posted to 21 PoW Camp at Chieti as Camp Commandant in the early days of August 1942, and I remained there for about two months. I was not satisfied with my appointment as Camp Commander, and I applied to my superiors in order to be relieved from this task. As I did not take too much interest in running the camp, I am not able to remember the names of members of my staff.'

Barela accepted that he had visited Farrell in the early hours of the morning shortly after his return to the camp and agreed that he had confined him to a small space in the courtyard, but claimed that that had been to 'avoid him getting in touch with any other PoWs'. He made no admission to having used threats, and said that after that first occasion, he had not seen Farrell for two or three days. Then, according to Barela:

I was called early in the morning, I do not remember by whom, and I was informed that there had been a noise in the cell, and that it was suspected that the prisoner was attempting to re-escape ... I believe that only Captain Croce and I entered the cell ... I had with me a bamboo cane which I always used to carry along. I was not in a calm mood, because I was worried about the reaction of my superiors. I told the prisoner, through Captain Croce, that I did not want to be awakened at such an unusual time. The POW answered that he did not want to be alone in his cell and I made it clear to him that he return to the camp as soon as the enquiry was completed. During this conversation, I gesticulated with my hands, but in spite of the fact that I was holding the cane, I did at no time strike the POW. I remained in the cell for 5 or 6 minutes, and then I returned to my room ... in the following days ... Captain Croce went several times to see the POW and obtained a statement from him explaining how he had escaped ... the prisoner was informed that he would not be charged for the theft of a bicycle that he had used during his escape. In spite of my promise to the POW that he would not be transferred, this was later done by order of the Army Corps at Bari...

Captain Croce, who was also being held pending investigations of war crimes, was interviewed about the allegations against Barela, and a witness statement was taken from him on 27 February 1946. Croce was not prepared to help Barela, and at the same time was keen to ingratiate himself with the British authorities and to minimize his own involvement. He confirmed that on the night of Farrell's return to the camp, Barela had visited Farrell and ordered him to stand in the confined space behind the guard room wall, and that he gave orders for the guards to shoot Farrell if he strayed outside the small area. In relation to the night of the beating, Croce confirmed that Farrell had been held against the wall of his cell at bayonet point, and continued:

The Commandant was in a very bad temper, and I saw him strike Lieutenant Farrell once or twice with the stick. I had a feeling that something like this was going to happen even before it took place, and as soon as I saw what the Commandant intended to do, I left the cell. I have the impression that after leaving the cell I heard Lieutenant Farrell call out as if in pain, but I did not stay in the vicinity and went back to bed as it was apparent that I was not needed as an interpreter. I would say that at the time I was somewhat confused as I had been dragged from bed to go to the cell and was still a little dazed ... The following morning, I again went with the Commandant to the cell to see Lieutenant Farrell. The Commandant said through me that he was sorry to hear that he [Lieutenant Farrell] had had a nightmare the previous night, but that these nightmares would continue until it was found out how he had managed to escape ...

According to Croce, Barela had even tried to persuade the Church of England padre, Major Chutter, to 'use his spiritual connections with Lieutenant Farrell in order to obtain information on his escape'. Chutter's own statement to the investigators does not quite agree with that, and his detailed account of what happened has already been set out. By mid-April 1946, the investigators had clear evidence from Farrell that Barela had assaulted him, plus the support of Croce. Even though Croce was a witness who was in many ways open to doubt (he was described in internal correspondence in the Judge Advocate's department as an extremely unpleasant and untruthful person), the prosecution were entitled to call him as to what had happened in the cell – even liars can on occasion tell the truth, and he gave direct evidence that Barela had assaulted Farrell. Significantly, Barela himself had admitted to entering Farrell's cell carrying a cane and to being extremely angry.

Unfortunately, Barela was very well connected – no doubt one reason for his arrogance and pomposity. Already, by 16 April 1946, the office of the Deputy Judge Advocate General, General Headquarters [GHQ], Central Mediterranean Forces, was warning London that they had 'recently received various representations on behalf of Barela, mainly from Italian Espiscopal sources, who appear to take a great interest in his welfare, and you may think it advisable that under the circumstances, the case against him should be dealt with as expeditiously as possible.' Barela's connections were applying pressure to secure his release. However, the investigators in the Judge Advocate's department were quite confident that they had a good case.

A question was also raised about Barela's health. It seems that this factor, together with the pressure that was being brought to bear, finally persuaded GHQ to drop the case against Barela. A staff minute and letter announced on 20 June that the case was not to be brought to trial: Barela was to be released. The Judge Advocate's department was angry at the decision, and undoubtedly wondered whether some improper pressure had had its effect on GHQ. On 17 July 1946, Brigadier H. Shapcott, Military Deputy at the Judge Advocate's department, wrote to GHQ protesting that the evidence provided a strong case against the ex-Commandant. Shapcott stressed the seriousness of the case, saying: 'At the time of the beating and ill-treatment, Barela was not only the Commandant of a prisoner-of-war camp, but also an officer of the rank of lieutenant colonel in the Italian army … may I ask you to reconsider your decision in this case … the trial could take place with very little delay.' Brigadier Shapcott received his reply in a letter from the Commander in Chief, Mediterranean Forces, dated 13 August 1946. It read as follows:

1. The principal factor which led to the decision not to bring Barela to trial was that he was in failing health, and that it appeared unlikely that he would be able to stand trial, or that any punishment inflicted by the court could be carried out.

2. Coupled with this was the fact that he has been in custody for over three months, and considerable pressure was being brought to bear on this HQ by the Ministry of Grace and Justice, by important business interests and by the Vatican for Barela's release. It was apparent that even if he was brought to trial, the weight of the evidence of character which the defence was prepared to bring would result in only a nominal sentence being awarded.

3. The Military resources of this theatre are so limited that it is necessary to restrict war crimes trials to those relating to serious offences in respect of which severe sentences are likely to be awarded, The Barela case does not fall in this category and could only be tried at the expense of more important cases; accordingly it was decided to drop it. This policy has been communicated to the War Office and it is not possible to change it unless the resources of the theatre in Judge Advocate General Staff and War Crimes Staff are increased.

4. Barela (and Croce) have been released and no further action is contemplated.

Readers will form their own view as to whether justice was done. They may feel that, in the aftermath of the war, Lieutenant Colonel Mario Barela, who had personally beaten up one of his prisoners, got away with it. Sadly, he was not alone.

Outerbridge

In due course, the RAF War Crimes Investigation Branch began an investigation into the killing of Jim Outerbridge, and once the war had been won, a number of the former Italian guards were arrested, including Barbarito and Papantonio. On 18 January 1946, Papantonio was interviewed by Sergeant K. Thompson of the RAF Police Special Investigation Branch, and made a statement under the criminal caution that was current at the time – namely that he was not obliged to say anything unless he wished to do so, but that anything he did say would be taken down and given in evidence. Papantonio denied firing any shots himself, and stated: 'I do not know who fired at the prisoner.' He claimed that although he had raised the alarm when he saw the prisoner climbing out of the window, by the time he got off the train on to the platform, the prisoner was already lying on the ground wounded, and he and his colleagues had been ordered to lift him back on the train, and had placed him in the guard's van. His account is difficult to reconcile with the fact that Commandant Massi rewarded his efforts with the sum of 100 lire.

For the investigators, the problems were those common to many such investigations after the war. One of the key witnesses, Pilot Officer Weaver, escaped before the end of the war and crossed through Allied lines, then returned to active duty and was killed. Lieutenant Eric Lawton survived a little longer. On 25 February 1945, a barrister called Wilfred Price, who was assigned to investigate Italian war crimes, interviewed him and prepared an affidavit for him, in which he identified Papantonio as Outerbridge's murderer. However, Eric Lawton returned to active service shortly thereafter and was killed in action on 6 April 1945, before he could sign and swear the affidavit. Lieutenant Pritchford, who may have had the best view of all of the killing of Jim Outerbridge, because he had put his head out of the window after Outerbridge's escape to watch events on the platform, was recorded as missing in Italy, and the war crimes investigators never managed to trace him.

Papantonio's photograph was sent to Lieutenant Edwin Lee, in the hope that he might be able to make a positive identification of him as the guard who had killed Outerbridge. However, when asked in May 1946, three years after the event, Lieutenant Lee not surprisingly replied that although Papantonio's face was familiar, he could not definitely say that he was the man who had fired the fusillade of shots that killed Outerbridge. At about the same time, on the night of 4/5 May 1946, there was a mass escape of Italians being held on suspicion of war crimes from a prison camp near Naples. Papantonio and Barbarito were amongst those who escaped, and there is no evidence that they were ever recaptured. In the absence of any living witnesses who could identify Papantonio as Outerbridge's killer, the prosecuting department concluded with considerable reluctance that any prosecution was doomed to failure. The investigation against Papantonio and Barbarito was eventually discontinued.

The author visited the place at which Jim Outerbridge was murdered in November 2013, to pay his respects. The journey north from Chieti to Cattolica is a long one, lasting a minimum of three hours today, and doubtless far longer in the wartime conditions of May 1943. It was easy to understand the mounting frustration that Jim Outerbridge felt, as he sat in his carriage with the villages and countryside passing by. The seaside belt on which Cattolica is situated is now extensively developed for the holiday trade and the station is no longer jointly named after nearby Gradara, which sits with its splendid castle atop a nearby hill. The station itself is surrounded by houses and commercial buildings, and both sides of the railway are fenced for safety. In November, Cattolica was virtually deserted, as all of the holiday hotels were closed. Therefore it was possible to spend a few quiet moments at the station and to place a British Legion cross with James Edwin Outerbridge's name on it on the platform where he was almost certainly killed – the northbound platform as the trains run today.

Croce

Complaints of ill treatment and cruelty came thick and fast against those who had been running Campo 21 as the various successful escapees returned home. However, the war in Italy continued, and initially the priority remained that of achieving victory. Allied troops did not reach Chieti until June 1944, after the fall of Monte Cassino and the German Gustav defensive line in May. The Italian staff in Campo 21, like all Italians, had had a number of choices after the Armistice. They could side with the Germans and Mussolini's new Fascist party, or join the resistance and partisans, or try to find their way south to 'free' Italy, or simply fade away into the hills and mountains. Croce was a man whom, according to Major Sell, the prisoners had wanted to lynch after the Armistice. He is the one man whom all prisoners in Campo 21 remembered afterwards, usually with hatred. It is not clear what Croce did immediately after the camp had been closed. He was still in contact with Rome, and Rome remained in German and Fascist hands. However, once the Gustav line collapsed and the Germans retreated to take up their second defensive line, the Gothic Line far to the north, Croce clearly decided that the 'writing was on the wall' for Fascism, and changed sides. The evidence suggests that his wife was living in Naples, now in Allied hands. There was a shortage amongst Allied forces of Italian interpreters, and in the autumn of 1944 Croce managed to obtain a job interpreting for his old enemies, the British. In September 1944, Captain Croce was attached to 2 Royal Tank Regiment during their operations against the Gothic Line. He remained with them until 22 November, acting as a liaison officer. During this time, in what was a supreme irony, he was permitted to wear the badge of the 2 Royal Tank Regiment on his battledress. Once Croce left 2 Royal Tank Regiment, he was meant to remove the badge, but in fact he never did and continued until the end of the war to wear it. Lieutenant Colonel Lascelles, the Commanding Officer, commented: 'Captain Croce proved to be quite useless in his duties, his energies being devoted to attempts to visit his wife in Naples rather than to the furtherance of the war effort; it was difficult to understand why he held commissioned rank. It was a relief to this regiment when he was posted away …'

Eventually, in 1946, as described above, an investigation started into possible war crimes in Campo 21. Barela, Massi and Croce were all arrested and held in custody. Some of what Croce had to say has already been set out. Croce did everything possible to exculpate himself, even claiming that after the Armistice he had been suspended by Colonel Massi because he had tried to help 12 prisoners of war to escape. There were difficulties, as always in the post-war situation, with gathering evidence. Eventually it was decided that there was not enough evidence to prosecute Croce, mainly because too many of the witnesses had died later in the war. The Judge Advocate General's department decided in May 1946 to let Croce go, but with the comment: 'Croce appears to be an extremely unpleasant and untruthful person, and it is regretted that sufficient evidence is not held in this Office to justify a charge against him.'

Campo 21

Campo 21 did not remain empty for long after evacuation. It became a transit camp for Allied prisoners captured in various parts of northern Italy – a staging post on their journey towards Germany. The German front line solidified in the late autumn along the river Sangro. It became known as the Gustav Line and included the stronghold of Monte Cassino. The Germans and Fascists held out there until May 1944, and Chieti finally fell to the Allies in June 1944. Tony Gregson revisited the camp with his wife in April 1953. Not very much had changed. He was able to surprise the Italian garrison by showing them the entrance to his tunnel, tunnel 2, which was still concealed under the drain hatch beside what had been his bungalow. I myself visited Campo 21 on 18 November 2013. Clouds covered the sun, it had been raining the evening before, and at about midday the temperature was only 15 degrees centigrade. The temperature dropped appreciably later in the afternoon, and by 1600hrs I needed a jacket and light sweater. That night, I was grateful for a warm coat.

The camp has been continually occupied by the Italian military since the end of the Second World War. Around it, a bustling modern community has grown up and the fields are long gone. However, the original 4-metre high walls are still there, with barbed wire and broken glass on the top, although houses and commercial premises now nestle up to them on all sides. After the war, the camp was used for a while by the Folgore, the Italian parachute brigade, but it has been occupied for many years now by the *Carabinieri*, the Italian military police, and it is currently the administrative base of the Comando Generale dell'Arma dei Carabinieri. I was welcomed by the current Comandante, Colonello Marco Mochi, who extended to me a very genuine welcome and every possible courtesy. For the prisoners of old, getting in was easy, but getting out very difficult. Thanks to Colonello Marco Mochi, I was able to walk out of the camp with ease at the end of my visit, and even enjoyed a salute from the *carabinieri* on duty at the main gate (perhaps rather in the fashion of Whitby playing the role of Croce).

The old camp is now a spacious, modern military facility. However, there is only a small garrison based there. Long gone are the days when 1,300–1,600 prisoners were squeezed into one part of the camp, together with their Italian guards. Although the main cookhouse has been replaced by a much larger modern building, all six of the original bungalow blocks are still there and the exteriors are very little changed. They now live up to the potential that they always possessed. The rear courtyards are tarmacked over and used mainly as a parking facility. The water tower remains, and is still in use to supplement the water supply when necessary, although effective plumbing has long since replaced the disaster of 1942/3. Beside the water tower there is now a small, ageing brick-built amphitheatre. The main well and the vegetable garden have gone, and that area is now an all-weather football pitch.

Bowes and Brown's cricket wicket, the asphalt road that ran down the centre of the camp, is also gone. In its place there is a wide concrete parade ground, uninterrupted by trees, which would have made a small but far easier playing surface. A cricket ball has not been bowled there since the summer of 1943 (so far as I am aware). As in 1953, when Tony Gregson visited, the Italian garrison knew nothing of the tunnel entrance in the rear courtyard of Gregson's bungalow. The drain hatch is still there, although the sump and the drain beneath it have been remodelled. It seems probable that some at least of that tunnel, and others, may still stretch from their original starting points towards the wall. Presumably, when the foundations of the buildings outside the wall were laid, the exit points of tunnels 1–4 were filled in.

It is still possible to see Chieti cathedral from the camp compound, although the fields that stretched up the hill are all now covered in buildings. The administration block for the camp is where it always was, and the main gate retains its curved entrance, although it now has a roof to keep off inclement weather. The buildings, with their polished marble floors, now look smart and well suited to both winter and summer weather.

Acknowledgements

I must first of all pay tribute to the work done by the Monte San Martino Trust, and its founder Cavaliere Ufficiale J. Keith Killby OBE, to commemorate the courage and self-sacrifice of the ordinary Italian people after 8 September 1943, which enabled so many Allied escaped prisoners of war to get home. I had the honour to be the Trust's chairman between 1997 and 2005, and have seen at first hand the excellent work that it continues to do. The Trust's library has provided me with invaluable material whilst writing this book.

I am also very grateful to the families of the various ex-prisoners who have helped me with my researches and given me permission to access and use records made and preserved by them, in particular the families of Arthur Green, Tony Gregson, Ronald Hill, Richard Edmonston Low, Mac McLucas, Gordon Norbrook, David Roberts, Jack Hodgson Shepherd, Frank Stone, Kenwyn Walters, Sam Webster and Bill Wendt. From this list, Jack Hodgson Shepherd deserves a special mention because his beautiful drawings of the camp, like those of Gordon Horner, really bring home what camp life was like. I must apologise to the families if I have failed to include in this book all of the decorations that these brave men won, or indeed the ranks that they eventually achieved. In most cases I have confined myself to the ranks that they held when they were in Campo 21, and the decorations of which I am aware that they held at that time. About 2,000 prisoners of various Allied nationalities spent time in Campo 21. It follows that there must still be very many stories from the camp that I do not know. However, I hope that I have succeeded in conveying fairly the nature of the camp and life within its walls, for worse or for better.

I must also take this opportunity to thank the very helpful staff at the Imperial War Museum and, most importantly, those who have donated their fathers' collections of wartime documents to that museum.

I am particularly grateful to George Hervey-Murray for allowing me to interview him at some length, and to Frank Osborne and Bob Walker Brown for extending the same courtesy to me some years ago.

My thanks go also to those who helped me to visit and inspect Campo 21 itself: Nino and Anne Fontecchio, and, most importantly, the Comandante of the Centro Nazionale Amministrativo dell'Arma dei Carabinieri, Colonello Marco Mochi, and his staff.

Once again I am indebted to the staff at my publishers Pen and Sword: Henry Wilson, my editor Jan Chamier, Matt Jones, Laura Wilkinson and her team, and Jon 'the Jacket King' Wilkinson.

Source Material

National Archives, Kew
Army Lists 1916–1946
FO 371/37273 Terms of the Italian Armistice
FO 916/652 Camp reports
KW 16/29 Red Cross/Protecting Power reports on Chieti
WO 32/18499 Complaints as to conditions, Driberg MP's questions, Finch allegation, Croce
WO 165/39 MI9 War Diaries
WO 208/3315 Escape reports: Cross, Johnson, Weaver,
WO 208/3316 Escape reports: Cooper, Whitby, Borradaile, Sudbury, Cameron, Uglow, Mather, Rickett, Hope, Wendt, Gore, MacLucas,
WO 208/3317 Escape reports: Hawkins, Boiteaux-Buchanan, Tills,
WO 208/3318 Escape reports: St Clair Erskine, Lodge, Bourhill, MacKay, Newman,
WO 208/3319 Escape reports: Tower, Murray
WO 208/3328 Escape/Liberation reports: Joscelyne, Earle
WO 208/3330 Liberation report: Haslehurst
WO 208/3327 Escape reports: Collarbone
WO 224/111 Red Cross Reports
WO 310/24 Killing of Outerbridge
WO 311/1192 Killing of Outerbridge
WO 311/1201 War Crimes: Farrell and general complaints, affidavits, Barela, Outerbridge
WO 392/21 Italian POW index

Imperial War Museum

Documents
Blair, D. A. 85/29/1
Bompas, W. M. G. 'Bill' 86/89/1
Bowden, K. J. 91/26/1
Freer Roger, M. 10984
Goody, J. 99/20/1
Green, Arthur Edward Chase 08/34/1
Hill, R. C. W. 253
Jenkins, John 98/21/1
McGinlay, A. O. 93/11/1
Pelley, Sir John 91/15/1
Sell, Harold Sydney 88/59/1
Shackleton 98/19/1
Shepherd, Jack Hodgson 95/1/1
Spooner, Pat 03/52/1

Audio Interviews
Bonnello 11959
Burdon-Taylor, Charles 'Bonzo' 10613
Carmichael 6207
Crabtree, Horace 9347
Fisher 15749
Flowerdew, Douglas 16315
O'Brien, Pat 14616
Pollak, Joe 31513
Rendell, Dennis Bossey 19055
Speares, John Alan 6395
Vickers, Thomas Douglas 13090
Audio transcripts:
Hood, Stuart 06287/04
Mumford, E. N. 00363/04

Personal Interviews
Hervey-Murray, George
Osborne, Frank
Walker Brown, Bob

Bibliography

Absalom, Roger 1991 *A Strange Alliance*, Accademia Toscana di Scienze e Lettere.

Bateman, G. C. 1986 *Diary of a Temporary Soldier*, privately published.

Bowes, Bill 1958 *Express Deliveries*, The Sportsman's Book Club.

Brown, Freddie 1954 *Cricket Musketeer*, Nicholas Kaye.

Davies, Tony 1985 *When the Moon Rises*, Leo Cooper.

Dodds, Arthur 1993 *Desert Harvest*, Dianthus Publishing Ltd.

English, Ian et al. 1997 *Home by Christmas*, available through the Monte San Martino Trust.

Foot, M. R. D. and J. M. Langley 1979 *MI9 Escape and Evasion 1939-45*, The Bodley Head.

Frelinghuysen, Joseph S. 1990 *Passages to Freedom*, Sunflower University Press.

Furman, John 1959 *Be not Fearful*, Anthony Blond.

Horner, Gordon 1948 *For you the War is Over*, privately published.

Graham, Dominick (Toby) 2000 *The Escapes and Evasions of An Obstinate Bastard*, Wilton 65, available from the Monte San Martino Trust.

Newby, Eric 1971 *Love and War in the Appenines*, HarperCollins.

Newby, Eric 1982 *A Traveller's Life*, William Collins and Sons Ltd.

Woods, Rex 1986 *One Man's Desert - the story of Captain Philip Gardner VC*, William Kimber.

Monte San Martino Manuscripts

Hawkins, G. W. B.

Joel, John H. (Solly)

Lodge, Ernest Fisher

Osborne, Frank

Pennycook, John

Pighetti, Dott. Luigi *The Hidden Heroes*

Spooner, Pat

Stern, Peter

Walker Brown, Bob, extract from *Mars and Minerva* magazine

Privately Held Manuscripts and Archives

Hervey-Murray, George: manuscript

Kenwyn Walters, J. E.: manuscript and diary

Lett, Gordon: diary and mixed archive including transcripts of and notes for the CNA lectures

Low, Richard Edmonston: manuscript *Escape into Italy*

Maides, John, Bulmer, Bill and Mick Wagner: manuscript *A Long Long Way to Go Home*

Stone, Captain F. W.: manuscript

Webster, First Lieutenant Samuel Redden, Junior: private family archive

Wendt, Flying Officer Bill: private family archive

Index